AUGSBURG EAGLE
A Documentary History
MESSERSCHMITT

# Bf 109

**William Green**

ASTON PUBLICATIONS LIMITED

Published in 1987 by Aston Publications
Limited, Bourne End House, Harvest Hill,
Bourne End, Bucks., SL8 5JJ

ISBN  0  946627  17  7

Printed in England by
Redwood Burn Limited,
Trowbridge, Wiltshire

Sole distributors to the UK book trade,
Springfield Books Ltd.,
Norman Road,
Denby Dale, Huddersfield,
West Yorkshire, HD8 8TH

Sole distributors for the USA,
Motorbooks International,
PO Box 2,
729 Prospect Avenue,
Osceola,
Wisconsin 54020,
United States

# Contents

# Introduction

The annals of military aviation are punctuated by technical innovations initiated spontaneously and independently in several countries almost simultaneously, and a supreme example in the development of the single-seat fighter was the marriage of the all-metal stressed-skin monocoque structure with the low-wing cantilever monoplane configuration, and the embellishment of this union with cockpit canopy and retractable undercarriage.

It was to be claimed that the Messerschmitt Bf 109 established this *nouvelle vogue*; that this German warplane was the progenitor of such fighters, which, in piston-engined form, were to attain their zenith during World War II. As are so many claims to precedence in technological development, these were exaggerations, yet both embodied an element of truth. The Bf 109 could not justifiably claim to be the *first* such warplane to fly, but it *was* the first to achieve service status, while its début undoubtedly helped stimulate international fighter evolution.

This creation of Willy Messerschmitt and Robert Lusser was certainly the world's most *advanced* single-seat fighter in the May of 1935 when it embarked on its flight test programme, a fact that was perhaps not immediately obvious. The success that attended its infancy was to be maintained during maturity; the genealogical processes facilitated by the design of its fundamental components resulting in the application of progressively more powerful engines and armament, enabling it to retain a position in the forefront of its class for three-quarters of a decade – no mean achievement during a period in which combat aircraft evolution throughout the world had accelerated to an unprecedented pace.

Several years before work on the Bf 109 had begun in the Augsburg drawing office of the Bayerische Flugzeugwerke, the more imaginative of fighter designers had predicted the early demise of the tried and tested biplane formula which had dominated the fighter scene since World War I and was still lauded by their more conventional colleagues. Some had already opted for the monoplane configuration before the 'thirties were born, but despite their search for increased performance by means of improved aerodynamic efficiency, few of the pro-monoplane faction believed that, without an inordinately heavy structure, the cantilever wing could withstand the extreme stresses to which a fighter was subjected in combat. External bracing permitted a lighter structure, and while reducing drag, such refinements as undercarriage retraction and a cockpit canopy introduced complexity and added weight with its adverse effect on manoeuvrability.

The year 1934, in which Messerschmitt and Lusser commenced the design of the Bf 109, was to be seen in retrospect as the dawn of a new era in fighter design; the era of the low-wing cantilever fighter monoplane with enclosed cockpit and retractable undercarriage. Almost simultaneously, official requirements for such an advanced and, by the standards of the day, sophisticated warplane had been framed in several countries, for it had suddenly become obvious that the performance of the fighter was being eclipsed by that of its natural prey, the bomber. Speed had finally taken precedence over manoeuvrability, and the visionaries had achieved a victory over the conventionalists. Yet the progeny of those imaginative requirements framed in 1934 were not the *first* such fighters as was widely believed.

Somewhat surprisingly, the Soviet Union had already gained the distinction of evolving the first cantilever low-wing fighter monoplane of all-metal construction with an enclosed cockpit and retractable undercarriage, Pavel O. Sukhoi having initiated the design of such a warplane in July 1932 at the TsAGI, or Central Aero and Hydrodynamic Institute, in Moscow. Developed under the aegis of Andrei N. Tupolev and employing an all-metal structure with sheet alloy skinning, this aircraft, the ANT-31 (or I-14), had flown on May 27, 1933. A little more than 15 weeks later, on September 14, 1933, another all-metal fighter monoplane embodying similar refinements, the Boeing Model 273 (XF7B-1), had made its initial flight several thousand miles away, but it is dubious if many of the design teams that began work on fighters of similar concept during the following year were aware of these events.

During the autumn and winter of 1934, the low-wing cantilever fighter monoplanes with retractable undercarriages and enclosed cockpits under design were legion. In parallel with the BFW team at Augsburg, Walter and Siegfried Günter were labouring in Ernst Heinkel's bureau at Warnemünde on the design of what was to be the Bf 109's principal competitor for orders from the still-clandestine *Luftwaffe*. In Britain, an ailing Reginald J. Mitchell was working at the Supermarine Aviation Works at Southampton on what was destined to be the Bf 109's most important opponent during much of the conflict that was to commence a half-decade later. The Vickers drawing offices at Weybridge were designing the Venom, and the Bristol and Gloster companies had begun work on fighters intended to meet the same F.5/34 requirement, all, like the Bf 109 and the Spitfire, employing all-metal stressed-skin monocoque structures. Slightly nearer to London, in Hawker Aircraft's Canbury Park Road factory, in Kingston-upon-Thames, Sydney Camm and his colleagues were immersed in the detail design of the future Hurricane.

Across the Channel in France, the Morane-Saulnier design team at Puteaux, led by R. Gauthier, had begun work on the M.S. 405, progenitor of the M.S. 406 which was to provide the Bf 109 with one of its *first* opponents of W.W. II, and which, like the Hurricane, was the synthesis of years of fighter design translated into the newly-fashionable configuration, retaining classic tubular metal construction with fabric skinning. In view of the growing popularity of light-metal stressed-skin monocoque structures, the retention of steel tube and fabric was somewhat surprising; particularly so in view of the fact that all the Morane-Saulnier fighter's competitors built to meet the requirements of the 1934 specification, the Loire 250, the Loire-Nieuport 161, the Dewoitine D.513, and the Bloch 150, were of stressed-skin monocoque construction.

On the other side of the Atlantic in the U.S.A., the *nouvelle vogue* in fighter design and construction had found its share of adherents as elsewhere. Don Berlin, the Chief Engineer of the Curtiss-Wright Corporation, was working on the Model 75 fighter, prototype construction of which began in November 1934, John Northrop and his team were developing the Model 3A (XP-948), and to compete with these for Army Air Corps contracts, Alexander Kartveli was evolving the Seversky SEV-1XP, all featuring stressed-skin monocoque structures.

These dozen or so fighter prototypes all flew between mid-1935 and mid-1936, performing their flight trials with varying degrees of success, and few of them progressing further than the experimental phase, but of those that *did* achieve production status, the Messerschmitt Bf 109 and the Supermarine Spitfire, which followed it into the air some nine months later, on March 5, 1936, were supreme and destined to be probably the only fighters of W.W. II to achieve truly legendary status. They were remarkably similar in concept. Both represented the smallest practical warplane that could be designed around a pilot, the chosen power plant and the specified armament, and while the Spitfire was slender and ballerina-like, the aesthetically less-appealing contours of the Bf 109 endowed it with an air of ruthless efficiency. By comparison with the Spitfire, however, the German fighter possessed a much higher wing loading, compensating for this to some extent by adopting the then-radical combination of automatic leading-edge slots and slotted trailing-edge flaps.

Both the Spitfire and the Bf 109 were inspired designs, but whereas the British fighter drew on experience gained with the Schneider Trophy racing floatplanes, the German fighter possessed no illustrious sires. Yet, despite undistinguished pedigree, the Bf 109 was a true thoroughbred. Its creators had made no concessions to the traditionalists, and had taken full advantage of the most advanced aerodynamic and structural techniques to achieve what, by the standards of the day, was considered to be the ultimate in performance.

The Bf 109 was brought to production status and placed in service more rapidly than any of its contemporaries, entering the inventory of the *Luftwaffe* early in 1937. By the summer of 1940, five years after its début, it was still superior to any fighter extant, with the possible exception of its principal opponent, the Spitfire, and even this formidable British fighter was at a disadvantage in climbing, diving and in level speeds below 20,000 ft. (6 100 m). The Bf 109 possessed its share of short-comings, as, indeed, has every warplane ever designed, the advanced features that it presaged demanding certain penalties; penalties widely publicized and greatly exaggerated by the Allies for wartime propaganda purposes.

In fact, the design team responsible for the Bf 109 had displayed exceptional skill, and its manufacturers proved no less competent in endowing this fighter with an aerodynamic finish superior to those of its British and French contemporaries. It was perhaps fortuitous but indeed fortunate for the *Luftwaffe* that so early in its existence the service obtained a warplane of the calibre of the Bf 109. It was to be built in larger numbers than any other combat aircraft before or since; it fought on every front to which the *Luftwaffe* was committed, and its postwar manufacture in Czechoslovakia and Spain endowed it with a record for production longevity unlikely ever to be bettered by a fighter.

The Bf 109 first fired its guns in anger in Spanish skies in the early summer of 1937, and for the last time eleven years later, in the summer of 1948, over the newly-created State of Israel. On the pages that follow, I have attempted to correlate technical evolution and service career, describing use by the multifarious air arms that were to include this fighter in their inventories, from first operational commitment with the *Legion Condor* to use by the fledgeling Israeli air force more than a decade later. Owing to its importance in the history of the Messerschmitt fighter in particular and in the annals of fighter warfare in general, coupled with the fact that it has hitherto gone little recorded, much emphasis has been placed on early operation of the Bf 109 in the internecine Spanish conflict. Conversely, use of the Messerschmitt fighter in the "Battle of Britain" has been confined to the salient aspects of its role in this epic conflict as I feel that its activities in British skies in the summer of 1940 have been more than sufficiently documented in depth elsewhere to render reiteration here superfluous.

Few warplanes can be said to have evinced characteristics associated with the nation that conceived them more than did the Bf 109, and few warplanes have enjoyed a more remarkable or distinguished career. It will always be remembered as one of the principal actors in the drama that unfolded in the skies over Europe and North Africa during the years 1939–45, and is assured of its niche in aviation's metaphorical hall of fame.

William Green

# The Eagle's aerie

To the more perceptive Augsburger sitting over his *Tassen Kaffee* in the Königsbau – on the Adolf-Hitler Platz off the Kaiserstrasse – on a morning early in September of 1935, the headlines of his *Völkischer Beobachter* or *Neue Augsburger Zeitung* must have seemed gloomy portents indeed, recording the manoeuvres of French armoured forces in the Champagne, anti-aircraft artillery exercises in the vicinity of Berlin, or the attendance of the *Führer* at the autumn manoeuvres of the VI Army Corps. The prognostications of Germany's new leaders and their exhortations to the workers to place before all else the massive rearmament programme announced by the *Führer* hardly made for light reading.

The year had already been eventful for Germany's youthful Third Reich. On March 1, the *Luftwaffe* – a clandestine force in direct contravention of the Treaty of Versailles for several years – had been officially proclaimed to the world at large, and on March 16, the *Führer* had denounced the Treaty itself. France had promptly concluded a Treaty of Alliance with the Soviet Union, being emulated two weeks later, on May 16, by Czechoslovakia, and on June 18, Britain and Germany had concluded a Naval Agreement which had immediately created a serious rift between the old Allies, Britain and France. Ominous clouds were indeed gathering over Europe.

Not so many kilometres from the Königsbau, at a small airfield between Augsburg and the little town of Haunstetten, an event had taken place that had *not* been announced by the headlines of the *Völkischer Beobachter* or *Neue Augsburger Zeitung*. Yet, from several aspects, it was to prove of greater importance to Germany than many of the events being recorded dramatically by the newspapers in bold, funereal Gothic type. A radically new warplane had been undergoing its initial flight testing at the Augsburg–Haunstetten airfield nearby; a weapon forged in Bavaria that, when tempered, was destined to play a major role in the shaping of events in Europe. This warplane, the designation of which would, within little more than a year, be known to virtually every Augsburger and, for that matter, almost every German, was Messerschmitt's Bf 109; a fighter whose absence in the inventory of the *Luftwaffe* four years later when Germany initiated hostilities would have had an incalculable effect on the course of the war in the air and, possibly, the war itself.

At Augsburg–Haunstetten, the Bayerische Flugzeugwerke had created an eagle; a warplane that was to evince all the characteristics of the true bird-of-prey. It could hardly have been foreseen, however, on July 30, 1926, when the Bayerische Flugzeugwerke A.G. (BFW) was created by the *Reichsverkehrsministerium*, the Bavarian State Government, and the banking house of Merck, Finck und Compagnie, with a capital of 400,000 *Reichsmark*, that within barely more than a decade BFW would be Germany's most important fighter design organization; that a new World War would witness nearly 40,000 aircraft of the company's design roll off the assembly lines of an immense complex of factories to represent some 43 per cent of the entire combat aircraft output of Germany's as yet unborn Third Reich.

The company founded in Munich in 1926 was not the first aircraft manufacturing concern to bear the name of Bayerische Flugzeugwerke, the Albatros-Werke G.m.b.H. having established a company of this name in Munich more than 10 years earlier, on February 20, 1916. However, the relatively brief career of the first BFW had proved unspectacular, its few original designs failing to attract production orders. The new BFW had no connection with its namesake, having been formed to take over the assets and liabilities of the Udet-Flugzeugbau G.m.b.H. at Ramersdorf, Munich.

The Udet-Flugzeugbau had been established on October 23, 1922, by Ernst Udet, Heinz Pohl, Erich Scheuermann, and Hans Herrmann, with an authorized capital of 100,000 *Reichsmark*. The primary purpose of the company was to build light sports and training aircraft to the designs of Hans Herrmann, and the Udet U 1 single-seat ultra-light monoplane had already flown five months earlier, on May 12, this serving as a prototype for the company's first product, the U 2, of which seven examples were built. The U 3 was a more powerful two-seat derivative of the U 2, and the U 4 was a single-seat equivalent of the U 3.

*The U 7 Kolibri (above) and the U 8 four-seat light transport (below) were among the less successful products of the Udet-Flugzeugbau, the predecessor of the Bayerische Flugzeugwerke*

Both the U 2 and U 4 enjoyed some successes in international events, and in 1923 the Udet-Flugzeugbau evolved the U 5 four-seat light transport parasol monoplane. The U 6 was a further refinement of the U 4, seven being built, and the U 7 *Kolibri* was an ultra-light high-wing single-seater, while the U 8 was a progressive development of the U 5 four-seat light transport, a few examples being built for *Aero Lloyd*. The most ambitious aircraft developed by the Udet-Flugzeugbau was the U 11 *Condor* transport, which, carrying three crew members

*The Udet U 12 Flamingo was the first aircraft to be built in quantity by the Bayerische Flugzeugwerke*

*The M 18c, a photographic version of Messerschmitt's four-seat light transport powered by a 240 h.p. Armstrong Siddeley Lynx engine*

and eight passengers, was powered by four 125 h.p. engines mounted as pushers beneath the shoulder wing. Completed early in 1925, the U 11 contributed to the financial difficulties in which the Udet-Flugzeugbau now began to find itself.

Substantial loans had been obtained from Merck, Finck und Co., and some financial support had been provided by both the *Reichsverkehrsministerium* and the Bavarian State Government, but the situation progressively worsened. What was to prove the company's most successful design, the U 12 *Flamingo* primary training biplane, had flown during the course of 1925, but was too late to affect the situation.

In the spring of 1926, by which time both Udet and Scheuermann had left the company, the Udet-Flugzeugbau began negotiations for the purchase of the old Bayerische Rumpler-Werke G.m.b.H. factory at Augsburg, but by the time the contracts were drawn up the situation had deteriorated still further. The Merck, Finck banking house alone had invested 800,000 *Reichsmark* in the company, and discussions between this concern, the *Reichsverkehrsministerium* and the Bavarian State Government resulted in the decision to form a new company to take over the economic ruins.

The *Reichsverkehrsministerium* provided 62·5 per cent of the capital, the Bavarian State Government providing 25 per cent, and the newly-established Bayerische Flugzeugwerke A.G. proceeded with the purchase of the Augsburg factory, a further 400,000 *Reichsmark* being borrowed from the *Reichsverkehrsministerium* (although this loan was later to be made an outright gift). A new management was created under Dr. Alexander Schruffer, and preparations were initiated at Augsburg for large-scale production of the U 12 *Flamingo* which it was pro-

*(Above) An M 23b two-seat sports aircraft powered by a 115 h.p. Siemens Sh 14A, and (below) an M 18d/See floatplane with a 300 h.p. Wright Whirlwind engine*

posed to modify from all-wood to mixed construction by the application of a welded steel-tube fuselage.

A disagreement with the new management had resulted in the dismissal of Hans Herrmann in the autumn of 1926, and the task of redesigning the U 12 fuselage for steel-tube construction was taken over by Karl Theiss, this resulting in the appearance of two derivatives of the U 12 in 1927, the BFW 1 *Sperber* and the BFW 3 *Marabu*. Neither progressed further than the prototype stage, and when quantity deliveries of the U 12 began from Augsburg the wooden fuselage was retained. In addition to being ordered in some numbers by the *Reichsverkehrsministerium*, the U 12 was also exported, 24 being delivered to Hungary where a further 40 were built under licence by Manfréd Weiss, 10 were delivered to Austria, and others were built under licence by Backmann in Riga, Latvia.

Although BFW was enjoying some success with the U 12, the concern lacked a competent and creative engineer to lead its design bureau, and it was proposed that an amalgamation should be arranged with another Bavarian aircraft manufacturer, the Messerschmitt Flugzeugbau G.m.b.H. of Bamberg, which was producing the highly-successful M 18 all-metal cantilever monoplane light transport. The M 18 had been designed by Dipl.-Ing. Willy Messerschmitt, a graduate of the Munich Technical High School, who, during the early 'twenties, had designed and built several successful gliders and sailplanes. In 1923 he had formed the Flugzeugbau Messerschmitt at Bamberg, and had built the S 15, S 16 *Bubi* and S 16a *Betty* motorized sailplanes before, in 1925, he had developed his first design intended from the outset for power, the M 17 *Ello* tandem two-seat monoplane.

From the experience gained with these aircraft, Messerschmitt had designed the M 18 light transport which initially provided accommodation for a pilot and three passengers. The prototype was of wooden construction but the production version featured an all-metal structure and a metal-skinned fuselage, and with a contract for 12 aircraft of this type from Theo Croneiss, who was in process of creating a domestic airline, the Nordbayerische Verkehrsflug G.m.b.H., the Messerschmitt Flugzeugbau G.m.b.H. had been established on March 25, 1926. The success of the M 18 had enabled Messerschmitt to obtain a subsidy from the Bavarian State Government, but the demands of the newly-formed BFW and the unfavourable economic conditions of the 'twenties rendered the financial support of two separate aircraft factories impracticable, and considerable pressure was brought to bear on Messerschmitt to merge his company with BFW.

Messerschmitt was loath to relinquish his independence, however, and it was finally agreed that the Messerschmitt Flugzeugbau G.m.b.H. would confine itself to design development but, while retaining all design rights and patents, would move to the BFW factory at Augsburg, BFW disbanding its design bureau and giving priority to the production of aircraft of Messerschmitt design. By these means, the two companies were able to maintain their separate entities while functioning as one, and the agreement was signed on September 8, 1927, the M 18b being moved to Augsburg.

Meanwhile, Messerschmitt had built the M 19 tandem two-seat sports monoplane for Theo Croneiss, and the first original Messerschmitt design to be built by BFW at Augsburg was the 10-seat M 20 transport which suffered an accident on its first flight on February 26, 1928, *Deutsche Lufthansa* (DLH) promptly cancelling a contract for this type. A second prototype was immediately built, and after being flown successfully by Theo Croneiss on August 2, 1928, the DLH reinstated the contract. By this time, the *Reichsverkehrsministerium* was coming under repeated attack for the extent of its investment of public funds in the aircraft industry, and had decided to sell its

*(Above) The second of the six Bf 108A monoplanes built specifically to participate in the 4th Challenge de Tourisme Internationale. This aircraft, D-ILIT, crashed shortly after the Challenge team commenced training. (Below right) Ernst "Udlinger" Udet, a good friend of Willy Messerschmitt, was initially unimpressed by the Bf 109 but eventually became its most ardent champion*

shareholding in the BFW. Messerschmitt persuaded the wealthy Strohmeyer-Raulino family to purchase 87·5 per cent of the shares, purchasing the remaining 12·5 per cent himself, and on July 1, 1928, a new board of directors took office with Otto Strohmeyer as chairman, management being shared by Messerschmitt and Fritz Hille.

The BFW now had an extensive development programme – *too* extensive as was soon to be realized. This included variants of the M 18, the M20b, the M 21 tandem two-seat primary training biplane intended as a successor to the *Flamingo*, the M 22 twin-engined bomber evolved at the behest of the *Reichswehr*, the M 23 tandem two-seat sports monoplane, and the M 24 eight-passenger transport. Only two prototypes of the M 21 were to be built, and the M 22 bomber was to be abandoned after the sole prototype crashed. The M 23 was to prove an unqualified success, but during the course of 1929 the financial situation of the BFW rapidly worsened. DLH cancelled a contract for 10 M 20b transports that had reached an advanced stage in construction, demanding repayment of deposits, and in 1930 the BFW showed a loss of 600,000 *Reichsmark*. With the DLH cancellation there was no option but to file a bankruptcy petition on June 1, 1931.

Although the Messerschmitt Flugzeugbau had ostensibly been absorbed by the BFW three years earlier, it still in fact retained design and patent rights, managed to raise 8,000 *Reichsmark* capital and, in co-operation with the BFW receiver, succeeded in forcing DLH to take delivery of the M 20b transports as well as the prototype M 28 high-speed postal monoplane that had been designed specifically to a DLH requirement. Messerschmitt also succeeded in obtaining an order to develop a new two-seat sports aircraft, the M 29, specifically for the 1932 *Europa-Rundflug*, and in December 1932 a basic agreement was reached with BFW's creditors to discharge the bankruptcy, this being made official on April 27, 1933.

### An Eaglet hatches

The Bf 109 was born on the Augsburg drawing boards of the Bayerische Flugzeugwerke A.G. early in 1934 to meet a requirement drawn up by the *Luftwaffenführungsstab*. The broad parameters of this requirement, together with prototype development contracts, had earlier been passed to Arado, Focke-Wulf and Heinkel, and Dipl.-Ing. Messerschmitt, who, with Rakan Kokothaki, was co-manager of the Bayerische Flugzeugwerke and unpopular with some of the more influential members of the *Reichsluftfahrtministeriums* (RLM), or State

Air Ministry, was informed semi-officially that no production contract would be awarded his fighter. Indeed, he was encouraged to refuse the development contract, and as he possessed no experience in the design of high-speed combat aircraft, Messerschmitt was fully aware that the consensus of opinion in the *C-Amt*, or Technical Office, was that, *should* his fighter ever materialize, it was inconceivable that it would offer serious competition for the progeny of the more experienced Arado and Heinkel teams.

That the State Secretary of Aviation, Erhard Milch, fully subscribed to this view is without doubt. Had he considered that the remotest chance existed of Messerschmitt's design proving superior to the other contenders in the fighter contest

*The M 35a (below), powered by a 150 h.p. Siemens Sh 14A engine, was the immediate predecessor of the Bf 108*

*(Above and below) An early production Bf 108B-1 Taifun powered by a 240 h.p. Argus As 10C engine*

he would certainly have refused to sanction the issue of the contract to the Bayerische Flugzeugwerke. The enmity between Willy Messerschmitt and Erhard Milch stemmed from 1929 and the cancellation by the latter, when Managing Director of DLH, of the contract for 10 M 20b transports. Messerschmitt believed the cancellation unjustified, and the quarrel between Messerschmitt and Milch had been bitter. By the time the Bayerische Flugzeugwerke was resurrected, Milch, to whom the *Führer* was heavily obligated, had been appointed State Secretary of Aviation. As such he was permanent deputy to Hermann Göring, and, wielding considerable power, was determined to frustrate Messerschmitt's aspirations and restrict the Bayerische Flugzeugwerke to the licence manufacture of the designs of other companies.

In May 1933, the Bayerische Flugzeugwerke possessed only 82 employees, and Dipl.-Ing. Messerschmitt, anxious to maintain the nucleus of a design team, began to solicit work abroad. His co-manager, Kokothaki, succeeded in obtaining a contract from Rumania for the design of a six-passenger commercial transport from the Intreprindere Constructii Aeronautice Romane (ICAR) of Bucharest. Work on the design of this transport was initiated at Augsburg as the M 36, and simultaneously the design of a light cabin monoplane of advanced concept, the M 37, was begun, ICAR having evinced interest in such an aircraft as a possible production successor to the licence-built Raab-Katzenstein *Tigerschwalbe* trainer.

Prompted by State Secretary Milch, quick to grasp any opportunity to discredit Messerschmitt, *Oberstleutnant* Wilhelm Wimmer, in charge of the *C-Amt*, officially rebuked the management of the Bayerische Flugzeugwerke for accepting a foreign development commission. Milch was now hoist with his own petard, however, for Messerschmitt and Kokothaki protested vehemently that, as the *C-Amt* had not deigned to provide their company with any form of development contract, it had no recourse but to solicit commissions

abroad, the undeniable logic of this argument forcing the *C-Amt* to award the Bayerische Flugzeugwerke a development contract while doing nothing to enhance Messerschmitt's personal standing in official circles.

The RLM had concluded that the 4th *Challenge de Tourisme Internationale* to be held in August–September 1934 would provide an admirable opportunity to display the resuscitation of German aviation, plans being formulated for the entry of a strong German contingent. The previous *Challenge* had been held in 1932, the leading places in the contest having been taken by Poland with the RWD-6, and the Bayerische Flugzeugwerke was instructed to design and build six examples of a competition aircraft for inclusion among the German entries in the new *Challenge*.

Messerschmitt now had an opportunity to put into practice the latest techniques in structural and aerodynamic design which he was already in process of embodying in the M 37. Fortunately, in view of the strictly limited time allowed by the contract for completion of development of the competition aircraft, the M 37 broadly met the requirements of the specification, and in October 1933 metal was cut on what had now been officially designated the Bf 108.

Within a few weeks of this event, Messerschmitt was joined by Dipl.-Ing. Robert Lusser who had left Ernst Heinkel to take over the *Projektbüro* of the Bayerische Flugzeugwerke. Lusser had worked with Hans Klemm at Böblingen where he had been preoccupied with light sports and touring aircraft, and had parted company with Klemm in 1932 to accept leadership of Heinkel's sports aircraft design department. Another member of the Augsburg team was Hubert Bauer, who, as head of the experimental construction department and workshop manager, had joined Messerschmitt in 1929. Both Lusser and Bauer had major roles in the development of the Bf 108, the first flight of which took place almost simultaneously with the receipt by the Bayerische Flugzeugwerke of a fighter development contract, and this, too, was to owe much to Lusser and Bauer.

The first of the six Bf 108As (D-IBUM) was flown in the spring of 1934 at the company's airfield, the remaining five aircraft (D-ILIT, D-IZAN, D-IJES, D-IMUT, and D-IGAK) all being completed within four months. The Bf 108A was a remarkably advanced aeroplane, having an all-metal structure embodying flush-riveted stressed skinning, main undercarriage members which, operating mechanically through a worm gear, retracted outwards into wing wells, and a fully enclosed cabin. The small wing, which was of Messerschmitt-patented single-spar construction, carried Handley-Page leading-edge slots and trailing-edge slotted flaps to achieve the highest possible lift coefficient, and the result was a speed range of almost five to one.

Initial flight trials exceeded the most sanguine of expectations, and at this juncture Messerschmitt was offered a professorship in aeronautical design at the Danzig Technical University. In order to ascertain if there was still as much prejudice against him in official circles, he informed the *C-Amt* of the offer, and enquired if any importance was attached to his work for the future. He was promptly informed by *Oberstleutnant* Wimmer that his person was officially considered to be of no importance to the industry, and that, therefore, he would do well to accept the appointment in Danzig.

Fortunately for the *Luftwaffe* and to the annoyance of State Secretary Milch, Messerschmitt's friends prevailed upon him to refuse the professorship, these friends including *Oberst* Fritz Loeb who had by now been appointed to the Technical Office, Wimmer, who was to be succeeded by Ernst Udet on June 10, 1936, eventually being assigned to the *Luftkommando-Amt*, the forerunner of the *Luftwaffengeneralstab*.

While the situation of the Bayerische Flugzeugwerke was improving, the number of employees increasing to 524 by the

*A Bf 108B Taifun imported into the U.K. in 1939 (and registered G-AFRN) which was impressed by the R.A.F. in May 1941 as DK280*

end of 1933, orders having been received for the licence manufacture of 30 Dornier Do 11s and 24 Heinkel He 45s, and the fighter development contract now permitting some increase in the design staff, no less antagonism was being displayed towards Dipl.-Ing. Messerschmitt. Both factory and official trials with the Bf 108A had progressed favourably during the spring and early summer, but shortly after the *Challenge* team began training flights on the new aircraft one of the Bf 108s (D-ILIT) crashed.

The manager of the team, Theo Osterkamp, promptly insisted that the Bf 108 was unsafe, and incited two other team members, Hans Seidemann and Fritz Morzik, to adopt an unruly attitude towards both the aircraft and Messerschmitt himself. Fortuitously, *Oberst* Loeb was in Augsburg at the time, and intervened on Messerschmitt's behalf, pointing out that the Bf 108 had been thoroughly tested at Rechlin and had met with the full approval of the official test pilots. Furthermore, he flew to Berlin and proposed to State Secretary Milch that Osterkamp be replaced as team manager. Although Milch officially took no action in the matter, no further complaints were voiced against the Bf 108, four examples of which participated in the *Challenge* which commenced on August 31, 1934.

Despite the largest team – 15 aircraft were entered of which two were withdrawn, one of these being the Bf 108A that crashed at Augsburg – which included most of the leading pilots of the Third Reich, the German contingent failed to capture first and second places which went to Poland and the RWD-9. Third place was taken by the German team with a Fieseler Fi 97, and the fifth and sixth places went to Theo Osterkamp and Werner Junck respectively, both flying 250 h.p. Hirth HM 8U-powered Bf 108As (D-IMUT and D-IJES). A 218 h.p. Argus As 17-powered Bf 108A (D-IGAK) flown by Carl Francke took tenth place.

Although it had not taken any of the first places in the contest, the Bf 108 had put up a very creditable performance, and had, in fact, proved itself the fastest participant. Messerschmitt's team had already initiated the design of a slightly enlarged and more capacious derivative, the Bf 108B, which was to appear in 1935 and gain international acclaim as the *Taifun* (Typhoon) four-seater, but by this time Messerschmitt, Lusser, and their growing Augsburg team, were preoccupied with the design of the single-seat fighter for which the *C-Amt* (by now known openly as the *Technische Amt*) had so reluctantly awarded the Bayerische Flugzeugwerke a development contract as the Bf 109.

Design of the Bf 109 had, in fact, been initiated in March 1934, before the the Bf 108A flew, and the latter served to reassure Messerschmitt and Lusser of the feasibility of the combination of aerodynamic and structural features that they were embodying in their fighter, which, while by no means revolutionary, was undeniably audacious in design. Having been informed from the outset that no production order was likely to follow the development contract, the Augsburg team had nothing to lose by carrying the state-of-the-art to what it considered to be the ultimate. Had the team acceded to the proposals of the conventionalists, compromise would have been necessary, and compromise, in Messerschmitt's view, inevitably resulted in mediocrity. Thus, he was uncompromising in his approach to the fighter that saw birth on the Augsburg drawing boards during the summer and autumn months of 1934.

Like the Bf 108 that immediately preceded it, the Bf 109 was an all-metal low-wing cantilever monoplane with flush-riveted stressed skinning. The fuselage was an oval-section light-metal monocoque; the single-spar wing featured automatic slots on the outer portions of its leading edges, and the inner portions carried slotted flaps on the trailing edges; the main undercar-

riage members were fully retractable, and the cockpit was enclosed by a hinged canopy. None of these features was in itself radical. The Dornier Do H *Falke* single-seat fighter monoplane had utilized *all-metal* construction as early as 1922; the Short Silver Streak of 1920 had employed *stressed metal skinning*; fighters with *metal monocoque* fuselages had appeared from time to time during the 'twenties; wing *leading-edge slots* and trailing-edge *slotted flaps* had been featured by the Handley Page H.P.21 fighter of 1923, and the early 'thirties had seen Grumman fighters combining enclosed cockpits with retractable undercarriages. What *was* radical was the combination of all of these features in the one airframe.

The *Luftwaffenführungsstab* fighter requirement demanded a monoplane configuration, an armament of two 7,9-mm MG 17 machine guns, emphasized high rates of roll and turn, complete structural integrity in a power dive, and also stressed the importance of perfect spinning behaviour. The importance attached to spinning characteristics resulted from the unsuitability of the Dräger-type mask used by fighter pilots for oxygen feed under pressure, and thus, when flying near the fighter's stalling altitude, the possibility of the pilot blacking out always existed, the aircraft then entering a spin. If, after a few turns and before the pilot regained full consciousness, a flat spin developed, recovery was difficult if not impossible.

In so far as the power plant was concerned, both Junkers and Daimler-Benz were engaged in the development of powerful liquid-cooled 12-cylinder engines of inverted-vee type – a configuration dictated both by considerations of good visibility for the pilot in a single-engine installation and ease of mounting. The former company's Jumo 210 was selected in the autumn of 1934 for initial installation, after a provisional mock-up had been completed around the abortive 700 h.p. water-cooled BMW 116, with provision for mounting interchangeability with the Daimler-Benz DB 600, which was at an earlier stage in development. Within these broad parameters the Bf 109 was evolved.

Metal on the Bf 109 prototypes had been cut late in 1934, and in early May of the following year, the first of these, then known as the Bf 109a, was being readied for initial taxying trials at Augsburg–Haunstetten when Messerschmitt received a visit from Ernst Udet. Udet, who had still to accept a commission in the *Luftwaffe* and was visiting the factory in a private capacity, was promptly shown the Bf 109a, but after a cursory examination of the aircraft, he turned to Messerschmitt and said: "This machine will never make a *fighter!*"

Udet, like so many other German pilots of the period, still believed an open cockpit, fixed undercarriage and biplane configuration to be prerequisites in the design of any successful fighter, and his prejudice, which Messerschmitt was aware would be shared by many pilots unwilling to accept the demise of the lightly loaded and readily forgiving biplane, was anything but encouraging. In the event, within the year, Udet was to become the most ardent of champions of the Bf 109.

# The contenders

The Bf 109a (*Werk-Nr.* 758) began taxying trials with its main undercarriage legs temporarily braced by a cross member which was removed after the completion of the first phase of high-speed ground tests. The undercarriage retraction mechanism had been extensively tested on a ground rig but the damping effect of the oleos proved insufficient and demanded modification before, late in the May of 1935, the prototype was flown for the first time by Messerschmitt's senior test pilot, Hans-Dietrich "Bubi" Knoetzsch. As the planned Jumo 210 was not available for installation, the first prototype, by this time known as the Bf 109 V1 (the system of *Versuchs* numbers having been universally adopted by the German aircraft industry) and registered D-IABI, was fitted with a Rolls-Royce Kestrel V 12-cylinder upright-vee liquid-cooled engine rated at 695 h.p. for take-off and 640 h.p. at 14,000 ft. (4 267 m), and driving a two-bladed fixed-pitch Schwarz wooden airscrew. With the completion of initial factory trials, the Bf 109 V1 was ferried, via Leipzig, to the *Erprobungsstelle* (Proving Centre) at Rechlin by Knoetzsch. On touching down at Rechlin the starboard main undercarriage leg attachment point broke, but fortunately damage to the airframe was superficial and repairs quickly effected.

*1he Bf 109a (later Bf 109 V1) Werk-Nr. 758 during initial trials at Augsburg-Haunstetten, first flight taking place on May 28, 1935*

The *E-Stelle* test pilots looked askance at the Bf 109 V1, with its steep ground angle and resultant poor view for taxying, its sideways-hinging cockpit canopy, and its automatic wing leading-edge slots. They were also suspicious of its high wing loading of 24 lb./sq. ft. (117,18 kg/m²). Messerschmitt patiently explained that the ground angle had been selected in order to obtain the steepest practicable incidence and, therefore, the highest lift coefficient when landing, and that the slots were fitted to provide improved aileron control near the stall. These slots were perhaps the most radical innovation in fighter design presented by the Bf 109, and there was general concern regarding the possibility of the slots opening inadvertently during aerobatics. However, Knoetzsch's demonstrations and the fact that the Bf 109 V1 clocked 290 m.p.h. (467 km/h) – 17 m.p.h. (27 km/h) faster than the maximum speed registered during the initial evaluation phase by the similarly-powered but larger and heavier He 112 V1 – visibly impressed RLM officials at Rechlin.

Nevertheless, the appreciably lower wing loading of 20·3 lb./sq. ft. (99,1 kg/m²) offered by the Heinkel fighter, coupled with the broader track of its undercarriage, and superior view for taxying and landing, were considered more acceptable by most of the *E-Stelle* pilots than the higher climbing, diving and level speeds of the fighter offered by the Bayerische Flugzeugwerke, and when the Bf 109 V1 was ferried back to Augsburg–Haunstetten, the He 112 remained firm favourite as the first monoplane to see service with the *Jagdfliegern*.

Construction of the second and third prototypes of the Bf 109 had meanwhile been proceeding, and with the availabil-

ity of a Jumo 210A engine in October 1935, the Bf 109 V2 (*Werk-Nr.* 759) was completed. Registered D-IUDE, the Bf 109 V2 differed from its predecessor in only minor respects, apart from the engine installation. The main undercarriage oleo legs were strengthened, as were also the attachment points and hydraulic jacks, strengthening plates were riveted on over the wheel wells, a gun-cooling intake was introduced above the engine on the spinner line, and provision was made for the installation in the fuselage nose for two MG 17 machine guns with 500 r.p.g., although this armament was not fitted in the second prototype, being installed for the first time in the Bf 109 V3 (*Werk-Nr.* 760 D-IOQY) in which provision was also made for an engine-mounted 20-mm MG FF/M cannon, this being accompanied by a cropped spinner.

The Bf 109 V2 commenced flight trials in January 1936 with a Jumo 210A engine rated at 680 h.p. at 2,700 r.p.m. for take-off and 610 h.p. at 2,600 r.p.m., but owing to power plant delivery delays, it was not joined in the test programme by the V3 until the following June. By this time there was a marked change in the attitude of the *Luftwaffenführungsstab* towards the Bf 109, this being reflected by the noticeably more cordial attitude of the RLM towards Dipl.-Ing. Messerschmitt himself, and the placing of an order with the Bayerische Flugzeugwerke for a pre-production series of 10 fighters.

The increasing favour with which the Bf 109 was being viewed in official circles was due to several factors, one of which was the revelation by German Intelligence in June 1936 that Supermarine had received a production contract for 310 Spitfires. Although the Spitfire had flown for the first time some nine months later than the Bf 109, the rapidity with which it had been ordered into production impressed the *Luftwaffenführungsstab*, as did the close similarity in concept between Messerschmitt's fighter and its British counterpart. More important in influencing the Fighter Acceptance Commission, however, were the results of flying trials at Augsburg–Haunstetten, Rechlin and Travemünde, which, in large measure, had dispelled many of the earlier doubts regarding the Bf 109's more sophisticated features, such as its automatic slots. Thus, from a rank outsider the fighter from Augsburg had become the odds-on favourite by the time the definitive evaluation trials were held at Travemünde in the autumn of 1936.

The He 112 still possessed its share of supporters, some enjoying considerable influence, and rumours that the Bf 109 suffered vicious handling characteristics and basic structural weaknesses were assiduously fostered, but the comparative trials left few doubts in the minds of the Acceptance Commission of the superiority of Messerschmitt's contender which was demonstrated extremely effectively by Dr.-Ing. Hermann Wurster. Gerhard Nitschke demonstrating the Heinkel fighter was, on the other hand, at a serious disadvantage in that he was flying the He 112 V4 which, differing from earlier prototypes in major respects, had only attained an early stage in its flight development and could not, therefore, be flown in full accordance with the rules laid down by the Acceptance Commission.

The Messerschmitt test pilot's remarkable demonstration of the spinning capabilities of the Bf 109, the series of flick rolls that he performed at low altitude across the airfield, the obvious ability of the fighter to snap into and out of any rolling position and remain, as one witness put it, "as steady as though on rails", the structural integrity suggested by the terminal velocity dive from 24,600 ft. (8 050 m), and the tight turns within the boundaries of the airfield made a considerable impression

*The He 112 V1 D-IADO, the first prototype of the Bf 109's principal competitor powered by a Kestrel engine*

on the Commission, and a decision in favour of the Bf 109 was taken. Dipl.-Ing. Carl Francke, who had flown the Bf 109 V2 over the 11th *Olympiad* in Berlin in August, and was in charge of the official flight evaluation of the competing fighters at Travemünde, fully concurred with the Commission's decision which, after they had flown the fighter, was endorsed by *Oberst* Ernst Udet and his comrade of World War I, the future *General der Jadgflieger*, *Major* Robert *Ritter* von Greim.

## Heinkel's competitor

Prior to the definitive choice of the Bf 109 by the *Reichsluftfahrtministerium* in 1936 to fulfil the single-seat fighter monoplane requirement, the contest had become the subject of discord within both governmental and industrial circles. Each principal contender – the Bf 109, with its light, relatively simple structure, delicate if angular lines and apparent fragility, and Heinkel's He 112, characterized by curvaceous solidity and robust but complex and heavy structure – had its adherents; both factions were vocal, and dissension was in no way mitigated by the intense personal dislike that existed between (now) Dr.-Ing. Willy Messerschmitt and Dr.-Ing. Ernst Heinkel.

The selection of the Bf 109 became the subject of much adverse criticism, usually from those not fully conversant with all the factors governing the selection. Subtle propaganda was directed against the Messerschmitt-designed fighter, but time was to prove this to result from personal prejudices and jealousies, and was also to establish the wisdom of the RLM choice. The Bf 109 possessed the hallmark of the thoroughbred, and was to progress from prototype to initial service model fundamentally unchanged. In marked contrast, its principal competitor, the He 112, was to suffer seemingly interminable experimentation and change. Indeed, other than a superficial relationship in overall configuration, the fighter that was eventually to emerge in production form as the He 112 was to bear no resemblance to the prototype initially flown under this designation.

The demise of the lightly loaded and highly manoeuvrable biplane was accepted as imminent but, nevertheless, there was understandable prejudice against the monoplane in the *Jagdstaffeln*. The numerous traditionalists in the ranks of the fighter pilots vigorously lauded the biplane's manoeuvrability; there were very few visionaries to decry the narrowing performance gap between the biplane fighter and its natural prey, the bomber. The Heinkel team of Walter and Siegfried Günter was strongly influenced by the opinions of the conventionalists in the *Luftwaffenführungsstab*; Willy Messerschmitt and his Chief Designer, Robert Lusser, on the other hand, made no concessions. Thus, the Günter brothers' concept for the *Luftwaffe's* second-generation fighter was inevitably less advanced than that of their contemporaries working at Augsburg.

Both low-wing cantilever monoplanes with retractable undercarriages, designed around the new Jumo 210 engine and making provision for interchangeability between this power plant and the DB 600, the fighters differed in virtually every other respect. In an attempt to provide a wing loading acceptable to former biplane pilots, the Heinkel fighter featured an inordinately large, broad-chord, semi-elliptical wing spanning 41 ft. 4 in. (12,60 m) and possessing a gross area of 249·72 sq. ft. (23,2 m²). The appreciably lighter and smaller Messerschmitt design had angular, almost equi-tapered wing surfaces grossing only 174 sq. ft. (16,17 m²), and thus, although nearly 18 per cent heavier than its rival, the He 112's 30 per cent greater wing area offered a loading of some 3·7 lb./sq. ft. (18,08 kg/m²) less than that of the Bf 109 prototype. However, to improve aileron control near the stall, the Bf 109 had automatic leading-edge slots, and whereas the He 112 had

orthodox plain flaps, those of the Messerschmitt fighter were slotted.

Striving for minimum drag, Messerschmitt and Rethel had given their fighter the slimmest possible fuselage, enclosing the pilot's cockpit with a hinged canopy. The narrow, cramped cockpit and the limited headroom resulting from the canopy, the poor forward view for taxying resulting from the fighter's steep ground attitude, and the fact that the canopy, hinging along the starboard side, could not be opened to obtain a view forward or aft along the fuselage sides, were hardly features that appealed to the traditionalists. The He 112, on the other hand, with its deeper fuselage permitting the pilot to be seated in a more generously proportioned cockpit higher over the wing, coupled with the anhedral angle of the inboard wing portion and an open cockpit, offered a substantially better view on the ground. Furthermore, its sturdy mainwheel legs provided a much wider track than the rather more elegant cantilever legs attached to the fuselage of the Bf 109, and therefore superior ground stability, but at 5,093 lb. (2 310 kg), the loaded weight of the He 112 was substantially greater, and its heavier structure was more complex to build.

The Ernst Heinkel Flugzeugwerke had, like the Bayerische Flugzeugwerke, received a contract for three prototypes of its fighter monoplane, and as the Jumo 210, which had successfully completed bench-running and had been placed in production at Dessau, was not immediately available for installation, the *Technische Amt* of the RLM had instructed Heinkel, as it did Messerschmitt, to install the Rolls-Royce Kestrel V in the first prototype. This, the He 112 V1 (D-IADO *Werk-Nr.* 1290), was completed in the summer of 1935. In a generally similar performance category to that of the Jumo 210, and weighing much the same, the Kestrel V drove a two-bladed fixed-pitch wooden airscrew.

The first prototype was joined in November 1935 by the He 112 V2 (D-IHGE *Werk-Nr.* 1291) and, five weeks later, by the He 112 V3 (D-IDMO *Werk-Nr.* 1292), both powered by the Jumo 210C rated at 640 h.p. at 2,700 r.p.m. for take-off and having a maximum continuous rating of 540 h.p. at 8,860 ft. (2 700 m).

At this stage there was little doubt as to which of the two fighter designs was favoured. Indeed, the rather more sophisticated Bf 109 was considered the outsider in the contest. The factory test programme was undertaken initially by *Flugkapitän* Gerhard Nitschke, who had succeeded *Flugkapitän* Werner Junck as Heinkel's Chief Test Pilot shortly before testing of the He 112 began, and several *Luftwaffe* and RLM pilots visited

*The He 112 V2 D-IHGE with clipped wings and Jumo engine which crashed during spinning trials*

*The He 112 V3 D-IDMO was flight tested in the spring of 1936 with a smaller, redesigned wing, and a single-piece sliding cockpit canopy*

Travemünde to fly the new fighter, including Dipl.-Ing. Francke. It was soon realized by the Günter brothers, however, that wing area was over generous, one of the most serious shortcomings of the fighter being a poor rate of roll, and the aircraft having somewhat sluggish characteristics in most aerobatic manoeuvres. It was also now appreciated that the thick, high-lift wing section offered serious disadvantages, and estimated that its profile reduced attainable maximum speed by 15–18 m.p.h. (24–29 km/h). As drag was undoubtedly destined to rise with the introduction of gun troughs, etc., and the problem of an already overweight structure would be compounded by the addition of service equipment, work was initiated on the design of a new wing of reduced thickness/chord ratio. The near-straight leading edge gave place to an ellipse which it was anticipated would reduce drag and improve handling qualities.

As an interim measure, the tips of the wings of the He 112 V2 and V3 were clipped to reduce overall span by some 40 in. (103 cm), and three-blade constant-speed airscrews were fitted. The new wing was fitted to the He 112 V3 for flight testing in the spring of 1936, overall span and gross area being reduced to 37 ft. 8¾ in. (11,5 m) and 232·5 sq. ft. (21,6 m²). At the same time as the new wing was fitted, the V3 received a single-piece sliding cockpit canopy, a modified rudder, a pair of 7,9-mm MG 17 machine guns mounted in the forward fuselage and firing through troughs on each side of the engine, a modified exhaust system in which the individual ejector stubs gave place to a single collector tube on each side, and a redesigned radiator bath.

Meanwhile, initial evaluation of the competing fighters had not resulted in the anticipated choice of the He 112 over the other contenders as the new single-seat fighter of the *Luftwaffe*, but in the placing of an order with both Heinkel and the Bayerische Flugzeugwerke for a pre-production series of 10 fighters for further development purposes, the definitive selection of a fighter for quantity production being deferred pending the outcome of further trials at Travemünde in the autumn of 1936. The fourth prototype, the He 112 V4 (D-IZMY), which was, in fact, the first pre-production airframe, was the first aircraft to fly with the new wing from the outset, and was considered as the first A-series prototype, this participating in the Travemünde trials. Before these trials began, however, *Flugkapitän* Nitschke had been forced to bale out of the He 112 V2 during spinning tests.

The He 112 V4 was powered by a Jumo 210Da engine with two-speed supercharger and offering 720 h.p. for take-off and

670 h.p. for five minutes at 12,795 ft. (3 900 m), a two-bladed controllable-pitch airscrew being fitted. Carrying a similar twin-gun arrangement to that of the V3, and weighing 3,472 lb. (1 575 kg) empty and 4,806 lb. (2 180 kg) and 4,916 lb. (2 230 kg) in normal and maximum loaded condition, the V4 also featured a markedly smaller tailplane, but although both handling characteristics and performance were now decidedly improved, the Heinkel fighter had not, owing to the necessary redesign of its wing and tail surfaces, attained a comparable stage in development to that of the Bf 109 when it arrived at Travemünde in the autumn of 1936 for the definitive evaluation trials. It was not possible, therefore, for *Flugkapitän* Nitschke to demonstrate the He 112 V4 in full accordance with the rules laid down by the Acceptance Commission, a fact which gave the Messerschmitt-designed fighter a distinct advantage.

Another factor favouring the Bf 109 was the previously-mentioned change of attitude within the *Luftwaffenführungsstab* and the *Technischen Amt* towards the fighter monoplane that had come about during the period of time that had elapsed between the début of the first prototypes of the He 112 and Bf 109 and the final Travemünde trials. At the outset, it had been widely believed that the Bf 109 had little to commend it, apart from a simple and economic structure offering ease of manufacture. In the spring of 1936, when Reginald J. Mitchell's ideas on interceptor fighter design finally crystallized in the shape of the Spitfire, it was seen that these closely paralleled those of Messerschmitt and Lusser, knowledge leading to increasing importance being attached to ultimate speed. There could be no doubt that, in this respect, the Bf 109 had the edge over the He 112. Furthermore, many of the initial doubts concerning the handling characteristics and the value of the "new fangled" wing leading-edge slots had been dispelled by such highly-experienced fighter pilots as Robert *Ritter* von Greim, Ernst Udet, and Dipl.-Ing. Francke.

Thus, by the time the final demonstrations took place, the Messerschmitt and Heinkel fighters had changed places as favourite for production orders. It was conceded that general stability in flight was comparable for both fighters, that there was little to choose between them in climb rate, and that the He 112 was only marginally slower than its competitor. The general concensus of opinion was that the Heinkel fighter offered better ground handling characteristics, although this was contested by Messerschmitt, who pointed out that it was preferable to transfer landing shocks direct to the static centre of the aircraft rather than via the wings to the fuselage.

In every other respect, the Bf 109 proved itself markedly superior to the He 112. It was easier to handle in aerobatics; its roll rate was higher as the elliptical wings of the Heinkel fighter had a greater roll-damping moment than the tapered trapezoid wings of the Bf 109; the automatic wing leading-edge slots resulted in the Bf 109 reacting more satisfactorily as a result of a sudden stall and holding tighter turns than could the He 112, and the Bf 109 could out-dive the Heinkel with ease.

Perhaps most impressive were the spinning characteristics of the Bf 109, which were demonstrated at Travemünde by Dr.-Ing. Hermann Wurster, who had succeeded "Bubi" Knoetzsch as Messerschmitt's Chief Test Pilot. Considerable importance was attached to the spinning behaviour of a fighter, and the test programme at Travemünde called for the fighter to be spun 10 times to port and 10 times to starboard. During one demonstration with the c.g. in the rearmost position, Wurster spun the tail-heavy fighter 17 times to port and 21 times to starboard without a hint of a flat spin. He then performed a terminal velocity dive from 24,600 ft. (7 500 m), pulled out safely just above the ground, and even demonstrated a *Männchen*, or "Tailstand", which was demanded by Dr. Jodl-bauer, one of the principal members of the Acceptance Commission, and the choice between the fighters was no longer in any doubt.

Despite the decision in favour of the Bf 109, Ernst Heinkel believed that the possibility of an order from the *Luftwaffe* for his fighter still existed, and persisted with its development, and in December 1936, the He 112 V4 was transported to Spain for operational evaluation by the *Legion Condor*. After its return to Germany it was demonstrated at Zürich-Dübendorf during the international flying meeting in July 1937, and it was exhibited at the aviation exhibition held in Milan in that year. It was also demonstrated to the Finnish Air Force at Helsinki, but by that time, development of the A-series had given place to the He 112B, Dipl.-Ing. Heinrich Hertel, Heinkel's Technical Director and Chief of Development, having instituted a complete redesign of the fighter in the hope that the Ernst Heinkel A.G. could still fulfil at least a part of the German air arm's demand for warplanes in this category.

Meanwhile, three further A-series airframes had been completed, the He 112 V5 essentially similar to the V4, the He 112 V6 (D-ISJY) which embodied further redesign of the radiator bath and taller vertical tail surfaces, and the He 112 V8 (D-IRXO) which was delivered as a test-bed for Daimler-Benz engines, being fitted with a DB 600Aa rated at 1,000 h.p. at 2,350 r.p.m. for take-off and 910 h.p. at 13,120 ft. (4 000 m).

The He 112 V8 actually preceded the He 112 V7 (D-IKIK *Werk-Nr*. 1935) which was both the first B-series airframe and a DB 600 test-bed. It had become patently obvious to Dipl.-Ing. Hertel that the He 112 was underpowered if, in its existing form, it was to compete successfully with the Bf 109. Messerschmitt's lightweight structural design concepts had proved eminently successful, and thanks to its simple construction, development of the Bf 109 had progressed far more rapidly than that of the He 112.

Taking a leaf from Messerschmitt's book, Hertel stripped the He 112 fuselage of its heavy framing and, with weight-consciousness paramount, completely redesigned the structure. At the same time, considerable effort was expended in improving aerodynamic cleanliness. The fineness ratio of the fuselage was slightly increased, overall length being stretched to 30 ft. 6 in. (9,30 m) from 29 ft. 2⅓ in. (8,90 m), and both the wing planform and structure were changed, the highly efficient, truly elliptical planform being of 182·986 sq. ft. (17,0 m²) area, a reduction of some 20 per cent by comparison with the A-series wing, and the heavy two-spar structure giving place to a single main spar with two auxiliary spars.

The empty weight of the He 112 V9 (D-IGSI), which was the first true prototype of the He 112B, was 3,571 lb. (1 620 kg), and at a loaded weight of 4,960 lb. (2 250 kg), wing loading was 27·1 lb./sq. ft. (132,3 kg/m²), which was closely comparable with contemporary versions of the Bf 109. Wing span was only 29 ft. 10¼ in. (9,10 m), which was less than the overall length of the fuselage, and with an immense root chord endowing the wing with an aspect ratio of only 4·86 to 1, the Heinkel fighter now possessed a truly unique planform. The He 112 V9 flew in July 1937 powered by a Jumo 210Ea engine with two-speed supercharger and driving a two-blade constant-speed airscrew, power ratings being similar to those of the Jumo 210Da.

*(Above right and below) The He 112 V4 on display at Zürich-Dübendorf in July 1937. This aircraft had previously undergone operational evaluation in Spain with the Legion Condor*

*The He 112 V8 D-IRXO, an A-series airframe used primarily as a Daimler-Benz test bed*

For its relatively modest power, the He 112 V9's performance was very respectable, comparing favourably with that of the early production Hurricane I, which, although larger and heavier, could call on 1,030 h.p. from its Merlin II engine. The wing had a flush-riveted stressed skin, and the similarly-covered fuselage was an oval-section monocoque built up on Z-section frames with "top-hat" stringers. The cockpit was enclosed by an aft-sliding glazed canopy which offered outstanding all-round vision, and armament comprised two wing-mounted 20-mm MG FF (Oerlikon) cannon and a pair of fuselage-mounted 7,9-mm MG 17 machine guns.

By the time the He 112 V9 commenced its flight test programme, the Bf 109B had already made its service début. Ernst Udet, newly promoted to the rank of *Generalmajor*, and Chief of the *Technischen Amt* for nearly a year, visited Marienehe at Heinkel's request to witness a demonstration of the new prototype, but while he admitted that the fighter was better in some respects than the Bf 109, he saw little point in occupying production space with two aircraft types of virtually identical performance intended to fulfil one task. The discussion terminated with Udet's suggestion that, if Heinkel was so anxious to continue development of the He 112, he should solicit export orders wherever he could, for no production order would be forthcoming from the *Luftwaffe*. Messerschmitt's fighter had been selected as standard equipment and the decision was irrevocable.

## The back-up fighters

At an early stage in the fighter programme it had become obvious that the final choice lay between the contenders from Heinkel and the Bayerische Flugzeugwerke; that the progeny of the other companies awarded development contracts, the Arado Flugzeugwerke and the Focke-Wulf Flugzeugbau, were

to be considered as back-up programmes to safeguard against failure of both favourites.

The Arado team, led by Dipl.-Ing. Walter Blume (Ing. Walter Rethel, the designer of previous Arado fighters, having joined Messerschmitt and the Bayerische Flugzeugwerke), possessed no experience in all-metal aircraft construction, nor in the design of retractable undercarriages. In the belief that the increased drag of fixed gear would be compensated for by the reduction in weight resulting from the elimination of retraction mechanism and the cut-outs in the wing structure for wheel wells, Walter Blume elected to employ a cantilever low-wing configuration, with close-cowled fixed main undercarriage members, the cantilever legs being kept to minimum length by the adoption of an inverted-gull wing form. In the event, a miscalculation was to result in the airframe weighing in at a substantially higher weight than had been anticipated, this increased weight more than absorbing the saving effected by the use of a fixed undercarriage.

Designated Ar 80, the fighter employed a single box-spar type wing with light alloy covering for the upper surfaces and fabric covering for the undersurfaces. As little experience existed with modern stressed-skin monocoque structures, the Ar 80 employed a welded steel-tube fuselage covered forward by detachable light metal panels and aft by lateral light metal strips riveted to the formers. The first prototype, the Ar 80 V1, was fitted with a Rolls-Royce Kestrel VI rated at 525 h.p. for take-off and 640 h.p. at 14,000 ft. (4 267 m), and commenced its flight test programme in the early spring of 1935. Unfortunately, during one of the first test flights the pilot lost control at low altitude, the aircraft crashing and being written off.

A second prototype, the Ar 80 V2 (D-ILOH), was at this time awaiting delivery of a Jumo 210 engine, but the loss of the first prototype necessitated the hurried completion of the Ar 80 V2 with a Kestrel V which, rated at 695 h.p. for take-off, drove a two-bladed fixed-pitch wooden airscrew. Trials with the Kestrel-engined Ar 80 V2 were disappointing. Structural weight was excessive, empty weight at 3,593 lb. (1 630 kg) being 16 per cent greater than anticipated, and at the normal loaded weight of 4,630 lb. (2 100 kg) the fighter was underpowered. Furthermore, drag was appreciably higher than had been calculated, with the result that maximum speed was barely 255 m.p.h. (410 km/h) at 13,120 ft. (4 000 m).

Early in 1936, the Ar 80 V2 was re-engined with a Junkers

*The He 112 V9 D-IGSI was the first true prototype of the B-series fighter. Its performance compared closely with that of the Bf 109B but the Messerschmitt fighter had already made its service début by the time the He 112 V9 commenced its flight test programme*

*The Ar 80 V2, seen in its original Kestrel-engined form, proved incapable of offering serious competition to either Bf 109 or He 112, being substantially overweight and suffering excessive drag*

Jumo 210C, but this resulted in only a marginal improvement in altitude performance, low-altitude performance and initial climb proving inferior. Arado estimated that the provision of a constant-speed airscrew in place of the fixed-pitch unit would boost maximum speed to 264 m.p.h. (425 km/h) at 13,120 ft. (4 000 m), but the Ar 80 V2 was evaluated both at the *Erprobungsstelle* Travemünde and, subsequently, at the *Erprobungsstelle* Rechlin, and as a result of these trials Arado was informed that no good purpose could be served by the further development of the design. By this time, the construction of a third prototype, the Ar 80 V3 (D-IPBN) had been completed. This, in an effort to reduce structural weight, abandoned the inverted gull wing configuration in favour of a simpler wing with constant dihedral from root to tip. The Ar 80 V3 was powered by the Jumo 210C, and was the first prototype to be equipped with a constant-speed airscrew, but the full performance envelope of the aircraft remained to be explored when further work on the Arado fighter was abandoned.

While few members of the *Luftwaffenführungsstab* suffered any serious doubt that the fighter of the future would be a low-wing cantilever monoplane, elementary caution dictated careful evaluation of possible alternative configurations. Thus, in view of the exceptional promise being shown by Focke-Wulf's Fw 56 *Stösser* auxiliary fighter and advanced training parasol monoplane, the *Technische Amt* had suggested to the company's Technical Director, Dipl.-Ing. Kurt Tank, that the Focke-Wulf submission to meet the new fighter specification should utilize a similar wing arrangement; a scaled-up, more powerful *Stösser*, embodying state-of-the-art aerodynamic and structural refinements. Tank was made fully aware that all competing projects would be low-wing cantilever monoplanes, but the suggestion of the *C-Amt* presented him with the challenge of evolving a parasol monoplane which, by means of careful aerodynamic design, could offer a performance comparable with those of its low wing competitors.

The parasol monoplane with a retractable undercarriage was, in so far as the history of military aircraft design was concerned, to be included among the true *rarae aves*. Indeed, the number of warplanes of this configuration were to be counted upon the fingers of one hand, and but two of these had been single-seat fighters. By the late 'thirties, any configuration other than those of low- or mid-wing cantilever monoplane was to be considered *passé* for the land-based single-seat fighter, but early in 1934, when the *Luftwaffenführungsstab* finalized its single-seat all-metal fighter monoplane requirement, the parasol arrangement still possessed its adherents who believed the markedly superior field of vision it afforded the pilot worth the

sacrifice of the few knots shaved from the fighter's performance by the drag of the necessary bracing struts.

Tank allocated primary design responsibility for the Fw 159 to *Oberingenieur* R. Blaser, and from the outset accent was placed on aerodynamic cleanliness in an attempt to compensate for the higher drag inherent in the specified configuration. In so far as the basic parasol fighter monoplane configuration was concerned, Blaser and his team found no shortage of design precedents, but only *two* such fighters embodying a *retractable* undercarriage were known to have flown, the Dayton-Wright XPS-1 and the shipboard Curtiss XF13C-1, the latter having been tested initially as a *biplane*.

*Ernst Heinkel (left) and Udet who was largely responsible for the thwarting of the former's ambition to supply the Luftwaffe's next fighter*

Like its competitors, the Fw 159 was designed to take either the Jumo 210 or DB 600 12-cylinder inverted-Vee liquid-cooled engine, which was a prerequisite of the specification, and utilized an oval-section light metal monocoque fuselage, and a metal-skinned parallel-chord wing comprising a main box-spar and an auxiliary spar carrying the ailerons and flaps occupying the entire trailing edge apart from the cut-out above the fuselage. Of modified NACA section, the relatively low thickness/chord ratio wing was carried above the fuselage by splayed N-struts, single inclined aerofoil-section struts on each side bracing the main spar to the lower fuselage longerons.

The pilot was seated beneath an aft-sliding hood, and all fuel was housed by a single tank forward and below the cockpit, a releasable panel enabling the tank to be jettisoned in an emergency. Particularly careful attention was given to ease of maintenance, almost the entire forward fuselage being covered

*(Above) The Fw 159 V1 which suffered an undercarriage failure resulting in its destruction at the end of its first flight. Although embodying several novel features, the Fw 159 could not seriously compete with the low-wing monoplanes against which it was pitted. (Below) The design of the Fw 159 placed emphasis on ease of maintenance, and featured numerous hinged access panels seen open on the Fw 159 V3*

mechanism of this was, it was to prove the "Achilles Heel" of the Focke-Wulf fighter. The main legs were double-jointed, providing a form of levered suspension under compression, and each unit had an auxiliary oleo strut which, during the retraction process, compressed the lower main leg joint, the upper joint breaking and the entire unit being raised vertically through fairing doors barely larger than the wheel diameter. Although complex, the system was a model of ingenuity, and on test rigs the mechanism functioned flawlessly. The first of the three prototypes, the Fw 159 V1, completed in the spring of 1935, was mounted on blocks, and its undercarriage raised and lowered repeatedly. The legs retracted and extended with absolute precision, and after the successful completion of taxying trials on the airfield at Bremen, preparations were made for initial flight trials.

The Fw 159 V1 was fitted with a Jumo 210A engine rated at 680 h.p. at 2,700 r.p.m. for take-off and driving a Schwarz fixed-pitch three-bladed wooden airscrew. The aircraft took-off on its first flight with *Flugkapitän* Wolfgang Stein at the controls. The undercarriage retracted perfectly, and Stein completed initial handling tests, made two moderately high-speed runs across the airfield, and entered the landing pattern. To the onlookers it appeared that the undercarriage had extended correctly, but Stein suddenly opened the throttle, raised the flaps and flew across the field with the undercarriage down. It was then seen that the main leg joints had only partly extended, Stein having been warned of the predicament by the undercarriage lights indicating that the legs had failed to lock.

He circled the field time and time again, constantly operating the undercarriage mechanism in a fruitless attempt to lock the legs in position. The first prototype had not been fitted with fuel tank jettisoning equipment, and there was no alternative but to circuit the field until the fuel was exhausted and then risk a landing. Various suggestions were daubed in whitewash on the concrete hard-standing, the Fw 159 V1 having no R/T equipment, including the proposal that Stein should attempt a slow loop and work the hand pump during the final stage of the loop in the hope of utilizing centrifugal force to lock the legs. Nothing proved of avail.

by hinged panels providing ready access to power plant, armament and ancillary equipment.

Perhaps the most novel feature of the Fw 159 was its retractable undercarriage, but highly ingenious though the

Stein had taken off with full fuel, this being sufficient for two hours' flying and less than 30 minutes' flight testing had been undertaken when the undercarriage fault had been discovered. He was therefore forced to circuit the field for some 90 minutes before attempting to land. He finally approached the field in a long glide with the undercarriage partly extended. The legs immediately snapped off on making contact with the ground and the aircraft somersaulted twice before coming to rest on its back. The Fw 159 V1 was a write-off but, miraculously, Stein suffered no more than superficial bruising.

It was subsequently ascertained that the engineers responsible for the design of the undercarriage had miscalculated its drag when extending, and the oleo-hydraulic mechanism possessed insufficient power to counter the drag and lock the legs in position. Thus, the second prototype, the Fw 159 V2 (D-INGA), completed shortly after the abortive first test flight of the initial prototype, was fitted with substantially reinforced oleo-hydraulic undercarriage actuating mechanism. In other respects, apart from a lengthened tailwheel leg and uncowled tailwheel, it was identical to its predecessor, and flight testing began in earnest. The handling characteristics of the Fw 159 proved not dissimilar to those of the Fw 56 *Stösser*, but stalling speed was on the high side, climb rate was lower than had been calculated, and the turning circle was considered to be poor.

The third prototype, the Fw 159 V3 (D-IUPY), differed from the V1 and V2 in having a Jumo 210B engine which, rated at 600 h.p. for take-off, afforded 640 h.p. for five minutes at 8,860 ft. (2 700 m). The three-blader was replaced by a two-bladed airscrew, also of wooden fixed-pitch Schwarz type, the cockpit canopy was revised, a three-panel glazed hood being introduced and the light metal fairing aft of the cockpit, previously attached to the hood, was fixed, and armament was installed. This comprised two 7,9-mm MG 17 machine guns with 500 r.p.g., these being installed in the upper decking on the forward fuselage and synchronized to fire through the airscrew disc. Provision was made for mounting a 20-mm MG FF (Oerlikon) cannon to fire through the airscrew hub, although this was never installed as the MG FF proved unsuitable for engine mounting.

During the course of 1936, the Fw 159 V2 was fitted with the twin-MG 17 armament, the fairing aft of the cockpit was fixed, and the two-panel glazed hood arranged to slide over the fairing, the three-bladed fixed-pitch wooden airscrew was replaced by a Junkers-Hamilton two-bladed variable-pitch metal airscrew, and the Jumo 210Da engine with two-speed supercharger was installed. The Fw 159 V3 was also fitted with a two-blade variable-pitch metal airscrew and, eventually, a fuel-injection Jumo 210G engine rated at 700 h.p. for take-off and 730 h.p. at 3,280 ft. (1 000 m), but by this time (late summer of 1937) the *Reichsluftfahrtministerium* had long since selected the Bf 109 for the re-equipment of the *Jadgflieger*. Both the Fw 159 V2 and V3 had been evaluated at the Travemünde *Erprobungsstelle* during the spring and early summer of 1936, but the preference of the *Luftwaffenführungsstab* for the low-wing cantilever monoplane evinced from the outset of the fighter programme had already been strengthened as a result of the initial testing of the He 112 and Bf 109, coupled with developments abroad.

The Focke-Wulf fighter was not given really serious consideration as a contestant, being viewed by the Travemünde *Erprobungsstelle* staff as some sort of half-way house between the fighter biplane whose demise was now accepted as imminent and the aerodynamically efficient low-wing fighter monoplane of the future; lacking the manoeuvrability of the former and the performance of the latter. The Fw 159 had, in fact, little to commend it. In the form tested at Travemünde, it was barely lighter than the similarly-powered He 112 yet it possessed a substantially higher wing loading, which, at 22·83 lb./sq. ft. (111,46 kg/m²), was only marginally lower than that of the 600 lb. (272 kg) lighter Jumo 210-engined Bf 109.

Despite the effort expended by *Oberingenieur* Blaser's team to reduce aerodynamic drag, the Focke-Wulf fighter could not seriously compete with its Heinkel and Bayerische Flugzeugwerke competitors in most aspects of performance, and it was improbable that the ingenuity displayed in the complex undercarriage design would have found an appreciative audience among field maintenance personnel. Although the Fw 159 was deleted from the fighter contest, flight testing and development continued into 1938, and with the fuel-injection Jumo 210G engine, the Fw 159 V3 clocked a maximum speed of 252 m.p.h. (405 km/h) at 14,765 ft. (4 500 m).

*The last prototype of the Focke-Wulf contender for Luftwaffe orders, the Fw 159 V3 D-IUPY, was eventually fitted with a fuel injection Jumo 210G engine and a two-blade variable-pitch metal airscrew, and flight testing and development continued into 1938 despite the choice of the Bf 109 as standard fighter equipment*

# The Eaglet grows talons

Shortly after the decision had been taken to produce the Bf 109 for the *Jagdflieger*, a large aviation display was held at Rechlin in the presence of (then) *General der Infanterie* Göring, *Reichskriegsminister* von Blomberg, and the entire *Ingenieurkorps* of the RLM, the display culminating in a mock aerial battle in which a raiding force of bombers was to be intercepted by four He 51s, these in turn being attacked by *Oberst* Udet flying the Bf 109 V3. Udet duly took off, attacked and "shot down" each of the He 51s, and then, for good measure, intercepted and "destroyed" the entire formation of bombers.

*The Bf 109 V3 was the first prototype with a cropped spinner and provision for an engine-mounted cannon*

Despite such demonstrations, there was still much criticism of the choice of the Bf 109 in favour of the He 112, and the undercarriage of the Messerschmitt fighter suffered particularly from disparaging comment, the wider track undercarriage of the competitive Heinkel fighter being lauded. The track of the Bf 109's undercarriage was, in fact, no less than that of the He 51 with which the *Jagdstaffeln* were equipped. Owing to this narrow wheel track, in the event of a landing with only one leg extended, the Messerschmitt fighter could be held level for longer after touching down than could its Heinkel contemporary with its much wider wheel track, dropping a wing at an appreciably lower speed, and thus running less risk of a ground loop or nosing over. An incidental advantage offered by the undercarriage of the Bf 109 was that, being attached directly to the fuselage, it enabled a wing to be changed without any special jacks or supports.

The pre-production model was designated Bf 109B-0, although, in fact, all 10 pre-series aircraft were allocated *Versuchs* numbers. Thus, the Bf 109B-01 (*Werk-Nr.* 878 D-IALY) became the Bf 109 V4, the Bf 109B-02 (*Werk-Nr.* 879 D-IIGO) became the Bf 109 V5, the Bf 109B-03 (*Werk-Nr.* 880 D-IHHB) became the Bf 109 V6 *et seq*. The Bf 109 V4, alias Bf 109B-01, flown for the first time in November 1936, differed from its immediate predecessors in having a Jumo 210B engine with increased reduction ratio and offering 640 h.p. at 2,700 r.p.m. for five minutes and a maximum continuous output of 540 h.p. at 2,600 r.p.m. Provision was made for an armament of two MG 17 machine guns. This was followed by the similarly-powered V5 (D-IIGO) and V6 (D-IHHB) in December, these replacing the fixed-pitch Schwarz airscrew with one of variable-pitch VDM type. Another change was the provision of three cooling slots in the engine cowling in place of the single intake immediately aft of the spinner, and like the V4, these aircraft featured a revised production-type windscreen and some revision of the wing structure in the vicinity of the wheel wells permitting the discarding of the external stiffening plates. Armament comprised three MG 17 machine guns and the cropped spinner first introduced on the V3 was adopted.

Considerable impetus was now placed behind both production and improvement of the Bf 109 fighter. Tooling for the initial production model, the Bf 109B or *Bertha*, had commenced at Augsburg–Haunstetten in the late autumn of 1936, with the first airframes following closely on those of the 10 pre-production machines assigned to the development programme. The expansion of the Bayerische Flugzeugwerke facilities had begun in 1935, the company having received in that year contracts for the licence manufacture of 90 Arado Ar 66s, 115 Gotha Go 145s, 70 Heinkel He 45s, and 35 He 50s, as well as for 32 Bf 108Bs.

A new assembly hangar had been erected a little more than a mile from the Augsburg–Haunstetten airfield, but the scale of production envisaged by mid-1936 dictated an appreciably greater increase in plant capacity than proved acceptable to the Municipality of Augsburg. Thus, on July 24, 1936, a new company was formed as the Messerschmitt G.m.b.H., and this acquired land at Regensburg for the erection of a new assembly plant. The speed with which the factory was built and tooled may be gauged from the fact that within 16 months production of the Bf 108B had been transferred in its entirety to Regensburg. Simultaneously, the experimental shops and the drawing and administrative offices at Augsburg were greatly expanded.

The first Bf 109B left the Augsburg–Haunstetten assembly line in February 1937, by which time the premier *Luftwaffe* fighter *Geschwader*, JG 132 "*Richthofen*", had been designated the first unit to receive the new combat aircraft, and had been assigned the task of working up the Bf 109 to combat status. It was intended that II *Gruppe* at Jüterbog-Damm would be the first to convert, followed closely by I Gruppe at Döberitz. However, the re-equipment of at least part of *Jagdgruppe* 88 in Spain took precedence owing to the mastery over the unit's He 51s being displayed by the Soviet I-15 and I-16. Thus, after a hurried conversion course, II/JG 132 personnel were posted to Spain to where 16 Bf 109Bs were delivered for assembly at Tablada aerodrome, Seville, in March 1937.

The oval-section light metal monocoque fuselage of the Bf 109B was manufactured in two halves and joined longitud-

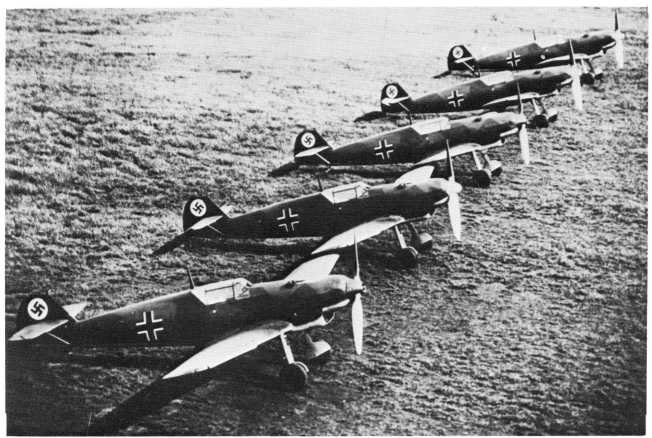

*(Above and below right) Initial production batches of Bf 109B fighters fitted with the interim two-bladed wooden Schwarz fixed-pitch airscrew photographed at Augsburg-Haunstetten awaiting Luftwaffe acceptance during the spring of 1937. The first home-based unit to equip with this fighter was JG 132 "Richthofen"*

inally top and bottom, each half being constructed of longitudinal stringers and vertical panels, the latter having flanged edges to form Z-frames which were pierced for the stringers. The single-spar wing was attached to the fuselage at three points, two on spar flanges and one at the leading edge, and the entire trailing edges were hinged, slotted ailerons outboard and slotted flaps inboard, automatic slots being carried by the outboard leading edges. The tailplane was braced to the fuselage by a single strut on each side, and the main undercarriage members were raised outward into the wings by hydraulic jacks. The oil cooler intake was removed from the radiator bath and a separate intake provided beneath the port wing.

Power was provided by a Jumo 210Da engine which, with a two-speed supercharger, 87 octane A2 fuel and driving a two-bladed wooden Schwarz fixed-pitch airscrew, offered 720 h.p. at 2,700 r.p.m. for take-off, maximum continuous sea level outputs being 610 and 545 h.p. at 2,600 and 2,500 r.p.m. respectively. At its rated altitude of 8,860 ft. (2 700 m), the Jumo 210Da offered 640 h.p. for five minutes, and maximum continuous outputs of 575 and 510 h.p. at 2,600 and 2,500 r.p.m.

The fuselage tank of 55 Imp. gal. (250 l) capacity was contoured behind and beneath the pilot's seat, the pilot was provided with a Carl Zeiss *Reflexvisier* C/12C reflector sight, and the armament comprised two 7,9-mm MG 17 machine guns mounted on the engine crankcase with their muzzles protruding into blast troughs in the upper nose decking with 500 r.p.g. Provision was also made for the installation of short-range single-waveband FuG 7 R/T equipment, but this was considered to be a dispensable luxury and was not fitted to the Bf 109Bs despatched to Spain.

*(Above) A Bf 109B photographed during acceptance trials in the early summer of 1937, and (below) Bf 109Bs of II/JG 132, the first Gruppe to convert to the fighter*

## Blooded over Spain

Towards the end of February 1937, with the conclusion of the Battle of Jarama in a somewhat pyrrhic victory for the Republican forces who had thwarted the Nationalist aim of cutting the Madrid–Valencia high road, *Generalmajor* Hugo Sperrle, in overall command of Germany's *Legion Condor* committed to the Spanish Nationalist cause, finally succeeded in convincing Berlin that, however unpalatable, the fact that his Heinkel

*An early Bf 109B with Schwarz fixed-pitch airscrew and uncropped spinner*

He 51 fighter biplanes were manifestly inferior to the Soviet fighters which they were engaging in combat had to be accepted.

Throughout that winter, Sperrle's He 51-equipped *Staffeln* comprising *Jagdgruppe* 88 had been increasingly hard-pressed. The need to afford fighter cover for the strategic attacks by the bomber element of the *Legion* against such targets as the harbours of Cartagena, Alicante and Malaga, the steel plants and munitions factories in the northern provinces, and the armament centre at Albacete had stretched the German fighters to their limits. To cover these far-flung operations, the *Staffeln* had been switched from base to base, at times operating from León, Burgos, Vitoria, San Sebastian, Logroño, Saragossa, Teruél, Barahona, Avila, Escalona del Prado and Cordoba, these constant moves, themselves, imposing penalties on pilots and groundcrew alike, and as enemy fighter opposition escalated, the situation facing the German fighter force had assumed ever more serious proportions.

It had become imperative that the *Legion* receive an infusion of new Messerschmitt Bf 109B fighters, which had only that month begun to leave the Augsburg–Haunstetten assembly line, if the balance in the air war over Spain was to be redressed. As a result of Sperrle's report, the situation was viewed with such seriousness in Berlin, that, ignoring the protests of the *Luftwaffenführungsstab*, precedence in re-equipment with the new fighter was assigned to a *Staffel* of *Jagdgruppe* 88 and fighters of the initial production batch were hastily crated and shipped to Spain.

The Bf 109 fighter was, in fact, no stranger to Spanish skies. A combination of misgivings concerning the potency of the He 51 and a desire to ascertain the capabilities of the radical new warplane under operational conditions had prompted the *Reichsluftfahrtministerium* to send three prototypes of the fighter, the V3, the V4 and the V5, to Spain, where they had arrived at the beginning of December 1936. The V4 and V5 had been briefly flight tested at Augsburg–Haunstetten before hurried disassembly for shipment to Spain.

On December 9, 1936, *Leutnant* Hannes Trautloft, at that time based with his He 51B *Staffel* at Vitoria, was ordered by the Chief of Staff of the *Legion, Oberstleutnant Freiherr* Wolfram von Richthofen, to proceed immediately to Tablada airfield, Seville, to flight test the Bf 109 V3 which had just been assembled. Trautloft, who was later to command *Jagdgeschwader* 54 *Grünherz* and end W.W. II with the rank of *Oberst* and 57 "kills", including four over Spain, was one of the old hands of the *Legion*. He had arrived in Spain on August 7, together with five other pilots and eight mechanics under the leadership of *Oberleutnant* Eberhard, to test fly and demonstrate the six He 51 fighters which had accompanied them aboard the *Usaramo*, these having been unloaded in Cádiz and transported to Tablada for assembly.

Upon arrival at Tablada airfield, Trautloft was informed that the Bf 109 V3 had suffered major damage during the previous day when an inexperienced pilot, assigned the task of taking the prototype up for its initial test flight after re-assembly, had over-corrected for the strong swing to port during take-off resulting from propeller torque and had ground-looped. The Bf 109 V4 was still being re-assembled and the arrival of the Bf 109 V5 was still awaited. Trautloft finally flew the Bf 109 V4 on December 14, but during the ensuing weeks, the aircraft suffered continuous minor problems, such as faulty undercarriage locking mechanism, a defective water pump, carburettor troubles and engine overheating, and several emergency landings were necessary. Thus, it was not until January 14, 1937, that Trautloft could finally ferry the fighter to the Madrid Front for operational trials. These were desultory and there are no records to indicate that the Bf 109 V4 actually joined combat, and seven weeks after its arrival in Spain, the prototype was returned to Augsburg, together with the Bf 109 V5, the Bf 109 V3 having been returned to Germany for repairs to the damage suffered during its abortive initial take-off from Tablada.

Although it would seem that little knowledge of the characteristics of the new Messerschmitt fighter in combat had been gained from the brief sojourn of the prototypes in Spain, much useful information on operational conditions was undoubtedly gleaned and it was with understandable eagerness that *Jagdgruppe* 88 awaited the arrival of its first Bf 109s. Almost indecent haste was meanwhile being displayed by Berlin in getting the new fighter to Spain and 12 aircraft (plus four spares) to re-equip a complete *Staffel* were shipped to and assembled at Tablada during March. The aircraft that arrived in Spain were among the first off the Augsburg–Haunstetten assembly line, and as the variable-pitch two-bladed metal propeller being manufactured under Hamilton licence and specified for the production standard fighter was unavailable, a Schwarz fixed-pitch wooden propeller had been fitted★ and certain aspects of performance had suffered as a consequence. However, such was the urgency attached to the delivery of the fighters to Spain that this degrading was considered acceptable in the circumstances and the intention was to fit Hamilton propellers in the field immediately such became available.

The 2.*Staffel der Jagdgruppe* 88 was designated the first component unit to convert to the Bf 109B. The *Staffelkapitän*, *Oberleutnant* Lehmann, relinquished the unit to *Oberleutnant* Günther "Franzl" Lützow and its He 51B fighters were handed to the Spanish Nationalist air arm, these, together with the He 51Bs that had previously been operated by 4./J 88, which was

now disbanded, providing the nucleus of the equipment of three newly-formed Spanish squadrons, 1-E-2, 2-E-2 and 3-E-2.

"Franzl" Lützow was a strong personality and a dedicated combat pilot who, after his tour in Spain, during which he was to be credited with five "kills", was to return to Germany as *Ausbildungsleiter* of *Jagdfliegerschule* 1, an appointment in which his Spanish experience in fighter tactics was to prove invaluable. He was to fall foul of Hermann Göring owing to his outspoken views on the needs of the *Jagdflieger*, which the *Reichsmarschall* was to consider tantamount to mutiny, and was to lose his life in an Me 262 near Donauwörth on April 24, 1945, at which time he was credited with 108 "kills", including those gained over Spain. Largely as a result of his efforts, the conversion of 2./J 88 to the Bf 109B was achieved remarkably rapidly.

Despite the appreciably higher performance and very different handling characteristics that the Bf 109B presented pilots versed in the art of flying the unsophisticated He 51 biplane, no very serious accidents occurred during the conversion programme. The pilots expressed some concern initially over the rather alarming tendency of the Messerschmitt to drop the port wing during take-off and just before touch-down, but with

★ Bf 109B fighters fitted with the Schwarz and VDM-Hamilton propellers have been referred to as Bf 109B-1s and B-2s respectively, but there is reason to suppose that these suffix numbers were applied retrospectively, there being no contemporary evidence to substantiate their use at the time.

*(Above right and below) An early production Bf 109B (6-15) of the Legion Condor photographed after being captured intact by Republican forces when, as recounted on page 34, its pilot exhausted his fuel and landed on a road between Azaila and Escatron. It was subsequently thoroughly evaluated clandestinely by a French mission*

*The Bf 109B of Hauptmann Gotthardt Handrick, Gruppen-kommandeur of J 88. Note the five Olympic rings decorating the spinner of this aircraft (6-56)*

experience the 2./J 88 pilots found that judicious use of the rudder almost eliminated this caprice on the part of the fighter. Noticeable aileron shudder occurred when the slots were opened at high speed and the phenomena of the high-speed stall was encountered for the first time by many of the pilots, necessitating practice turns at varying speeds and turn rates to accustom them to the symptoms of an approaching stall. Coarse use of the controls at high speed sometimes produced violent aileron judder and the high axis of the fighter resulted in a tendency to swing pendulum-fashion, a movement having to be countered by application of rudder.

Familiarity with the aircraft and its eccentricities brought confidence in the capabilities of the Bf 109B, however, and the conviction by 2./J 88 pilots that they were now mounted on a fighter that was potentially the master of their Soviet opponents. Although ostensibly operational on its new fighters by late April, 2./J 88 did not join the remaining two He 51-equipped *Staffeln*, 1. and 3./J 88, in the Nationalist offensive against Bilbao in the north, which terminated on June 18 in Bilbao's famous "Iron Ring" being broken and the town falling to the Nationalist forces, but with the transfer of *Jagdgruppe* 88 from Vitoria to Herrera de Pisuerga, a small field some 60 miles (100 km) south of Santander, to cover the further Nationalist advance westwards on Santander and beyond to Gijón, the Bf 109Bs of 2./J 88 joined up with the other component *Staffeln*.

Herrera was most noteworthy for its excessive dust, each and every take-off being visible for miles around owing to the immense clouds of dust that it produced. The Bf 109Bs were painted light RLM grey over all upper surfaces and pale blue over the under surfaces – a finish which, with but one or two individual exceptions, was retained by the Messerschmitts committed to Spain throughout the duration of the conflict – and retained the *Zylinder Hut* (Top Hat) emblem that had earlier

been adopted for the He 51Bs on which the *Staffel* had originally been formed. The outstanding performance of which the Messerschmitt fighter was capable was jocularly attributed to that extra *Zylinder* (cylinder). Very little aerial activity took place during the first few days that the *Jagdgruppe* occupied Herrera and the *Legion* was officially resting prior to a resumption of the Asturian offensive.

The resumption of the Nationalist offensive in the north, however, was pre-empted on July 6 by a Republican offensive west of Madrid aimed at relieving pressure in the north. The Republican forces advanced 11 miles (18 km) southwards, capturing the small town of Brunete and threatening to cut off the entire Nationalist Central Front sector, from Madrid to Toledo. News of the dangerous situation on the Central Front was received late in the evening of July 8 by the *Jagdgruppe* Headquarters at Herrera. *Oberleutnant* Lützow's 2./J 88 personnel, quartered in a train nearby the field, received the alarm at midnight, and the *Staffel* was ordered to transfer to Avila, west of Madrid, where it was to be ready for operations the next morning. "Franzl" Lützow subsequently recalled that an advance element left on the 220-mile (350-km) journey over country roads between Herrera and Avila within little more than half-an-hour, together with the fuel truck; a locomotive was organized at the nearest railway station and the ground-crew, with hurriedly-packed spares, servicing equipment and tents, were steaming such an hour later. At first light, the Bf 109Bs took-off, being at a state of readiness shortly after midday, the fuel truck having been delayed on the journey to Avila.

The situation on the Madrid Front was hourly becoming more dangerous. The entire *Legion Condor* had been recalled southwards, the *Gruppenstab* and He 51Bs of *Oberleutnant* Douglas Pitcairn's 3./J 88 being deployed to Villa del Prados and *Oberleutnant* Harder's 1./J 88 being assigned to Escalona. For many of the less experienced pilots, the long flight to the south was none too easy due to the inaccuracy and extremely small scale of the only maps available. Upon their arrival, 1. and 3./J 88 were immediately committed to the ground support role, attacking troop concentrations and light anti-aircraft batteries with fragmentation bombs, 2./J 88 being intended primarily to escort massed bomber raids. At airfields in the vicinity of Madrid – Camposoto, Campo X, Barájas, Guadalajara, Alcalá, Manzanares, etc. – the Republicans had gathered virtually the entire complement of *Escuadra núm* 11 to provide air support for their offensive. This comprised the I-16-equipped *escuadrillas* of *Grupo núm* 21 and the I-15-equipped *escuadrillas* of *Grupo núm* 26. The orders of the *Escuadra* were to establish air superiority from the outset and retain it throughout the battle.

---

### Bf 109B Specification

**Power Plant:** One Junkers Jumo 210Da 12-cylinder inverted-vee liquid-cooled engine rated at 720 h.p. for take-off, 680 h.p. for five min. at 8,860 ft. (2 700 m), and 610 h.p. maximum continuous.

**Performance:** (At 4,310 lb./1 955 kg) Maximum speed, 255 m.p.h. (410 km/h) at sea level, 260 m.p.h. (418 km/h) at 3,280 ft. (1 000 m), 276 m.p.h. at 8,200 ft. (2 500 m), 289 m.p.h. (465 km/h) at 13,120 ft. (4 000 m); normal cruise at 4,740 lb. (2 150 kg), 217 m.p.h. (350 km/h) at 8,200 ft. (2 500 m); maximum range, 430 mls. (690 km); time to 19,685 ft. (6 000 m), 9·8 min.; service ceiling, 26,900 ft. (8 200 m).

**Weights:** Empty, 3,318 lb. (1 150 kg); maximum loaded, 4,740 lb. (2 150 kg).

**Dimensions:** Span, 32 ft. 4½ in. (9,87 m); length, 28 ft. 0⅔ in. (8,55 m); height, 8 ft. 0½ in. (2,45 m); wing area, 174·053 sq. ft. (16,17 m²).

**Armament:** Two 7,9-mm Rheinmetall MG 17 machine guns with 500 r.p.g.

Heavy fighting raged around the Brunete salient and the Bf 109Bs of 2./J 88 were soon in the thick of the almost continuous mêlée taking place in the skies above. Three or four times each day, the Bf 109Bs had to fly escort missions for the Ju 52/3m bombers and for reconnaissance aircraft, these always being flown at altitudes between 19,500 and 23,000 ft. (6 000 and 7 000 m), and enemy fighters being almost invariably encountered. From the outset, the Bf 109Bs came up against the I-16s of Ivan Lakeev's *escuadrilla* operating from Alcalá and Aleksandr Minaev's *escuadrilla* based at Barájas. These initial encounters did not establish conclusively the superiority of either German or Soviet fighter. The Messerschmitt was marginally the faster of the two aircraft at all altitudes, possessed a superior ceiling and was capable of out-diving its opponent, whereas the I-16 enjoyed a better rate of climb and was appreciably more manoeuvrable, being able to out-turn the Bf 109B with ease. According to Andres Garcia La Calle★, who commanded the first Spanish I-15 *escuadrilla* and was eventually to be credited with 11 confirmed "kills", the I-16 was superior to the Bf 109B in every way up to an altitude of approximately 9,840 ft. (3 000 m), but above that altitude the Soviet fighter had no chance whatsoever against its German counterpart given pilots of comparable capability. A single *Rotte*, or loose pair, of Messerschmitts, he comments, was capable of nullifying the effectiveness of a formation of two or three *escuadrillas* of I-16s simply by being present a thousand metres above the Republican aircraft.

It was Republican practice to patrol in large formations with the novices at the rear, and with the Bf 109s above, the formation leaders did not dare to turn as the formation then lost its cohesion, the novices inevitably straggling and the Bf 109s immediately pouncing on the stragglers in a dive. When this assault on the rear of the formation *was* witnessed by other pilots, there was little that could be done as the Messerschmitts could not be caught owing to their superior dive characteristics. As often as not, however, the I-16 formation would land back

★ La Calle was later to publish his memoirs under the title of *Mitos y Verdades* in Mexico where he died in 1975.

at its base totally unaware that it had sustained losses. The answer was to lure the Bf 109s down to a level at which they could be mastered by the I-16s, but this was not easily accomplished and thus the influence of the Messerschmitt fighter on the air war was to be out of all proportion to the number of German aircraft of this type committed. Such use of the German fighters was, of course, subsequent to the July fighting over the Brunete area in which they were blooded.

The Republicans claimed the destruction of a Messerschmitt for the first time on July 8, alleging that the *Legion* fighter had been brought down after a formation of five I-16s led by Yevgeny S. Ptukhin, C.O. of *Escuadra núm* 11, had been bounced by six Bf 109s, and that, in the mêlée that followed, Ptukhin had been firing at a Messerschmitt when an I-15 (supposedly flown by a Yugoslav volunteer, Bozhko Petrovich) had interposed itself between the Soviet and German fighters and, to Ptukhin's annoyance, delivered the *coup de grâce*. The *Legion* did not admit the loss of this Bf 109B over the Madrid Front and, in any case, little credence could be attached to the claim as, at that time, 2./J 88 and its Messerschmitts were still a long way away at Herrera! Neither was the loss of a Bf 109B admitted that was to be claimed nine days later, on July 17, by Frank Tinker, an American volunteer flying with the *1a Escuadrilla de Moscas*, as his seventh "kill", the first admitted loss being that of *Unteroffizier* Höness, who, responsible for the destruction of a Tupolev SB bomber during one of the first sorties of 2./J 88 from Avila, was shot down while attacking another SB. Another loss was suffered on July 20, when *Unteroffizier* Harbach was seen to bale out of his Bf 109B. Fortunately, his parachute drifted across the Nationalist lines and he returned safely to Avila by the evening. On the other hand, 2./J 88 had begun to build up a score with its new Messerschmitts, among the first claims being those of *Leutnant* Rolf Pingel, who later as *Kommandeur* of I *Gruppe* of *Jagdgeschwader* 26 on the Channel coast, was to achieve some notoriety as a result of inadvertently delivering a near-intact Bf 109F to Britain on July 10, 1941, claimed the destruction of one bomber and one fighter, and those of *Unteroffizier* Buhl, *Oberfeldwebel* Hilmann and *Feldwebel* Boddem (later to be killed in action over Spain

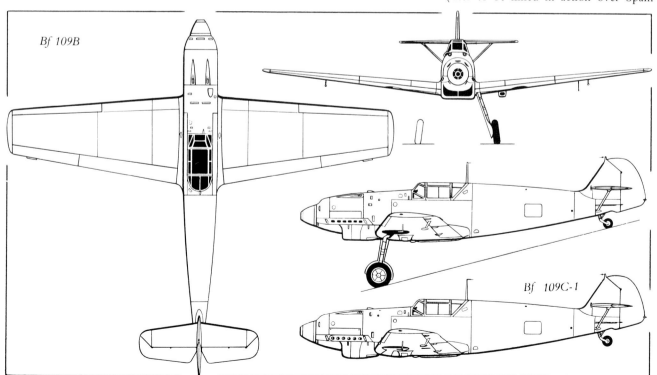

Bf 109B

Bf 109C-1

with the rank of *Leutnant*) who each accounted for a fighter.

Apart from the continuous escort sorties flown from Avila by 2./J 88, the *Staffel* had to fly standing patrols in defence of the airfield as a result of a Republican bombing attack on the base and from which the precious few Bf 109Bs fortunately emerged unscathed. Furthermore, the intense heat, which, at times reached 46°C (115°F) in the shade, rendered maintenance work and refuelling and re-arming the aircraft extremely arduous. At night, during which the searchlights over Madrid, 37 miles (60 km) to the east, were clearly visible, the temperature fell to only some 30°C (86°F) and the personnel slept in the open beneath mosquito netting.

On July 14, the Republican advance was halted, but furious aerial activity continued and, on July 18, a Nationalist counter-offensive was launched, the Bf 109Bs of 2./J 88 being assigned the task of breaking up the heavy Republican bomber attacks on Nationalist lines of communication behind the front. The success of the Messerschmitts was reflected by the greatly increased attention paid to their Avila base by Republican bombers. During one such raid, on July 23, hurriedly scrambled Bf 109Bs broke up the attacking bomber formation, *Feldwebel* Boddem bringing one of the bombers down and the others scattering their loads over the surrounding landscape without a single splinter landing on Avila airfield. Nevertheless, in reporting the attack that same evening, Republican radio claimed the destruction of no fewer than 20 aircraft!

Between July 24 and 27, the Battle of Brunete finally petered out and, on July 30, *Jagdgruppe* 88 returned once more to Herrera de Pisuerga. In the meantime, on July 20, the *Gruppenkommandeur*, *Hauptmann* von Merhart, had been recalled to Berlin and his place taken by *Hauptmann* Gotthardt Handrick★ who was later to become *Kommodore* of *Jagdgeschwader* 26 and, eventually, *Kommandeur* of 8 *Jagddivision* in Vienna. On August 14, the offensive against Santander was resumed once more and over this front the Nationalists now enjoyed complete air

---

★ *Oberleutnant* (later *Hauptmann*) Handrick had won the Modern Pentathlon Gold Medal at the XI Olympic Games held in Berlin in the previous year and decorated the spinner of his Bf 109B with the five Olympic rings. His aircraft was also personalized with a stylized "H" in the centre of the black disc on the fuselage sides and also the "Top Hat" emblem of 2.*Staffel* as the *Stabskette* was assigned to 2./J 88 for operational purposes.

*The Bf 109 V4 (D-IALY) above was, in fact, the first pre-series aircraft, the Bf 109B-01. (Below) A Bf 109B serving as a fighter trainer in Spain in 1948*

superiority, outnumbering the defending forces three or four to one. The Bf 109Bs of 2./J 88 were primarily occupied with top cover missions for the bomber element of the *Legion*. The opposing Republican fighters were operating under serious disadvantages. Apart from their numerical inferiority, they were forced to fly from airfields that were too close to the front line to permit adequate warning of impending enemy attack, and the one I-16-equipped *escuadrilla*, which operated primarily from La Albericia, evaded combat with 2./J 88 whenever possible. On August 26, Santander finally fell and the Nationalists continued the drive westward along the Asturian Biscay coast, *Jagdgruppe* 88 keeping pace with the advancing ground forces, occupying small, primitive, often barely more than semi-prepared strips around Santander and, subsequently, Llanes.

Meanwhile, additional Bf 109B fighters had been arriving at Tablada airfield for assembly – the number of Messerschmitt Bf 109 fighters of this sub-type sent to Spain was eventually to total 45 – and during September 1937, 1./J 88 relinquished its He 51Bs and converted to the monoplane, a new 4./J 88 being established with the biplanes for close support tasks and "Franzl" Lützow being transferred as *Staffelkapitän* to 1./J 88, presumably to ease conversion to the new fighter, his place being taken as *Staffelkapitän* of 2./J 88 by *Oberleutnant* Joachim Schlichting, who, as *Gruppenkommandeur* of III/JG 27, was to be shot down over the Thames on September 6, 1940, and taken prisoner.

After the fall of Santander and the overrunning by Nationalist forces of the entire northern area, the surviving Republican fighters had been evacuated to Carreño, an airfield on the extreme northern promontory by Gijón. It was from here that the last operational mission in the north was flown by Republican fighters; a mission that was to result in the first major encounter between I-16s and the newly-mounted 1./J 88. Six I-16s – three of them flown by Soviet pilots – and three I-15s, the only airworthy survivors of the Republican air component in the north, took-off from Carreño to intercept a *Legion* force of He 111s escorted by six Bf 109Bs of 1./J 88. While the I-15s attacked the bombers, the half-dozen I-16s took on the escorting Messerschmitts, and during the course of the ensuing battle, one of the Soviet pilots, I. Yevseviev, was to claim the destruction of one of the Bf 109Bs which he shared with his wingman, and one of the Spanish pilots, Francisco Tarazona Torán, was to claim another.

The successful conclusion of the northern campaign made feasible a resumption of Nationalist endeavours to capture Madrid, and to this end, early in November, the *Legion* transferred to fields around El Burgo de Osma and Almazán for the forthcoming offensive against Guadalajara, and a relatively inactive period of rest, recuperation and reorganization followed. *Generalmajor* Sperrle was recalled to Germany and his place as C-in-C of the *Legion Condor* was taken by *Generalmajor* Volkmann and, at lower level, Joachim Schlichting completed his tour of duty and *Oberleutnant* Wolfgang Schellmann took over as *Staffelkapitän* of 2./J 88. Schellmann was to become one of the most successful of *Legion* pilots, claiming 12 "kills"; he was to become *Kommodore* in turn of JG 2 "*Richthofen*" and JG 27 and was to lose his life in June 1941, being executed by Soviet forces after bailing out near Grodno as a result of his aircraft suffering damage from fragments of an I-16 which he had destroyed.

In their first months of operations over Spain, there could be little doubt that the Bf 109B fighters of *Jagdgruppe* 88 had acquitted themselves well. Combat attrition had been relatively light in view of the numerical scale of the missions flown, and despite their limited numbers, the Messerschmitts had made a very significant contribution to Nationalist efforts in Spanish skies.

# An Eagle evolves

While the Bf 109 was being "blooded" in action with understandably little publicity over Spain, the Propaganda Ministry in Berlin, while considering it impolitic to publicize the activities of the *Legion Condor*, had every intention of capitalizing on the capabilities of the Messerschmitt-designed fighter to raise German aviation prestige abroad, and the 4th International Flying Meeting held at Zürich-Dübendorf between July 23 and August 1, 1937, provided the ideal opportunity to furnish the world with a practical demonstration of the Bf 109's potentialities. The German team included no fewer than five Bf 109s, and none was, in fact, a completely standard production model, comprising the Bf 109 V7 (*Werk-Nr.* 881 D-IJHA), the Bf 109 V8 (*Werk-Nr.* 882 D-IPLU) and Bf 109 V9 (*Werk-Nr.* 883) fitted with the fuel-injection Jumo 210Ga engine, the Bf 109 V14 (D-ISLU) fitted with the new Daimler-Benz DB 600Aa engine, and the similarly-powered Bf 109 V13 (D-IPKY).

Ernst Udet had hoped to win the Circuit of the Alps in the single military aircraft category with the Bf 109 V14, but an engine failure necessitated a forced landing in which the aircraft was completely written off, although Udet himself was uninjured. Nevertheless, this event, which covered the circuit Dübendorf–Thun–Bellinzona–Dübendorf, was won by *Major* Hans Seidemann flying the Bf 109 V8, the 228-mile (367-km) distance being covered in 56 min. 47 sec. at an average speed of 241 m.p.h. (388 km/h). The trophy for the fastest speed over the same circuit by a team of three aircraft was won at an average speed of 233·5 m.p.h. (376 km/h) by the trio of Jumo-engined Bf 109s. The individual record for speed four times around a 31-mile (50-km) circuit was established by Dipl.-Ing. Carl Francke in the Bf 109 V8, the same pilot winning the Climb and Dive Competition in the Bf 109 V13 by climbing to

9,840 ft. (3 000 m) and diving to 500 ft. (150 m) in 2 min. 5·7 sec.

So impressive were these results that several of the competitors withdrew from the contest, and the claims made by the Propaganda Ministry on behalf of the Bf 109 had been fully vindicated. The statement that the fighter was already in *large-scale* service was an exaggeration, however, for apart from the Bf 109Bs serving with the *Legion Condor* in Spain, only I and II

*(Above) The Bf 109 V7 (D-IJHA) at Zürich-Dübendorf and (below) a Bf 109B fitted with a fuel-injection Jumo 210Ga engine which was to be standardized for the Bf 109C*

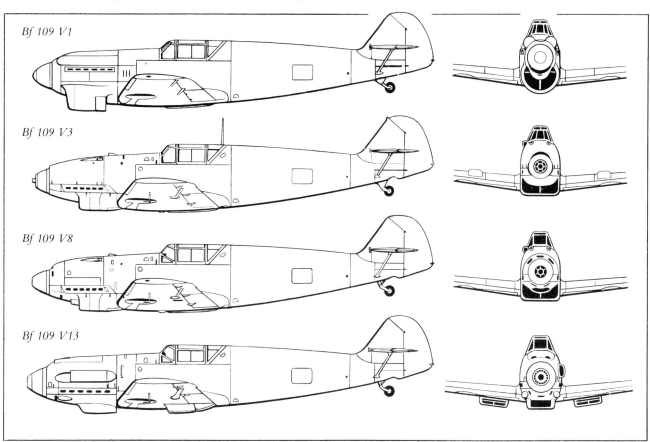

Bf 109 V1

Bf 109 V3

Bf 109 V8

Bf 109 V13

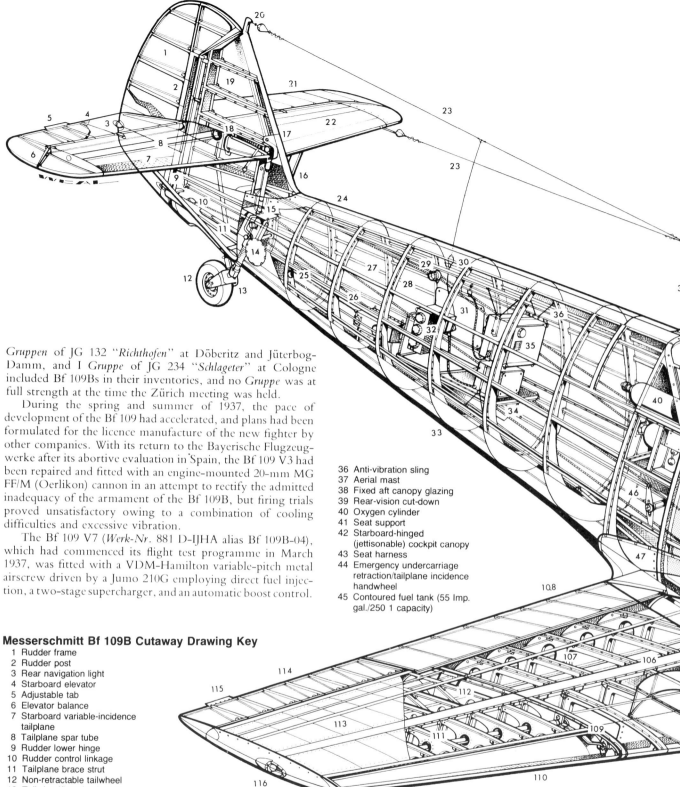

Gruppen of JG 132 "Richthofen" at Döberitz and Jüterbog-Damm, and I Gruppe of JG 234 "Schlageter" at Cologne included Bf 109Bs in their inventories, and no Gruppe was at full strength at the time the Zürich meeting was held.

During the spring and summer of 1937, the pace of development of the Bf 109 had accelerated, and plans had been formulated for the licence manufacture of the new fighter by other companies. With its return to the Bayerische Flugzeug-werke after its abortive evaluation in Spain, the Bf 109 V3 had been repaired and fitted with an engine-mounted 20-mm MG FF/M (Oerlikon) cannon in an attempt to rectify the admitted inadequacy of the armament of the Bf 109B, but firing trials proved unsatisfactory owing to a combination of cooling difficulties and excessive vibration.

The Bf 109 V7 (Werk-Nr. 881 D-IJHA alias Bf 109B-04), which had commenced its flight test programme in March 1937, was fitted with a VDM-Hamilton variable-pitch metal airscrew driven by a Jumo 210G employing direct fuel injection, a two-stage supercharger, and an automatic boost control.

36 Anti-vibration sling
37 Aerial mast
38 Fixed aft canopy glazing
39 Rear-vision cut-down
40 Oxygen cylinder
41 Seat support
42 Starboard-hinged (jettisonable) cockpit canopy
43 Seat harness
44 Emergency undercarriage retraction/tailplane incidence handwheel
45 Contoured fuel tank (55 Imp. gal./250 1 capacity)

### Messerschmitt Bf 109B Cutaway Drawing Key

1 Rudder frame
2 Rudder post
3 Rear navigation light
4 Starboard elevator
5 Adjustable tab
6 Elevator balance
7 Starboard variable-incidence tailplane
8 Tailplane spar tube
9 Rudder lower hinge
10 Rudder control linkage
11 Tailplane brace strut
12 Non-retractable tailwheel
13 Tailwheel/leg shock strut
14 Shock strut/control link access
15 Tailplane incidence screwjack
16 Port tailplane brace
17 Tailfin root fairing
18 Tailplane spar attachment/carry through
19 Tailfin structure
20 Aerial stub
21 Port elevator
22 Port tailplane
23 Aerials
24 Monocoque fuselage structure
25 Lift point
26 Control cables

27 Fuselage stringers
28 Frame
29 Tailplane incidence control
30 Aerial lead-in
31 Radio access door (port)
32 Relay box
33 Fuselage skinning
34 Radio equipment tray
35 FuG 7 radio pack

46 Elevator control quadrant
47 Wingroot fairing
48 Control cables
49 Diagonal brace strut
50 Starboard control console
51 Pilot's seat
52 Heelrest
53 Rudder pedal assembly
54 Seat adjustment lever

55 Control column
56 Instrument panel
57 Canopy lock/release
58 Revi C/12C reflector sight
59 Windscreen
60 Two 7,9-mm MG 17 machine guns
61 Machine gun barrels
62 Port flap
63 Flap control rod

Direct fuel injection enabled the power plant to function equally well in any position, a distinct advantage in a fighter aircraft, and the Jumo 210G offered 700 h.p. for take-off and 730 h.p. at 3,280 ft. (1 000 m), with 675 h.p. being available at 12,500 ft. (3 800 m). This version of the engine had not been ready for production installation, however, when deliveries of the Bf 109B had begun, all fighters of this model retaining the Jumo 210Da, with the Jumo 210G being installed only in the Bf 109C series, although the VDM-Hamilton airscrew was introduced at an early stage in production deliveries.

The Bf 109 V7 and V8 had effectively begun life as development aircraft for the Bf 109C, which, by the spring of 1937, was envisaged as the definitive Jumo 210-engined production variant of the fighter. Both the V7 and V8 featured a repositioned oil cooler intake ahead of the radiator bath beneath the nose, and additional auxiliary cooling slots, but the definitive Bf 109C, which dispensed with the latter and introduced a redesigned and deeper radiator bath, standardized on an oil cooler position similar to that employed by the Bf 109B.

As the difficulties with the engine-mounted MG 17 machine gun were still unresolved, the Jumo 210Da-powered Bf 109 V8 introduced a pair of wing-mounted MG 17s installed immediately outboard of the undercarriage wells. This change was

effected without major redesign of the wing structure, the breech of the gun being positioned behind the spar and thus obviating the need for a large cut-out in the spar web, bulky ammunition tanks being dispensed with in favour of 500-round belts which were fed into a forward-hinging panel, guided by chutes out to the wingtip, back to the wing root and finally to the gun by an arrangement of rollers. The barrel itself was housed by a tube which funnelled cooling air around it, through the spar web and into the breech compartment, escaping through a slot between the rear diaphragm and the flap. Firing trials led to some stiffening of the inboard wing leading edge, and a minor flutter problem was rectified by balancing the ailerons, but tests were successful, and the installation was adopted as standard for the Bf 109C-1. Armament was later removed, the Jumo 210Da gave place to a Jumo 210Ga and, with these changes, the Bf 109 V8 participated in the Zürich meeting in July 1937, as previously mentioned. The Bf 109 V9 was essentially similar to the V8 in its original form, but the wing-mounted machine guns gave place to 20-mm MG FF cannon after its appearance at Zürich where it had been flown without armament.

The development of this installation was to be somewhat protracted, and, in the event, was not to be standardized until

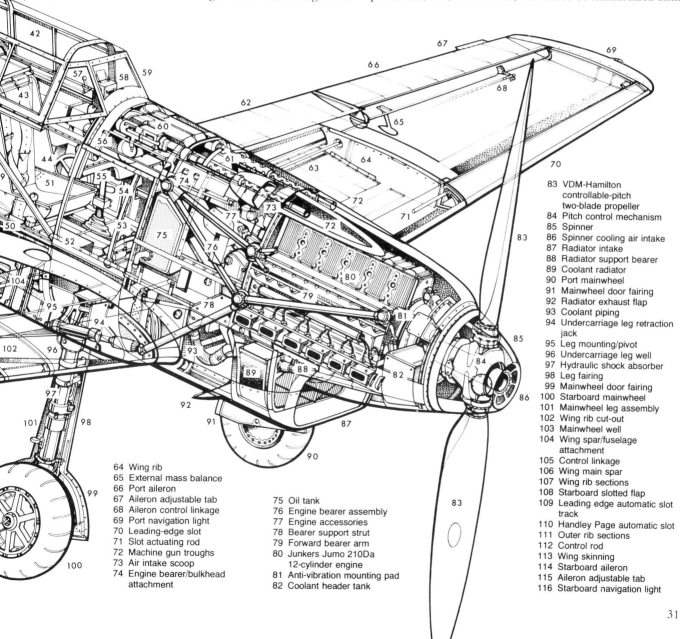

83 VDM-Hamilton controllable-pitch two-blade propeller
84 Pitch control mechanism
85 Spinner
86 Spinner cooling air intake
87 Radiator intake
88 Radiator support bearer
89 Coolant radiator
90 Port mainwheel
91 Mainwheel door fairing
92 Radiator exhaust flap
93 Coolant piping
94 Undercarriage leg retraction jack
95 Leg mounting/pivot
96 Undercarriage leg well
97 Hydraulic shock absorber
98 Leg fairing
99 Mainwheel door fairing
100 Starboard mainwheel
101 Mainwheel leg assembly
102 Wing rib cut-out
103 Mainwheel well
104 Wing spar/fuselage attachment
105 Control linkage
106 Wing main spar
107 Wing rib sections
108 Starboard slotted flap
109 Leading edge automatic slot track
110 Handley Page automatic slot
111 Outer rib sections
112 Control rod
113 Wing skinning
114 Starboard aileron
115 Aileron adjustable tab
116 Starboard navigation light

64 Wing rib
65 External mass balance
66 Port aileron
67 Aileron adjustable tab
68 Aileron control linkage
69 Port navigation light
70 Leading-edge slot
71 Slot actuating rod
72 Machine gun troughs
73 Air intake scoop
74 Engine bearer/bulkhead attachment

75 Oil tank
76 Engine bearer assembly
77 Engine accessories
78 Bearer support strut
79 Forward bearer arm
80 Junkers Jumo 210Da 12-cylinder engine
81 Anti-vibration mounting pad
82 Coolant header tank

*(Above and below) A Bf 109C-2 serving with 1./JG 137 at Zerbst, this being one of the new units hastily formed in the summer of 1938*

the introduction of the E-series of the fighter, although it was to be applied to some Bf 109C-1s at the factory as a retrospective modification (with which they became Bf 109C-3s). The MG FF cannon was inserted further outboard in the wing than the MG 17 machine gun with the rear of the breech block passing through the spar web and a 60-round ammunition drum inboard of the gun and ahead of the spar, the necessary depth for the drum being catered for by provision of a detachable blister fairing in the wing under surface.

The Bf 109 V10 was initially flown with the Jumo 210G engine, but in June 1937 this had been replaced by an early example of the Daimler-Benz DB 600Aa affording 960 h.p. at 2,350 r.p.m. for take-off and a maximum continuous output of 775 h.p. at 2,200 r.p.m., and the Bf 109 V11, V12, V13 and V14, all B-series airframes, which had also been allocated to power plant trials, were similarly modified. While the frontal area of the DB 600 differed little from that of the Jumo that it replaced, it was appreciably longer and substantially heavier. Nevertheless, the airframe aft of the firewall remained essentially unchanged, the c.g. being restored by redesign of the cooling system, the deep radiator bath beneath the nose giving place to partially buried ducted wing radiators situated well aft of the c.g. and providing greater cooling area with minimum effect on drag. The necessary ducting naturally imposed no small weight penalty but this was more than compensated for by the increase in power afforded by the Daimler-Benz engine.

Some local strengthening and increases in skin thicknesses were necessitated by the higher loads, heavier main spar forgings were introduced, the main undercarriage attachment points and oleo legs were strengthened, and a small oil cooler formed a part of the lower segment of the engine cowling, all portions of which were attached to the exhaust manifold shroud. The DB 600Aa drove an electrically-operated VDM controllable-pitch three-bladed metal airscrew and was carried on two cantilever bearers attached to the mainframe at four points. A long supercharger intake was positioned above the exhaust manifold on the port side of the engine cowling.

In November 1937, a fourth *Gruppe*, II/JG 234 *"Schlageter"* at Düsseldorf, began converting to the Bf 109B, collecting its first aircraft on the 13th of that month, and by the end of the year deliveries from the Augsburg–Haunstetten plant were being supplemented by deliveries from the Gerhard Fieseler Werke at Kassel which had initiated production of the Bf 109B under licence.

Deliveries of the Bf 109C-1, or *Clara*, began in the early spring of 1938, this variant having the Jumo 210Ga engine with deeper radiator bath and revised exhaust exits, and four MG 17 machine guns, two in the fuselage with 500 r.p.g. and two in the wings with 420 r.p.g. As with the earlier production model, some of the first Bf 109C-1s off the line were shipped to Spain for service with the *Legion Condor*, and during the course of the summer, I/JG 132 began to exchange its Bf 109Bs for the newer model. Production of the C-series fighter was, in the

*A Bf 109B serving with one of the Jagdfliegerschulen during the summer of 1939. This obsolescent model of the Messerschmitt-designed fighter lingered on in Luftwaffe first-line service until the early months of 1940*

*(Above and below right) Bf 109D fighters awaiting Luftwaffe acceptance at the Bremen factory of the Focke-Wulf Flugzeugbau in 1938. Focke-Wulf was one of two licensees of the Dora, the other being the Erla Maschinenwerk at Leipzig-Heiterblick. The Bf 109D was essentially an interim model pending availability of the Daimler-Benz engine*

event, strictly limited, and the Bf 109D, or *Dora*, delivered in parallel was destined to become the Jumo-engined model manufactured in largest numbers.

The Bf 109D was a hybrid in that it reverted to the carburettor-equipped Jumo 210Da engine of the Bf 109B series but retained the four-gun armament of the Bf 109C-1, and by the end of 1937, the Erla Maschinenwerk at Leipzig-Heiterblick had reached an advanced stage in tooling for the D-series fighter and the Focke-Wulf Flugzeugbau at Bremen had also received a contract for the licence production of the Bf 109D. A batch of five Bf 109Ds reached 3./J 88 in Spain in August 1938, three were to be supplied to Hungary early in the following year and 10 were also to be delivered to Switzerland. Without exception, however, the potential foreign purchasers of the Bf 109 were interested primarily in the newer Daimler-Benz-engined models, but the Swiss had expressed willingness to accept an initial batch of 10 Bf 109D fighters primarily for familiarization training in preparation for delivery of the more potent Bf 109E to their *Fliegertruppe*.

The first Bf 109D was to reach Switzerland on December 17, 1938, the 10th and last arriving on January 19, 1939, the fighters being ferried from Augsburg–Haunstetten to Switzerland by Swiss pilots and fitted with only rudimentary instrumentation, lacking both armament and radio which was to be installed after the arrival of the aircraft in Switzerland. The Swiss Bf 109Ds were eventually to be fitted with four 7,45-mm machine guns, those mounted in the upper decking of the forward fuselage having 480 r.p.g. and the wing-mounted weapons 418 r.p.g.; were to be issued to the *Fliegerkompagnie* 15 at Payerne and withdrawn from first-line service shortly after the completion of deliveries of the Bf 109E-3 and relegated to the conversion training role in which they were to serve for many years, the last being scrapped in 1949.

Such was the success that had meanwhile attended the

Bf 109, and, in consequence, the international acclaim received by (now) Prof. Dr.-Ing. Willy Messerschmitt, that the management of the Bayerische Flugzeugwerke was understandably

---

### Bf 109C-1 Specification

**Power Plant:** One Junkers Jumo 210Ga 12-cylinder inverted-vee liquid-cooled engine rated at 700 h.p. for take-off, 730 h.p. at 3,280 ft. (1 000 m), and 675 h.p. at 12,470 ft (3 800 m).
**Performance:** (At 4,405 lb./1 998 kg) Maximum speed, 261 m.p.h. (420 km/h) at sea level, 292 m.p.h. (470 km/h) at 14,756 ft. (4 500 m); normal cruise at 5,062 lb. (2 296 kg), 214 m.p.h. (344 km/h) at 10,170 ft. (3 100 m); maximum range, 405 mls. (625 km); time to 16,400 ft. (5 000 m), 8·75 min.; service ceiling, 27,560 ft. (8 400 m).
**Weights:** Empty, 3,522 lb. (1 597,5 kg); maximum loaded, 5,062 lb. (2 296 kg).
**Dimensions:** Span, 32 ft 4½ in. (9,87 m); length, 28 ft. 0⅔ in. (8,55 m); height, 8 ft. 0½ in. (2,45 m); wing area, 174.053 sq. ft. (16,17 m²).
**Armament:** Four 7,9-mm Rheinmetall Borsig MG 17 machine guns, the two fuselage-mounted weapons each with 500 r.p.g. and the two wing-mounted weapons each with 420 r.p.g.

*The Bf 109 V13 (above) was employed, as recounted on this page, to raise the world air speed record for landplanes on November 11, 1937, various aerodynamic refinements having been introduced and a specially-boosted engine installed. (Below left) The first Bf 109D delivered to Switzerland for the Fliegertruppe. It ground-looped during a crosswind landing when arriving at Dübendorf, breaking its undercarriage*

anxious to capitalize on this fame, and readily agreed to the appointment of Messerschmitt as Chairman and Managing Director. On July 11, 1938, the name of the company was changed to that of Messerschmitt A.G., and all patents owned by the Messerschmitt G.m.b.H. formed two years earlier were transferred to the renamed company.

The fame of Messerschmitt and the Bf 109 had been furthered in the previous year, on November 11, 1937, when Dr.-Ing. Hermann Wurster had raised the world air speed record for landplanes to 379·38 m.p.h. (611 km/h) with the Bf 109 V13, covering, in accordance with the then existing F.A.I. regulations, a 1·86-mile (3-km) course twice in each direction at an altitude not exceeding 245 feet (75,00 m). For the record flight the Bf 109 V13 was fitted with a specially-boosted DB 601 engine capable of delivering 1,650 h.p. for short periods, an elongated spinner, a strengthened and aerodynamically refined cockpit hood and a high polish to reduce skin friction. Wurster's feat did much to raise German aviation prestige as, for the first time, a German pilot flying a German aircraft had captured the world air speed record for landplanes.

The year 1938 was an important one for both the *Luftwaffe* and for its new fighter. Production of the Jumo 210-engined Bf 109 was to continue throughout the year, although development was by now concentrated on variants of the basic design powered by the more powerful Daimler–Benz series of 12-cylinder inverted-vee liquid-cooled engines. Difficulties involving the adequate cooling of an engine-mounted MG 17 machine gun had been largely resolved, and the Bf 109C-2 had been proposed, supplementing the quartette of MG 17s carried by the C-1 with a fifth engine-mounted weapon, but this remained a project.

Having gained international acclaim as a result of its success at Zürich-Dübendorf and acquisition of the world air speed record for landplanes, the Messerschmitt was continuing to receive somewhat more localized acclaim in Spain where the civil war was still being waged. The operations of the two Bf 109B-equipped *Staffeln* had been somewhat desultory for a time owing to something of a lull in the air war that, unbeknown to the *Jagdgruppe*, was to be a prelude to the gruelling Battle of Teruél to commence on December 15, 1937. As a consequence, attrition during this period was light, but of the few casualties suffered by the Bf 109B *Staffeln*, one was of particular significance: on December 4, while escorting He 51s attacking Bujaraloz airfield, *Feldwebel* Polenz flying 6-15 still fitted with its original Schwarz fixed-pitch propeller, ran out of fuel and landed on a road between Azaila and Escatron. Thus, the Republicans acquired an intact specimen of the Messerschmitt fighter, although its loss was never to be admitted by the *Legion*. In addition to the Bf 109B, the Republicans had succeeded in capturing an airworthy example of the He 111B bomber (25-32) and news of the acquisition of these enemy combat aircraft was quickly transmitted to Paris by the French air attaché, *Colonel* Quir-Montfollet, the result being an official but *clandestine* approach to the Spanish Republicans by the French government for permission to evaluate the German warplanes.

At this time, the French Premier, Camille Chautemps, had just closed the Franco-Spanish border, thus halting the flow of Soviet war material sent by this route to the Republican forces. The Republican government, anxious to foster the goodwill of the French government and persuade it to allow the frontier to be re-opened – an event that was to take place on March 17, 1938 – agreed to a French technical mission secretly visiting Spain to examine and test fly both the Bf 109B and the He 111B.

The French mission, which included *Ingénieur Général* du Merle, who was responsible for fighter equipment in the *Service Technique de l'Aéronautique*, *Commandant* de Briey, an armament specialist, and *Capitaine* Rozanoff, the most experienced test pilot of the *Centre d'Essais en Vol*, arrived in Barcelona on January 31, 1938. The captured Bf 109B of *Feldwebel* Polenz was at this time at the Sabadell airfield where a detailed examination of the fighter was carried out by the French technicians and flight testing was performed by Rozanoff, who, by the time the mission returned to Paris on February 13, had accumulated 30 hours of flying in the two German types. During these tests, the ASI of the Bf 109B was calibrated by flying a measured stretch along the straight road between Tarragona and Reus, and the French delegation was highly impressed with the fighter's performance. Very detailed reports were subsequently prepared and submitted by the members of the mission, Rozanoff's report on the flying characteristics of the Bf 109B making a point of the excellent level speed and dive capabilities of the fighter, but stressing the negative influence exerted by the engine's torque in a climbing turn to starboard. In view of the tension then existing between France and Germany, the reports were classified *Très Secret* and, in consequence, were never to be distributed to French fighter design bureaux which could have gained considerable benefit from the information that they contained.

The Nationalists were now preparing for a resumption of the offensive with the launching of an attack on the Aragón front but were pre-empted by a Republican offensive in the Teruél sector on December 15. To relieve pressure in the area, those forces, including the *Legion*, gathering along the Guadalajara front were quickly redeployed to the new danger point, *Jagdgruppe* 88 being reassigned to Calamocha, some 50 miles (80 km) from the fighting area. Although intensive effort was applied, the aviation of neither side proved very effective during the Battle of Teruél, primarily owing to the appalling weather. At Calamocha the temperature dropped to −20°C (−4°F) and the engines of the Bf 109Bs had to be regularly run up during the night to prevent seizing. On December 29, the Nationalist counter-offensive was launched and Republican air activity increased, although inclement weather strictly limited the number of sorties mounted by both sides.

On January 18, 1938, *Oberleutnant* Schellmann, *Staffelkapitän* of 2./J 88, opened his score by claiming an I-16 and *Unteroffizier* Woitke brought down an I-15. Teruél, itself, was occupied by Republican forces on January 22, but the fighting continued on into February, and on the 7th of that month, a mixed formation of Bf 109Bs from both 1. and 2.*Staffeln* led by the *Gruppenkommandeur*, *Hauptmann* Handrick, and flying escort to *Legion* bombers over the Teruél salient, sighted a formation of 22 Republican Tupolev SB bombers – the largest such group encountered to that date. There was no sign of any Republican fighter cover and the Bf 109Bs had accounted for several of the bombers before the *escuadrillas* of I-16s joined the mêlée. The battle degenerated into a far-ranging free-for-all which lasted only five minutes before the Republican fighters broke off combat, disappearing in the direction of Valencia, but during the action, the Messerschmitts had accounted for 10 of the SB bombers and two I-16 fighters without suffering a loss themselves. On the same day, the greatest individual success of the entire conflict was gained by a *Jagdgruppe* 88 pilot. The Calamocha airfield had suffered a number of attacks from SB bombers and during one such attack on February 7, *Leutnant* Wilhelm Balthasar succeeded in shooting down three of the bombers and an escorting fighter within the space of six minutes to bring his score over Spain to seven confirmed "kills". Balthasar, as *Staffelkapitän* of 7./JG 27, was later to gain a measure of fame as the most successful pilot of the French campaign, claiming the destruction of one enemy aircraft per day for 21 consecutive days and becoming the second fighter pilot to be decorated with the Knight's Cross. He was later to become *Kommandeur* of III/JG 3 and was to lose his life on July 3, 1941, when, as *Kommodore* of JG 2 "*Richthofen*", his fighter shed a wing during combat.

The Battle of Teruél raged on until the final recapture of the town by the Nationalists on February 21. Throughout the battle, the two Bf 109B-equipped *Staffeln* had claimed the destruction of some 30 enemy aircraft without loss to themselves.

On March 9, 1938, the Nationalists finally launched their long-planned offensive in the Aragón, the first phase being an attack to the south of the Ebro River and the second being an attack to the north of the Ebro. Within eight days, the Nationalist forces were to occupy 2,700 square miles (7 000 km²) of

territory. The *Legion* moved its combat group forward, the Bf 109Bs being deployed to Escatrón, and from here, on March 27, they attacked Lerida airfield in concert with the He 51s of 3./J 88, whose *Staffelkapitän* was by now *Oberleutnant* Adolf Galland, who had arrived in Spain during the previous May and had replaced *Oberleutnant* Pitcairn at the head of 3.*Staffel* late in 1937. A number of I-16s were destroyed on the ground on this occasion and despite an increasing interdiction role against Republican airfields, casualties suffered by the Bf 109B *Staffeln* remained light, only one Bf 109B being lost during attacks on the airfields at Bujaraloz, Candasnos and Caspe, and in the area around Belchite on April 1.

But the effectiveness of the *Legion* had now begun to decline, its strength being sapped by the continuous operation of its aircraft under arduous conditions without provision of adequate replacements. Deliveries of replacement Bf 109s from Germany were insufficient to make good the attrition suffered by 1. and 2./J 88 from all causes; spares were in short supply and satisfactory maintenance was becoming increasingly difficult with the result that readiness standards were falling.

On April 15, the Nationalist offensive finally cut the Republic in two when Nationalist forces reached the Mediterranean at Vinaroz and Benicarlo. The *Legion* was promptly transferred to bases in newly-occupied territory around Saragossa and along the Ebro valley, *Jagdgruppe* 88 being among the most forward-based units, being redeployed to La Cenia, some 15 miles (25 km) inland from the Ebro delta. The main emphasis was now concentrated on the push southwards, along the Mediterranean coast, and bitter resistance was encountered, both on the ground and in the air. The He 51s of 3. and 4.*Staffeln* suffered particularly heavy losses from 20-mm Flak, and these losses reached such alarming proportions during May that, for the first time since their inception some 14 months earlier, ground support operations were suspended. During this time, *Hauptmann* Handrick had a Ju 87A *Stukakette* under his command, but even this could only be employed when accompanied by a strong fighter escort.

On May 18, *Hauptmann* Handrick, patrolling along the coastline in company with the *Gruppen-Adjutant*, sighted 12 Tupolev SB bombers covered by between 15 and 20 I-16s. In one quick firing pass, during which he expended some 70 rounds from his twin MG 17 machine guns, he hit one of the I-16s which burst into flames and entered a vertical dive. The crash site was occupied shortly afterwards by advancing Nationalist forces who discovered that the dead pilot had been an American. A few days later, the Republicans mounted counter-attacks at Tremp and Balaguer, and three I-16-equipped *escuadrillas* were flown from the Levente to Catalonia to support these operations, the 1ª *Escuadrilla* being deployed to Reus, the 3ª to Vendrell and the 4ª to Monjos, these units posing formidable opposition for *Jagdgruppe* 88.

Meanwhile, the difficulties facing the He 51-equipped *Staffeln* had remained unresolved and a shortage of pilots in these units persisted. Galland, by now, had completed his tour of duty in Spain, but the appointment of a successor as *Staffelkapitän* of 3./J 88 proved something of a problem. One potential replacement promptly lost his life in an aerial collision and the ineptitude of another was such that he was immediately returned to Germany. However, the loss of another He 51 by 3./J 88 on June 9 was destined to be its last while mounted on the biplane, for the *Staffel* was now withdrawn from operations for conversion to the Messerschmitt, and Galland relinquished his command to *Oberleutnant* Werner Mölders. Mölders was destined to become the *Legion's* top scorer, surpassing *Oberleutnant* Harro Harder, who, one of three brothers all of whom became fighter pilots and lost their lives in W.W. II, had gained 11 "kills" before completing his tour in Spain at the end of

December 1937, and topping *Oberleutnant* Wolfgang Schellmann's score of 12 "kills".

Five Bf 109Cs had reached Tablada airfield in April, and these had been despatched to La Cenia to provide the nucleus of the equipment of the re-formed 3./J 88. As previously noted the Bf 109C embodied two noteworthy changes over the Bf 109B; the Jumo 210Da carburettor engine was replaced by a fuel-injection Jumo 210Ga, affording a nominal increase in maximum output, and the twin fuselage-mounted 7,9-mm Rheinmetall Borsig MG 17 machine guns with 500 r.p.g. were supplemented by a pair of similar weapons with 420 r.p.g. in the inner wing bays with their breeches aft of the mainspar. The arrival of these four-gun Messerschmitts was no coincidence as, during the previous month, the Republicans had begun to receive a four-gun version of the I-16 – the Type 10 which was to be referred to as the *Super-Mosca* – and Nationalist intelligence was fully aware of the arrival of the more heavily-armed version of the Polikarpov fighter which, in the event, was not to make its combat début until the series of air battles that preceded the second Ebro campaign initiated on July 25.

On June 10, 2./J 88 had destroyed two I-16 fighters and a single SB bomber without loss and had enjoyed even greater success on June 13, when the *Staffel*, in concert with 1./J 88, had claimed the destruction of no fewer than five I-15s and two I-16s over Castellón de la Plana, which was to fall to the Nationalist forces after fierce opposition two days later, on June 15. On the day prior to the capture of Castellón, however, the fortunes in the fighter conflict had been reversed when *Leutnant* Plieber was wounded in combat, writing off his Bf 109B in a forced landing after regaining his base, and *Leutnant* Henz had made a forced landing in Republican territory to the north of the Mijares River. Henz's Bf 109B had been captured intact by Republican troops and, according to Francisco Tarazona Torán, who was ordered to take a lorry from the nearest Republican fighter base and supervise the retrieval of the Messerschmitt, he had only just begun a preliminary examination of the machine when six Bf 109s appeared and strafed the grounded aircraft until it burst into flames.

By early July, the Nationalists had arrived at the gates of Sagunto and were on the point of launching a drive on Valencia. Although not yet at full strength, 3./J 88 now reappeared on operations with its newly-acquired Bf 109Cs, and its *Staffelkapitän*, *Oberleutnant* Mölders, achieved the first of a succession of "kills" on July 15, bringing down an I-16, and repeating his success two days later – he was to be credited with the destruction of 10 I-16s and four I-15s by the time he gained his final "kill" of the conflict on November 3. On July 18, five I-16s and five I-15s were shot down by Bf 109s fighting in concert with CR.32s in a battle over Segorbe, the losses sustained by the Nationalist combatants being three CR.32s of the Italian *Gruppo* XXIII "*Asso di Bastoni*". However, the fighting was not all so one-sided, for on the same day, 25 I-16s drawn from the 2ª, 3ª, 4ª and 5ª *escuadrillas* were to claim two Bf 109s and eight CR.32s without loss.

On the next day, July 19, Mölder's 3./J 88 encountered 18 Tupolev SB bombers over the Sagunto zone, escorted by three I-16 *escuadrillas*. *Oberleutnant* Mölders promptly gained his third "kill" and three other German pilots, Ebbighausen, Hein and Tietzen, each claimed an enemy aircraft. The following day witnessed Schellmann of 2./J 88 shoot down two I-16s as his seventh and eighth "kills", and on July 23, all available Bf 109s of the three *Staffeln* of *Jagdgruppe* 88 were scrambled to oppose some 40 I-15s and I-16s over Viver, claiming six "kills" without loss to themselves.

On the night of July 24–25, Republican forces crossed the River Ebro at a number of places between Mequinenza and Amposta in a bid to relieve the threat to Valencia, thus initiating the second Ebro campaign which was to see nearly four months of some of the bloodiest and fiercest fighting of the entire Civil War. This was to become a relentless battle of attrition in men, materials and supplies, and was to see six Nationalist counteroffensives repulsed by Republican troops occupying a bridgehead south of the river. The bomber element of the *Legion* was continuously engaged in destroying bridges across the Ebro in daylight, which were promptly repaired by the Republicans each night, and all three Bf 109 *Staffeln* were committed, their

*One of the five Bf 109Cs that reached the Legion Condor in April 1938 to provide the nucleus of the fighters for the re-equipped 3./J 88. It will be noted that this aircraft, dubbed "Luchs" (Lynx) by its pilot, displays three "kill" marks on the tail fin. The Bf 109C was powered by the fuel-injection Jumo 210Ga engine*

*(Above) One of the five Bf 109Ds (6-51 to 6-55) that supplemented the Bf 109Bs and Bf 109Cs of 3./J 88 from August 1938 is seen in the foreground in this photograph, another (below right) being seen at La Cenia. The Bf 109D differed from the Bf 109B primarily in having four-gun armament*

principal task being the escort of the *Legion* bombers whose raids decimated some remaining Republican divisions.

By this time, 3./J 88 had been brought up to strength by the arrival, early in August, of five Bf 109Ds at La Cenia. Various changes now took place in the command structure of the *Legion*, the principal of which being the return to Germany of the *Gruppenkommandeur*, Gotthardt Handrick, and his replacement by *Hauptmann* Walter Grabmann, followed, in November, by the recall of *Generalmajor* Volkmann and the transfer of command of the *Legion* to its erstwhile Chief of Staff, *Generalmajor Freiherr* Wolfram von Richthofen.

The second Ebro battle saw continuous and intensive aerial warfare which lasted throughout the remainder of August, through September and October, and eventually terminated on November 16, when the bridgehead on the southern side of the river was finally reduced. During their first two days of participation in the Ebro fighting, the Bf 109s had accounted for seven I-16s and three SBs, and, from September 2, the Nationalist forces had secured a measure of air supremacy over the front that was not to be seriously challenged by the Republicans thereafter. But if it had lost supremacy, the Republican air arm was anything but a spent force, and on October 4, Mölders shot down an I-16 – probably that flown by Enrique Tébar Pérez – and lost the Bf 109 flown by Otto Bertram. Eleven days later, on October 15, Mölders was to claim two I-16s, a double which he was to repeat on October 31, to bring his score of confirmed "kills" to 13.

A factor of major significance to emerge from the second Ebro campaign was a further development in modern fighter tactics. The *Legion* had been using an element of two fighters known as the *Rotte*, or loose pair. Some 200 metres separated the two fighters and the primary responsibility of the number two, or wingman, was to guard his leader from a quarter or stern attack, the leader navigating and covering his wingman. It was during the bitter fighting over the Ebro bridgehead and at Mölders' instigation that 3./J 88 adopted the so-called *Vierfingerschwarm*, or "finger-four" formation as it was to be called when adopted years later by the R.A.F., this simply consisting of two pairs and endowing the Bf 109 *Staffeln* with extraordinary flexibility which was particularly successful when utilized during fighter sweeps over enemy-held territory. The basic tactic was to survive both W.W. II and the Korean conflict to this day.

Following the successful completion of the Ebro campaign, the *Legion* enjoyed four weeks of much-needed but purely

relative rest and recuperation, but its equipment was at low ebb and the Nationalist High Command, which attached considerable importance to the strengthening of the *Legion*, was all too well aware that a new and final offensive had to be mounted quickly if its gains were to be consolidated and the conflict brought to a speedy conclusion. As far back as the previous June, the then commander of the *Legion*, *Generalmajor* Volkmann, had reported to Berlin that the *Legion*'s material resources were virtually exhausted, but the need to provide for any aggressive British or French reaction to the impending Sudeten *coup* had mitigated against any major re-supply of the German forces in Spain, and Volkmann's report had been tacitly ignored. By the end of the Ebro campaign, the *Legion* was, by consensus, incapable of further sustained operations.

The Nationalist forces as a whole were in desperate need of the replenishment of their supplies and equipment, and the German government was able to take advantage of this plight. It agreed to fulfil Spanish requirements and also re-equip the *Legion* with the most modern aircraft available to the *Luftwaffe* if the Nationalist government accepted earlier proposals that German capital be permitted to participate in Spanish iron ore mining, imported German mining machinery to the value of 5 million *Reichsmark* and accepted the entire cost of the re-equipment and operation of the *Legion*, making all payments in iron ore of which the German war industry was acutely short.

Earlier, in June, an He 112B-0 had been delivered to La Cenia for evaluation by the Nationalists*. It was flown by the

★ The Japanese had ordered 30 He 112B-0 fighters, but after delivery of an initial batch of 12 to Japan, the *Luftwaffenführungsstab*, fearing a violent reaction from Britain and France to the Sudeten coup, had ordered the impressment of the remaining aircraft. By the time they had been released, the Japanese had cancelled the contract for the final 18 fighters and, anxious to dispose of them, Germany promptly offered to sell them to the Spanish Nationalists and, in the event, 17 were to be sent to Spain in November 1938.

leading fighter pilots, including the most successful Spanish Nationalist pilot, Joaquin Garcia Morato. Morato took the opportunity provided by his visit to La Cenia to fly a Bf 109C and as a result of his recommendations, the Nationalist government had requested that Bf 109 fighters be supplied for the re-equipment of its fighter component, which, by that time, was mounted almost exclusively on the CR.32 biplane. The supply of Bf 109s was agreed in principle and, in October, three Spanish pilots, José Muñoz, Miguel García Pardo and Javier Murcia, had been seconded to 3./J 88 to gain experience in preparation for the first Spanish Bf 109-equipped unit.

The end of the Ebro campaign had brought with it a temporary lull in the air war, all Republican fighter pilots having been officially ordered to avoid combat with their opposite numbers, and at this time, the three Spanish pilots left 3./J 88 to commence the task of organizing the new 5-G-5 *Grupo* which was to comprise one *escuadrilla* of He 112s commanded by García Pardo and one *escuadrilla* of Bf 109s led by Murcia, the intention being to transfer the well-worn Bf 109s from the three *Staffeln* of *Jagdgruppe* 88 to the latter unit, the German *Gruppe*

re-equipping with the markedly more advanced Bf 109E at Nationalist government expense.

Aid received in consequence of Spanish acceptance of the German terms for re-supply of the Nationalist forces was to prove a considerable factor in enabling the Nationalists to mount their major and, in the event last offensive of the Civil War, on December 23. Six Army Corps, comprising 19 divisions, stormed across the Ebro and Segre rivers and advanced on Barcelona. It was not until a few days after the Catalonian offensive had been launched, however, that the first two or three Bf 109Es reached La Cenia for operational trials, and this despite the utmost priority attached to the replacement of the war-weary fighters of *Jagdgruppe* 88, albeit priority resulting from considerations other than a German desire to increase the effectiveness of the air support afforded by the *Legion*. In so far as Berlin was concerned, the conflict in Spain was all over apart from the mopping up, but the vital importance attached to the acquisition of Spanish ore took priority over everything. The vehement protests of the *Luftwaffenführungsstab* over the precedence given to *Jagdgruppe* 88 over home-based *Luftwaffe* units in the supply of the Bf 109E were ignored and some of the first aircraft off the assembly line were hurriedly crated and shipped to Spain, although this new version of the Messerschmitt fighter was not to reach Spain in quantity until February 1939.

On the day that the Catalonian offensive was launched, 37 of the 55 Bf 109s that had been sent to Spain for use by the *Legion* were still in the first-line inventory of *Jagdgruppe* 88, 32 of these being based at La Cenia and five at León, and despite Volkmann's pronouncement of some six months earlier that the *Legion*'s equipment was virtually exhausted, the three Bf 109 *Staffeln*, with their weary fighters, played a major role in clearing Catalonian skies of all Republican resistance. In the meantime, further veterans of the *Gruppe* had returned to Germany: *Oberleutnant* Mölders had handed over command of 3./J 88 to *Oberleutnant* Hubertus von Bonin; *Oberleutnant* Schellmann had relinquished 2./J 88 to *Oberleutnant* Lojewsky and *Oberleutnant* Schlichting had been succeeded as *Staffelkapitän* of 1./J 88 by *Oberleutnant* Reents.

On January 8, 1939, the second phase of the Catalonian offensive was begun and the *Legion* was sent to provide support in the Navarre Army Corps' section, but there was now only limited Republican aerial opposition and *Jagdgruppe* 88 was largely confined to strafing the remaining enemy airfields. For example, on January 12, the Bf 109s flew missions against the airfields at Valls, El Vendrell and Villafranca del Panadés. On January 15, Tarragona fell to the Nationalists and four days later, the final attack on Barcelona began, the city falling on January 26. The main preoccupation of the Bf 109s was by now the prevention of Republican aircraft escaping south. Encounters with I-16s had become increasingly infrequent and on

*(Above and below) Bf 109E-1s and E-3s at Saragossa in March 1939, shortly after the re-equipment of 2./J 88 with this type. This Legion Condor Staffel was still in process of working up to operational status with its new equipment when the Spanish conflict ended*

*The Bf 109E fighters, seen here with the "Zylinder Hut" of 2./J 88, saw but brief service with the Legion Condor and only about 20 had been assembled when hostilities terminated, the aircraft promptly being transferred to the Spanish air arm with which some were to serve until the 'fifties*

January 31, 1./J 88 suffered a combat loss when a Bf 109 was shot down in a battle over the Franco-Spanish frontier, and on February 6, during a concentrated attack on Villajuiga airfield, near the French border, two Bf 109s were shot down by an I-15 flown by José Falco. One of the Bf 109s, flown by *Leutnant* Nirminger, crashed in the middle of the airfield, its pilot later being killed by the *Legion Condor* bombs, and the other, flown by *Leutnant* Friedrich, crashing on the road between Rosas and Port Bou.

By early March, *Jagdgruppe* 88 was based at Barcience (Torrijos) and it was from here that, on March 5, von Bonin, *Staffelkapitän* of 3./J 88, claimed the last "kill" for the *Legion* which was, incidentally, the last machine to fall in the Civil War, an I-15 over Alicante and von Bonin's fourth confirmed victory. Three weeks later, at 0600 hours on March 27, the *Legion Condor* flew its last operational sortie when aircraft of its *Kampfgruppe*, escorted by Bf 109s of the *Jagdgruppe* as a mere formality, flew unhindered over the enemy's front line. By 0800 hours all signs of resistance on the ground had ceased and, an hour later, the Nationalist infantry and tanks began advancing, with the Republican forces fleeing from their path. On the following morning, the *Legion's* combat Headquarters was ordered to advance from the village of Mora to a new situation 19 miles (30 km) south-east of Toledo, but during the course of that day, the internecine struggle finally came to an end with the surrender of Madrid and Valencia.

Between August 1936 and March 1939, the *Legion Condor* had lost 96 aircraft, approximately 40 of these losses having been the result of enemy action, and had suffered 150 personnel killed and 200 wounded, about half of those killed being aircrew. Up to October 31, 1939 – no reliable figures being available for the closing five months of the conflict – the *Legion* claimed the destruction of 335 enemy aircraft of which 58 were credited to the *Legion's* Flak arm. Estimates concerning the number of pilots passing through the ranks of the four *Staffeln* of *Jagdgruppe* 88 were to vary widely, from 150 to in excess of 250, but whatever the figure, the experience that was gained by those pilots that served with the *Legion Condor* and survived the experience to fly with the *Luftwaffe* in W.W. II was of incalculable value; evidence of this was afforded by the 30 plus pilots who flew with the *Jagdgruppe* in Spain that were to be decorated with the Knight's Cross, were to provide the backbone of the W.W. II *Jagdflieger* and were to rise in rank and positions of command to the very top.

Although the bulk of the 40 Bf 109E-1 and E-3 fighters shipped to Spain for the re-equipment of *Jagdgruppe* 88 had arrived too late to participate in the final offensive, 2./J 88 completed conversion to the new fighters during the closing weeks of the Civil War at Saragossa, to where the other two *Staffeln* were redeployed from Barcience on March 11, and when the conflict terminated on March 29, half of the Bf 109Es had been assembled. The 20 Bf 109Es that had been assembled were now gathered at Logroño, together with the 27 surviving Jumo-engined Bf 109s, and officially transferred by the *Legion* to the Spanish air arm.

At the time of the Austrian *Anschluss* of March 13, 1938, the *Luftwaffe* had possessed 12 *Jagdgruppen* (excluding *Jagdgruppe* 88 in Spain with *Legion Condor*) of which half had converted or were in process of converting to the Bf 109, these being I/JG 131 at Jesau, I/JG 132 at Döberitz, II/JG 132 at Jüterbog-Damm, I/JG 234 at Cologne, II/JG 234 at Düsseldorf, and I/JG 334 at Wiesbaden. Apart from I/JG 136 at Eger-Marienbad which was still flying the obsolete He 51C-2 while awaiting imminent delivery of Bf 109s, the remaining five *Gruppen* – I and II/JG 134 at Dortmund and Werl, I/JG 135 at Aibling, I/JG 137 at Bernburg, and II/JG 334 at Mannheim – were for the most part equipped with the Arado Ar 68E and 68F.

As tension increased with the approach of the planned recovery of the Sudetenland, a programme was hastily formulated by the *Luftwaffengeneralstab* for the rapid expansion of the fighter force, and on July 1, 1938, no fewer than eight new *Jagdgruppen* officially came into existence. These *Gruppen* (III and IV/JG 132 at Jüterbog-Damm and Werneuchen respectively, IV/JG 134 at Dortmund, II/JG 135 at Aibling, II/JG 137 at Zerbst, I/JG 138 at Aspern, III/JG 234 at Düsseldorf, and III/JG 334 at Mannheim) were hurriedly formed on obsolescent fighters, one of them, I/JG 138, being established with the personnel of the fighter squadrons of the Austrian *Luftstreit-kräfte* absorbed by the *Luftwaffe* with the annexation. Another *Gruppe*, III/JG 132 which had been formed on Ar 68Es, was transferred to Fürstenwalde from Jüterbog-Damm shortly after its creation, and converted to the He 112B-0, which, being readied for shipment to Japan, had been requisitioned for *Luftwaffe* use.

As at August 1, 1938, the *Luftwaffe's* first-line inventory included 643 fighters of which fewer than half were Bf 109s, but such was the impetus placed behind production by the hazardous plans of the *Führer* that output was rising more rapidly than

*With the return of the Legion Condor to Germany, the Bf 109Es were handed over to the Spanish air arm, subsequently serving with Grupo 6-G-6 (as seen here) and then with the 25 Grupo of the 23 Regimiento, finally being relegated to the Escuela de Caza at Moron de la Frontera*

the fighters could be absorbed by the *Jagdgruppen*. Arado at Warnemünde had phased into the Bf 109 production programme, which, in addition to Messerschmitt, already included Erla,' Fieseler, and Focke-Wulf, and an Ob.d.L. strength return for September 19, 1938, recorded a total of 583 Bf 109s of all types, and of these 510 were serviceable. A substantial number of these fighters had still to be issued to the first-line *Jagdgruppen*, and the Bf 109B, C and D were the only service models, despite the carefully fostered belief that the Jumo 210-engined versions of the fighter were being *phased out* in favour of the Daimler-Benz-engined models that had allegedly already supplanted them on the assembly lines. In fact, a serious bottleneck in the supply of the Daimler-Benz engines had necessitated the retention of the Jumo 210-engined Bf 109 in production.

With the scheduled launching imminent of Germany's first aircraft carrier, then known as "*Träger A*", on August 1, 1938, a shipboard unit, *Trägergruppe* 186, was formed at Kiel-Holtenau. This initially comprised 4.*Trägersturzkampfstaffel*/ 186 equipped with the Ju 87A dive bomber, and 6.*Trägerjagdstaffel*/186 equipped with the Bf 109B. The latter was to be joined in the summer of the following year by another Bf 109B-equipped *Staffel*, this being 5.*Trägerjagdstaffel*/186, the intention being that both *Staffeln* should eventually re-equip with a specialized shipboard version of the Bf 109 for operation from the *Graf Zeppelin* (as "*Träger A*" was christened when launched on December 8, 1938), but in the event, the *Trägerjagdstaffeln* were destined to be confined to shore-based operations.

On November 1, 1938, a major reorganization of the *Lufwaffe* took place, and for the first time the fighter component was divided into *leichten* (light) and *schweren* (heavy) *Jagdgruppen*, the latter eventually (from January 1, 1939) becoming *Zerstörergruppen*. The *leichten Jagdgruppen* were I/JG 130 (Jesau), I/JG 132 "*Richthofen*" (Döberitz), I and II/JG 234 "*Schlageter*" (Cologne and Düsseldorf), I and II/JG 133 (Wiesbaden-Erbenheim and Mannheim), I/JG 134 (Aspern), I and II/JG 231 (Bernburg and Zerbst), I/JG 233 (Aibling), I/JG 331 (Mähr Trubau), I and II/JG 333 (Herzogenaurach and Eger-Marienbad), and I/JG 433 (Böblingen). Apart from I/JG 130 which was operating both Bf 109C and Bf 109D fighters, and one or two *Gruppen* such as I/JG 133 awaiting re-equipment, all the *leichten Jagdgruppen* were equipped with either the Bf 109B or Bf 109C.

The *schweren Jagdgruppen* comprised I/s.JG 141 (Jüterbog-Damm) with Bf 109Ds. II/s.JG 141 (Fürstenwalde) with Bf 109Cs, I, II, and III/s.JG 142 (Dortmund, Werl, and Lippstadt) with a mixture of Bf 109Bs, 109Cs and 109Ds, and I/s.JG 143 (Illesheim) and I/s. JG 144 (Gablingen), both with Bf 109Bs. On January 1, 1939, with the redesignation of the *schweren Jagdgruppen* as *Zerstörergruppen*, JG 141 became ZG 1, the I *Gruppe* commencing conversion to the Messerschmitt Bf 110 shortly afterwards; JG 142 became ZG 26 "*Horst Wessel*"; JG 143 became ZG 52, and JG 144 became ZG 76, a II *Gruppe* being formed with the Bf 109B and the I *Gruppe* converting to the Bf 110.

40

# The birth of Emil

The nimbus that ostensibly enveloped the Bf 109 by 1938 had been strengthened when, in July of that year, the internationally-respected American pilot, Major Alford J. Williams, had provided the fighter with an unsolicited testimonial which was to see widespread publication. Al Williams, a close friend of Ernst Udet, visited Germany in his Grumman G-22 "*Gulfhawk*" biplane, and was permitted to fly a pre-production Bf 109E. Although an admitted pro-biplane pilot, Al Williams's subsequent report on the German fighter monoplane left no doubt concerning his enthusiasm for the capabilities of the aircraft to which he referred as the most advanced of any fighter in existence.

However, his comment that, given the choice, he would prefer the Bf 109 to either the Hurricane or Spitfire in combat was difficult to understand in view of the fact that he had had no opportunity to fly either British fighter for comparison purposes. His opinion was perhaps based on information provided in Germany. Of course, Major Williams was *not* told that the version of the Bf 109 that he had been permitted to fly was a substantially more powerful model than equipped the *Jagdstaffeln* then operating the Messerschmitt fighter.

From the outset of Bf 109 design development provision had been made for the installation of the new DB 600 series 12-cylinder inverted-vee liquid-cooled engines, work on which had been initiated by Daimler-Benz as early as 1932. Indeed, when framing its original fighter specification the *Luftwaffenführungsstab* had stipulated that interchangeability between the Jumo 210 and the DB 600 should be taken into consideration in meeting the requirement, and as early as June 1937, the Bf 109 V10 had had its Jumo 210G replaced by an early DB 600Aa. It thus became, to all intents and purposes, the first prototype for the Bf 109E. The V11, V12 and V13 (originally the last three pre-production Bf 109B–0 airframes) were similarly powered, the last mentioned aircraft later being re-engined with a specially-boosted DB 601 to capture for the Third Reich the world air speed record for landplanes, as already recorded.

These were to be joined during the course of 1937–38 by several pre-production examples of what was at that time envisaged as the definitive production model of the Messerschmitt fighter, the Bf 109E, these all being assigned individual *Versuchs* numbers, the Bf 109E–02 becoming the Bf 109 V14, the Bf 109E–03 becoming the V15, the Bf 109E–04 becoming the V16, *et seq*. Whereas the Bf 109 V14 (D-ISLU), which had crashed at Zürich-Dübendorf while being flown by Ernst Udet, had been fitted with a DB 600Aa engine, subsequent pre-production airframes, such as the V15 (D-IPHR) and V16 (D-IPGS), were fitted with the DB 601A, and it was the Bf 109E fitted with this power plant that was to equip virtually the entire German single-seat fighter force for the first 18 months of World War II.

There were three reasons for the decision that the DB 600 would not be installed in the production Bf 109. Firstly, the prime principle of the programme formulated for the development of the *Luftwaffe* in 1933 had been the allocation of priority to bomber production in order to create as rapidly as possible a deterrent force to discourage any interference on the part of Britain or France in German rearmament. Thus, priority in the allocation of available DB 600 engines was awarded the Heinkel He 111. By 1938, when a shift in production emphasis from bombers to fighters was scheduled to take place, Daimler-Benz was already phasing out the DB 600 in favour of the superior DB 601, and the decision was taken by the RLM to limit production of the DB 600 in order to concentrate resources on the more advanced DB 601. The third reason was the belief that

the DB 600 was not ideally suited for fighter installation as, by this time, the value of direct fuel injection has been fully established.

While the DB 601 possessed almost identical overall dimensions to those of the DB 600, and the cylinder bore, stroke and capacity remained unchanged, the carburettor of the earlier power plant gave place to a direct fuel injection system, the compression ratio was increased from 6·5 to 6·9, supercharging capacity was improved, and an automatically-controlled hydraulic coupling to the supercharger drive was introduced. Marginally more powerful than the DB 600, the DB 601A was rated at 1,175 h.p. at 2,480 r.p.m. for take-off and offered 990 h.p. at 2,400 r.p.m. and 775 h.p. at 2,200 r.p.m. at 12,140 ft. (3 700 m). The fuel injection system reduced fuel consumption, afforded better results from relatively low octane fuel, and, unlike a carburettor-equipped engine, enabled its power plant to function under negative *g* without cutting or spluttering. However, the advantages of the system brought with them several problems which took longer to resolve than had been anticipated when the decision has been taken to phase

*The Bf 109 V19 (D-IRTT) above and the Bf 109 V13 (D-IPKY) were initially pre-production E- and B-series airframes respectively. The V13 is seen at Zürich-Dübendorf*

*(Above) Two of the Bf 109B pre-series aircraft (probably V11 and V12) assigned to engine development tasks and repainted for a series of widely-circulated 1939 propaganda photographs. (Below left) The Bf 109 V11 (B-08) which was allocated to Daimler-Benz for flight trials with the DB 600 engine*

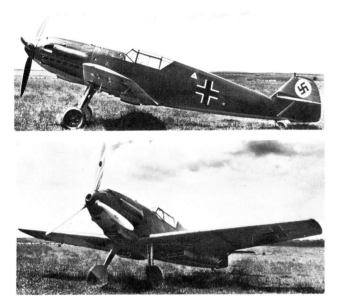

out the DB 600. In consequence, the DB 601 did not become available in quantity until late 1938, and therefore the Jumo 210-engined Bf 109 remained on the assembly lines for some six months longer than previously envisaged.

In general, the handling characteristics of the DB 601-powered Bf 109 were essentially similar to those of the Jumo 210-engined models of the fighter, despite the marked increases in loadings, although the turning circle suffered, and control was noticeably heavy at the upper end of the speed range. In other respects it handled well. Take-off with flaps lowered 20° was remarkably short, and initial climb rate excellent. Performance at altitude was good, and although the fighter stalled at quite high airspeeds, the stall was gentle, even under *g*, with no tendency to spin, and ample warning of its approach was provided by aileron vibration and buffeting. The ailerons were interconnected with the flaps, drooping 11° when the latter were lowered, the accompanying nose heaviness being compensated for by adjustment of the tailplane incidence, the range of movement of which was +3° to −8°.

By international standards, there was no denying that the performance of the DB 601A-powered fighter was remarkable and company test data prepared at the beginning of 1939 on the basis of trials with one of the initial production Bf 109E-1s revealed a maximum speed of 311 m.p.h. (500 km/h) at sea level, 317 m.p.h. (410 km/h) at 3,280 ft. (1 000 m), 329 m.p.h. (530 km/h) at 6,560 ft. (2 000 m), 335 m.p.h. (540 km/h) at 9,840 ft. (3 000 m), 345 m.p.h. (555 km/h) at 13,125 ft.

(4 000 m), 354 m.p.h. (570 km/h) at 16,405 ft. (5 000 m) and 351 m.p.h. (565 km/h) at 19,685 ft. (6 000 m). A fuselage tank following the contours of the pilot's seat accommodated 88 Imp. gal. (400 l) of fuel, which was sufficient for a 1·1-hour endurance at maximum continuous power at 19,685 ft. (6 000 m); absolute ceiling was 36,090 ft. (11 000 m), and the fighter attained an altitude of 3,280 ft. (1 000 m) in 1·0 min., 6,560 ft. (2 000 m) in 1·9 min., 13,125 ft. (4 000 m) in 3·8 min., 16,405 ft. (5 000 m) in 4·9 min. and 19,685 ft. (6 000 m) in 6·3 min. A 66-ft. (20-m) obstacle could be cleared on take-off within 350 yards (320 m) and landing distance from the same altitude was 749 yards (685 m), landing speed being 78 m.p.h. (125 km/h).

The use of direct fuel injection gave the Bf 109E-1 a considerable advantage. Negative *g*, such as occurred in sudden transition from level to diving flight and interrupted the fuel supply of fighters with engines possessing normal float carburettors, presented no problem, enabling the Messerschmitt fighter to out-dive its opponents. It retained the FuG 7 40-mile (65-km) range R/T equipment of earlier Bf 109s, together with the Carl Zeiss *Reflexvisier* (reflector sight) C/12C, but despite the appearance of armour on Soviet fighters encountered over Spain, no protection was provided either pilot or fuel tank.

Armament of the initial model comprised, like that of the Bf 109D-1, four 7,9-mm Rheinmetall Borsig MG 17 machine guns, two of these being mounted with a slight fore and aft stagger to accommodate the ammunition feed chutes in a light alloy cradle attached to the fuselage ahead of the cockpit and synchronized to fire through the airscrew disc (these being provided with 1,000 r.p.g.) and two being mounted as unsynchronized weapons in the wings (with 500 r.p.g.). However, the more lethal if slower-firing 20-mm MG FF cannon was by now generally favoured by the *Luftwaffenführungsstab* as a wing-mounted weapon (trials with the few Bf 109C-3s having proved generally satisfactory) and it had been decided to standardize on these as soon as the supply situation permitted, the model with wing cannon (and 60 r.p.g.) being assigned the designation Bf 109E-3, and the first examples of this sub-type followed closely on the heels of the initial production Bf 109E-1s. The Bf 109E-3 retained the twin fuselage-mounted machine guns and these, coupled with the pair of wing-mounted MG FF cannon, offered a combined weight of fire of 290 lb./min. (2,2 kg/sec).

In addition to the Daimler-Benz plants at Genshagen and Marienfelde, Henschel Flugmotorenbau at Altenbauna, and the Niedersachsische subsidiary of the Büssing-Werke of Braunschweig had tooled up for DB 601 production, and with the final clearance of the engine for service use late in 1938, delivery tempo of the initial DB 601-powered E-series fighter, the Bf 109E-1, increased rapidly, a substantial number of airframes having been stored pending power plant availability. By the time the first Bf 109E-1s left the assembly lines at the beginning of 1939, all production of the fighter by the parent company had been transferred from Augsburg–Haunstetten to Regensburg, thus enabling the former facility to concentrate on the Bf 110, and Focke-Wulf had phased out the Bf 109 programme in order to participate in production of the twin-engined *Zerstörer*.

In Austria, the Wiener-Neustädter-Flugzeugwerke (WNF) was preparing to manufacture the Bf 109E, and ground had been broken for a large new WNF-operated factory that was specifically intended for production of the Messerschmitt fighter, but the principal suppliers of the Bf 109 were by now the Erla Maschinenwerk at Leipzig and the Gerhard Fieseler Werke at Kassel. Between them, these two companies were to produce the bulk of the 1,540 Bf 109s accepted during the course of 1939, Messerschmitt's Regensburg factory contributing only 147 to this total.

Whereas total Bf 109 fighter production had barely exceeded 400 machines in 1938 (the entire German single-seat fighter output for the year, which included a small number of Ar 68s and He 112s, having been merely 450 machines), no fewer than 1,091 Bf 109s left the assembly lines between January 1, 1939, and September 1 when the codeword *Ostmarkflug* launched the aerial assault on Poland. This represented an average monthly output of 136·4 Bf 109s for the first eight months of 1939, and the Quartermaster-General's strength return to the *Oberbefehlshaber der Luftwaffe* at the time hostilities commenced included 1,056 Bf 109 fighters of which 946 were serviceable.

Throughout the spring and summer of 1939, the *Jagdstaffeln* were feverishly engaged in conversion to the Bf 109E from older fighters, and simultaneously new units were being formed. Some idea of the rapidity with which the Bf 109E was absorbed by the *Luftwaffe*'s operational inventory may be gained from the number of *Jagdstaffeln* mounted on this type and included in the order of battle September 1, 1939, although

a substantial proportion of the units were still operating earlier models of the fighter. It is of interest to note that on this date, too, five of the seven *Zerstörergruppen* still mounted on Bf 109s were temporarily assigned *Jagdgruppe* designations, these being II/ZG 1 (which became J.Gr. 101), I/ZG 2 (J.Gr. 102), III/ZG 26 (J.Gr. 126), I/ZG 52 (J.Gr. 152), and II/ZG 76 (J.Gr. 176), the designations of I and II *Gruppen* of ZG 26, which were flying Bf 109Bs and 109Cs, remaining unchanged as their conversion to the Bf 110C was imminent.

Bf 109-equipped units, the sub-type of the fighter with which they were operating and their numerical strengths (serviceable aircraft being indicated in parentheses) under the *Luftflotten* to which they were subordinated on the eve of hostilities were as follows:

*(Below) A Bf 109E-1 of 7./JG 51 "Mölders" shortly after redesignation from 1./JG 20 with which it was originally formed for the nocturnal intercept role. This unit subsequently served exclusively on day operations. (Above right) The Bf 109 V15 was the third E-series development aircraft, later being registered D-IPHR*

*A Bf 109E-1 of 2./JG 20 (later redesignated 8./JG 51) seen during exercises in the summer of 1939. Another aircraft of this unit is illustrated on page 65*

**Luftflotte 1:** I/JG 1 with 54 (54) Bf 109Es; I/JG 2 with 42 (39) Bf 109Es; 10.(*Nacht*)/JG 2 with 9 (9) Bf 109Cs; *Stab* and I/JG 3 with 51 (45) Bf 109Es; I/JG 20 with 21 (20) Bf 109Es and I/JG 21 with 29 (28) Bf 109Cs and 109Es (these two *Gruppen* having originally been scheduled for activation as night fighter units on November 1 but hurriedly pressed into service as day fighter units shortly before hostilities began); J.Gr. 101 (alias II/ZG 1) with 36 (36) Bf 109Bs, and J.Gr. 102 (alias I/ZG 2) with 44 (40) Bf 109Ds.

**Luftflotte 2:** *Stab* and I/JG 26 with 51 (51) Bf 109Es, II/JG 26 with 48 (44) Bf 109Es; 10.(*Nacht*)/JG 26 with 10 (8) Bf 109Cs; I and II/ZG 26 with 96 (92) Bf 109Bs and 109Ds awaiting conversion to the Bf 110C, and J.Gr. 126 (alias III/ZG 26) with 48 (44) Bf 109Bs and 109Cs.

**Luftflotte 3:** I/JG 51 with 47 (39) Bf 109Es; I/JG 52 with 39 (34) Bf 109Es; J.Gr. 152 (alias I/ZG 52) with 44 (43) Bf 109Bs; I and II/JG 53 with 51 (39) and 43 (41) Bf 109Es respectively, plus 1. and 2./JG 70 with 24 (24) Bf 109Es, and 1. and 2./JG 71 with 39 (18) Bf 109Cs and 109Es in process of formation as night fighter units.

**Luftflotte 4:** I/JG 76 with 49 (45) Bf 109Es.; I and II/JG 77 with 50 (43) and 50 (36) Bf 109Es respectively, and J.Gr. 176 (alias II/ZG 76) with 40 (39) Bf 109Bs and 109Cs.

In addition, the so-called *Luftwaffe-Lehrdivision* (Instructional Division), which had been formed on November 1, 1938, primarily for the development of operational tactics and techniques, included the *Stab* and I(*Jagd*)/LG 2 with 39 (37) Bf 109Es on strength, and 11.(*Nacht*)/LG 2 with 10 (9) Bf 109Es, while II/JG 186, comprising 5. and 6.*Staffeln* with 24 (24) Bf 109Bs was ostensibly under the control of the *Oberkommando der Marine*.

### Emil goes abroad

The high priority in the supply of the new Bf 109E to the *Legion Condor*, despite the urgency attached to the re-equipment of the *Jagdstaffeln* in Germany, resulted from considerations other than a desire to increase the effectiveness of the air support afforded the Nationalist forces by the *Legion* as previously recounted. Germany's acute shortages of such strategic materials as iron, chrome and copper ore, and of foreign currency,

dictated precedence being assigned to some export contracts irrespective of the pressing needs of the *Jagdstaffeln*. Considerable foreign interest had been aroused by the Bf 109 and Nationalist Spain had not been alone in expressing a desire to obtain this extraordinarily potent fighter. Several purchasing missions had visited the Messerschmitt A.G. and the RLM had perforce sanctioned the fulfilment of orders placed by the Yugoslav and Swiss governments.

In so far as Spain was concerned, with the end of the civil war the 20 Bf 109Es that had been assembled were gathered at Logroño, together with the 27 surviving Jumo-engined Messerschmitts, and officially transferred by the *Legion Condor* to the Spanish air arm. The Jumo-engined Bf 109s went to the León Air Park, the least worn of these subsequently being overhauled and utilized in the fighter training role. The Bf 109Es, which were dubbed *tripalas* (owing to their three-bladed airscrews) to distinguish them from the earlier models, or *bipalas*, had accumulated very few flying hours and, joined by the 20 additional fighters of this type still crated when fighting ceased, went, after the reorganization of the Spanish air arm in July 1939, to *Regimiento núm* 23 and equipped *Grupo núm* 25. Fifteen years later, after spending its final years in the training role with the *Escuela de Caza* at Morón de la Frontera, *Emil* was to be finally withdrawn from Spanish service.

Negotiations with Yugoslavia for the supply of Bf 109 fighters to the Yugoslav Royal Air Force, or *Jugoslovensko kraljevsko ratno vazduhoplovstvo* (JKRV), in fact began as early as January 1938, when Yugoslav Premier Stojadinović visited Germany with the primary purpose of acquiring modern weapons. The Yugoslav military attaché in Berlin had been highly impressed by the capabilities of the Bf 109 and when he and Premier Stojadinović met *Reichsmarschall* Göring to discuss planned Yugoslav weapon procurement, several dozen Bf 109s were a priority item on the list. Göring did his best to dissuade the Yugoslavs from persisting in their demand for the Messerschmitt fighter, commenting, "There is too much with which your pilots are unfamiliar in this new aircraft. They should convert by degrees to such fast warplanes or they will suffer many casualties, particularly during landings, and will develop a fear of really advanced fighters." The Yugoslavs remained adamant, however, and after the discussions had nearly broken down on the question of the supply of Bf 109 fighters, Göring finally relented, the iron, chrome and copper ore with which the Yugoslavs were to pay for the aircraft being of too vital importance to German industry to allow the sale to be endangered by what the Yugoslav military attaché somewhat naively believed, as he was subsequently to report, a matter of principle on the part of the *Reichsmarschall*. Nevertheless, some 15 months were to elapse before contracts for the supply of Messerschmitt fighters to the JKRV were to be finally ratified, the RLM constantly raising minor issues to delay signature.

Finally, on April 5, 1939, an initial contract for the supply to the JKRV of 50 Bf 109Es and 25 spare DB 601A engines was signed and 11 weeks later, on June 23, a supplementary contract was signed for a further batch of 50 Bf 109Es. The 6th Fighter Regiment (6.*Vazduhoplovni lovački pulk*) was designated the recipient of the German fighters and in the early autumn of 1939, the first three Bf 109E-3s were ferried from Augsburg to Zemun, Belgrade. Further fighters followed in small groups in the following months, ferried by JKRV pilots (on one occasion a group that had taken-off from Frankfurt landed on a Rumanian airfield as a result of poor navigation), but of the 100 aircraft ordered only 73 were actually delivered and spares backing proved so inadequate that many of these were to spend much of their brief service life grounded through lack of spares, sometimes being rendered unserviceable as a result of non-availability of as simple an item as a spare tyre.

The JKRV soon had cause to wonder if Göring had not, after all, been sincere in his attempt to dissuade them from acquiring the Messerschmitt as the 6th Fighter Regiment began to suffer numerous landing accidents, the major problem being the JKRV's lack of suitable transition aircraft between the simple and forgiving Hawker Fury biplane and the very much more sophisticated and somewhat more mettlesome Bf 109E. An attempt was made to utilize the Bf 108B Taifun four-seater as a transitional aircraft, but it sometimes proved necessary for former Fury pilots to convert to the more docile Hurricane for some 10 hours, following this period with about 20 hours on the Bf 108B before finally converting to the Messerschmitt fighter.

Various factors, including spares shortages, strictly limited the number of hours flown by the JKRV's Bf 109E-3s, and few Yugoslav pilots could be considered to have gained complete competence with the Messerschmitt by the time they were committed to combat – hardly any had any experience in flying the fighter in anything other than fair weather during daylight, and the JKRV pilot who tested his oxygen supply for the first time on the day that he also fired his guns for the first time in anger (and, incidentally, scored his first "kill", an He 111) was, if not typical, certainly not the most inexperienced of the JKRV's Bf 109E pilots.

The Swiss contract, which covered the immediate delivery of 10 Bf 109D-1s (see page 33) and an initial quantity of 30 Bf 109E-3s, had received the sanction of the RLM some months prior to the Yugoslav contract, and was to be shortly supplemented by a follow-on order for a further 50 fighters of this type. At this time, the Swiss *Fliegertruppe* had few modern combat aircraft, its few *Jagdfliegerkompagnien* flying antiquated Dewoitine D 27 parasol monoplanes, which, barely capable of 190 m.p.h. (306 km/h) and armed with a pair of rifle-calibre machine guns, were obviously incapable of putting up any realistic defence of Swiss air space. The Bf 109E-3s, like the earlier Jumo-powered Bf 109D-1s, were supplied to the *Fliegertruppe* without radio or armament and with only rudimentary

instrumentation, and the first example of this fighter reached Switzerland on April 14, 1939. A year was to elapse before, on April 27, 1940, the eightieth and last of the Bf 109E-3s ordered was to be delivered to the *Fliegertruppe*. These fighters were ferried to Switzerland by Swiss pilots until August 29, 1939, after which they were ferried by German pilots to the border airfield of Altenrhein and collected from there by Swiss pilots.

*A Bf 109E-3 of the Yugoslav 6th Fighter Regiment in 1940*

Delivery of the Bf 109E-3s to the *Fliegerkompagnien* was delayed by the need to install armament, radio, complete instrumentation, etc., but, nevertheless, when the *Fliegertruppe* was mobilized on August 30, 1939, 31 Bf 109Es had been taken into the inventory and were included on the strength of *Fliegerkompagnie* 6 at Thun and *Fliegerkompagnie* 21 at Dübendorf. These units, together with the Bf 109D-1s of *Fliegerkompagnie* 15 based at Payerne, were assigned the responsibility of maintaining "alarm patrols" of two fighters at constant readiness, but although Swiss air space had been violated 143 times by the aircraft of the combatants by the end of 1939, effective interceptions were few.

*(Below) A Bf 109E-3 with its ferry pilot shortly after its arrival at Zemun in the autumn of 1939. The Yugoslav Royal Air Force found the Emil troublesome, technical problems being exacerbated by inadequate spares backing. The Swiss, on the contrary, considered the Bf 109E-3 to be the most effective of their wartime aircraft, the third Swiss Emil being illustrated above right*

# A bird of a different feather

During the uneasy spring and summer months that preceded the assault on Poland and with it the commencement of World War II, Germany, much to the surprise of the international aviation fraternity, twice raised the world absolute speed record. The German Ministry of Propaganda had a field day, for never before had a nation gained this much-coveted record and raised it still higher within a month and with an entirely different aircraft. As with most pre-war records established in Germany, the demands of the Propaganda Ministry infused the feat with an element of subterfuge, and when the new records were announced and details submitted to the F.A.I. for ratification, the aircraft that had achieved such impressive speeds were referred to as the "He 112U" and the "Me 109R", and the use of specially-boosted engines was specifically denied. At that time, it was widely believed that the He 112 *was* in production for the *Luftwaffe*, if of less importance numerically than the Bf 109, and thus the impression was created that the high-speed aircraft were variants of standard *Luftwaffe* service fighters. Years were to elapse before the fact became widely known that neither "He 112U" nor "Me 109R" bore any relationship to the fighters allocated these numerical designations, other than common design teams and drawing boards, and the speed attained by the "Me 109R" was to stand as a record for piston-engined aircraft for 30 years.★

Fortuitously, both Ernst Heinkel and Willy Messerschmitt had set their sights on the absolute air speed record, and completely independently had striven to attain this goal, the efforts of one unbeknown to the other. The aim of the two aircraft manufacturers was, of course, known to *Generalmajor* Ernst Udet, as chief of the *Technischen Amtes*, and while he held the opinion that competition between the two could be ill-afforded by the industry, he was only too well aware of the mutual antipathy between Heinkel and Messerschmitt and the uncompromising ambition that they shared, and as he could neither disclose to one the intentions of the other or forbid either to pursue his aim without displaying favouritism, he chose to let matters take their course.

Whereas Heinkel adapted his new He 100 fighter for his attempt on the record, Messerschmitt's contender was designed from the outset solely for high-speed flying, making no concessions to operational tasks, and was thus the smallest and aerodynamically cleanest airframe that could be designed around a Daimler-Benz DB 601 engine and a pilot. As the *Projekt* 1059, Messerschmitt's proposals were put to the RLM in 1937, and a contract for design development and the construction of three prototypes was awarded on the basis that the programme be related to future fighter development and that the possibility of a fighter variant be investigated in parallel with design of the record contender.

Allocated the designation Me 209, the aircraft bore no similarity to the Bf 109 apart from being a low-wing cantilever monoplane. Appreciably smaller than the fighter, with a wing span of 25 ft. 7 in. (7,80 m) and an overall length of 23 ft. 9½ in. (7,24 m), the Me 209 possessed a gross wing area of only 114·097 sq. ft. (10,6 m²), the gross weight of 5,545 lb. (2 515 kg) thus endowing it with a wing loading of 48·746 lb./sq. ft. (237,2 kg/m²). Of all-metal stressed-skin flush-riveted construction, with hydraulically-operated main undercarriage members and a fixed tail skid attached to the base of a ventral fin, the aircraft featured a slot-type annular coil cooler intake immediately aft of the airscrew spinner, and a system of surface evaporation cooling for which 48.4 Imp. gal. (220 l) of water was provided by wing and fuselage tanks, the water being run through the engine cooling system and the steam led back into the wing where it was condensed before re-circulation.

The first prototype, the Me 209 V1 (*Werk-Nr.* 1185 D-INJR) was completed in June 1938, and after somewhat protracted ground running trials of the surface evaporation cooling system, the aircraft was flown for the first time from Augsburg-Haunstetten on August 1, 1938, by Dr.-Ing. Hermann Wurster, who, nine months earlier, had raised the world landplane speed record to 379·38 m.p.h. (611 km/h) in the Bf 109 V13. For the initial flight only sufficient fuel and coolant water for 15 minutes was carried, reducing take-off weight to 4,497 lb. (2 040 kg), and the undercarriage remained extended, but shortly after taking-off the engine temperature warning lights came on and Dr.-Ing. Wurster was forced to land.

His unfavourable report on the handling characteristics of the aircraft had been anticipated to some extent as ultimate speed had taken precedence over all other considerations in the design of the Me 209. Nevertheless, it was hardly to be expected that this potential record-breaker would prove to be, as Dr.-Ing. Wurster's successor, *Flugkapitän* Fritz Wendel, was subsequently to refer to it, a "vicious little brute" and a "monstrosity".

Initial handling trials produced the following list of complaints: (1) The engine runs unevenly; (2) the high temperature attained by the coolant fluid results in unsatisfactory cooling; (3) cockpit ventilation is inadequate and engine gases penetrate the cockpit, necessitating the constant use of an oxygen mask; (4) the undercarriage cannot be extended at speeds in excess of 155 m.p.h. (250 km/h); (5) the mainwheels tend to drop out of their wells during high-speed manoeuvres; (6) the fuel filler

★ Being raised to 488·78 m.p.h. (776,45 km/h) on August 16, 1969, by Darryl Greenamyer flying an extensively modified Grumman F8F-2 Bearcat.

*(Above and below) The Me 209V1, which was to hold the world air speed record for piston-engined aircraft for 30 years, was allocated the spurious designation of "Me 109R" for publicity purposes. (Opposite page) Messerschmitt and (left) Wendel*

caps tend to lift off at high speed; (7) the undercarriage hydraulic oil escapes from its reservoir and sprays the windscreen; (8) the take-off run is excessive and the take-off characteristics vicious; (9) visibility from the cockpit is severely limited; (10) marked instability manifests itself during the climb; (11) the rudder is inadequate to control the plane in a bank and the plane tends to nose down with any divergence from course; (12) when banking at full throttle the plane rolls over on its back; (13) stick forces are excessive and tiring; (14) at speeds in the vicinity of 100–105 m.p.h. (160–170 km/h) the controls soften up; (15) landing characteristics are extremely dangerous except under windless conditions; (16) on touching down, the plane swerves violently; (17) it is impossible to employ the brakes during the landing run as immediately they are applied the aircraft swerves from the runway.

Some of the more minor faults were rectified, but few of the more serious shortcomings of the design had been ironed out by February 8, 1939, when the second prototype, the Me 209 V2 (*Werk-Nr.* 1186 D-IWAH), made its first flight with Dr.-Ing. Wurster at the controls. Two months later, on April 4, 1939, the Me 209 V2 was being flown by *Flugkapitän* Wendel who was to undertake the record attempt in the third prototype. During his approach to Augsburg–Haunstetten over the Siebentischwald, the oil cooling system suddenly failed and, almost immediately the engine cut. Wendel had already lowered the undercarriage in preparation for landing, and the drag of this coupled with that of the unfeathered airscrew, resulted in the aircraft dropping like a stone. Wendel succeeded in getting the nose down and built up sufficient speed to clear the trees bordering the Haunstetterstrasse, but the aircraft was completely written off in the ensuing crash from which, surprisingly, Wendel emerged with barely superficial injuries.

Only five days earlier Messerschmitt had been surprised by the news that the He 100 V8 flown by Hans Dieterle had raised the absolute record to 463·92 m.p.h. (746,604 km/h), and although it had been intended to use the Me 209 V3 for the record attempt in July, plans were immediately revised, and the specially boosted DB 601ARJ (DB 601 V10) engine that had been delivered to Augsburg by Daimler-Benz was promptly

installed in the Me 209 V1 in order that the attempt should be made as quickly as possible. The DB 601ARJ had a maximum output of 1,550 h.p., this being obtained by increasing the r.p.m. to 3,000 and using methyl alcohol as an additive, and for a one-minute burst this power plant could afford 2,300 h.p.

Several days passed in awaiting favourable weather for the flight, and finally, on April 26, 1939, *Flugkapitän* Wendel took off in an attempt to beat the record established by Dieterle in the He 100 V8, succeeding in raising it 5·3 m.p.h. (8,53 km/h) to 469·22 m.p.h. (755,138 km/h) by a *tour de force*, the Me 209 V1 being aerodynamically inferior to the Heinkel record-breaker but its DB 601ARJ engine being boosted to give some 500 h.p. more for the vital seconds occupied by the record runs.

Ernst Heinkel, furious that he had not been appraised of Messerschmitt's plans by Udet, immediately initiated preparations for a further attempt on the record with the He 100 V8, being confident that his aircraft would reach 478 m.p.h. (770 km/h) given comparable conditions to those under which the Me 209 V1 had gained the record, but in July he was officially requested to desist from any further attempt to raise the record. The impression had been created abroad that the record had been gained by a version of the Bf 109 fighter and, as Udet put it, "It would be embarrassing if another fighter proves to be faster!"

# A fully-fledged Eagle

By the time the codeword *Ostmarkflug* launched World War II, the Messerschmitt Bf 109 was no longer an eaglet. It had grown to maturity in Spanish skies and was a fully-fledged eagle by any standards, having attained a more advanced stage of evolution than any comparable foreign contemporary. However, many of the units flying the Bf 109 on the eve of hostilities were not considered to be fully operational, still being in process of working up, and contrary to popular belief, fewer than 200 Bf 109s were included in the *Luftwaffe*'s Order of Battle against Poland. The limited deployment of Bf 109 units in the East was dictated by prudence on the part of the *Oberbefehlshaber* which contrasted markedly with the calculated risk represented by the assault on Poland.

This campaign was being undertaken with the knowledge that the *Luftwaffe*'s reserves of fuel, bombs and ammunition would be insufficient for any major effort in the West should Britain and France take joint action in support of Poland. The retention of the bulk of the *Jagdstaffeln* in the West was, therefore, deemed necessary as a safeguard against such an eventuality. Fighter reserves were dangerously low, and the only single-seat fighter units that could be spared for participation in the opening phases of the Polish campaign were the Bf 109Es of I(*Jagd*)/LG 2 and the Bf 109Bs of J.Gr. 101 (alias II/ZG 1) which formed a part of the 1.*Fliegerdivision*, the Bf 109Es of I/JG 1 and the Bf 109Cs and 109Es of I/JG 21 under the *Luftwaffenkommando-Ostpreussen*, and the Bf 109Ds of J.Gr. 102 (I/ZG 2) under the direct command of the *Fliegerführer zur besonderen Verwendung* (Air Force Commander for Special Duties).

The obsolescent P.Z.L. P.7 and P.11c fighters by which the *Luftwaffe* found itself opposed made little attempt to contest the supremacy enjoyed by the Bf 109, the activities of which were soon largely confined to the strafing of targets of opportunity,

and although the Western Allies had still made no move against Germany, it was not without some relief that the Ob.d.L. found it possible to withdraw westward the Bf 109s of I/JG 1 and I/JG 21 while the Polish campaign was still in progress. While the *Jagdstaffeln* engaged in the Polish conflict suffered few losses in aerial combat, operational attrition was, nevertheless, high, and the Quartermaster-General's loss return to the *Oberbefehlshaber* for the period September 1–28, 1939, listed 67 Bf 109s. Most of the fighters had fallen victim to groundfire, and almost as many again were considered to have been lost to strength as a result of more than 10 per cent damage.

Fortunately for the *Jagdstaffeln*, the lack of activity in the West provided ample opportunity to make good this attrition. The Messerschmitt fighter had drawn first blood in combat with the R.A.F. when, on September 4, 1939, a Bf 109E-1 of II/JG 77 had shot down a Wellington of No. 9 Squadron attempting an attack on the *Scharnhorst* and the *Gneisenau* lying off Brunsbüttel. Less than a month had passed when, on September 30, Bf 109Es of JG 53 shot down four out of five Fairey Battles of No. 150 Squadron engaged on armed reconnaissance over Saarbrücken, this leading to the restriction of the Battle to nocturnal activities.

Eleven weeks later, on December 18, the largest air battle in the West to that time took place when 24 Wellingtons of Nos. 9, 37 and 149 Squadrons attempting an armed reconnaissance sortie over the Schillig Roads, the Jade Estuary and Wilhelmshaven, were intercepted by Bf 109Cs of 10.(*Nacht*)/JG 26, Bf 109Es of II/JG 77, Bf 109Bs of J.Gr. 101, and Bf 110Cs of I/ZG 76 operating from Jever, Nordholz, and Neumünster. During the ensuing combat 12 of the Wellingtons were destroyed for the loss of two Bf 109s, and three other Wellingtons were written off in crash landings after crossing the British coastline. This disastrous sortie markedly influenced R.A.F. Bomber Command thinking and subsequent operations.

The first months of W.W. II on the Western Front, known to the British and French as the Phoney War and *Drôle de Guerre* respectively, and to the Germans as the *Sitzkrieg*, saw only limited skirmishes between the *Jagdstaffeln* and Allied fighters, and on the few occasions when Bf 109Es *did* encounter Morane-Saulnier M.S. 406s of the *Armée de l'Air* or Hurricanes of the British Advanced Air Striking Force (A.A.S.F.) the *Luftwaffe* was given no reason to modify its belief that in the Messerschmitt it possessed the best single-seat fighter extant. The obsolescent models of the Bf 109 were steadily phased out and replaced by the Bf 109E, the Bf 109B and 109C having been largely relegated to the *Jagdfliegerschulen* by the end of 1939, and the Bf 109Ds being transferred to the improvised *Nachtjagdstaffeln*.

The service career of the Bf 109D-1 with the *Luftwaffe* was naturally restricted by the fact that its performance had been eclipsed by many of the fighters included in the inventories of the opposing air forces, yet, before being finally phased out of the first-line inventory late in 1940, the Jumo-engined fighter appeared at times on the strength returns of a surprisingly large number of units. The Bf 109D had entered service in the spring of 1938 with the I *Gruppe des Jagdgeschwaders* 131 at Jesau, this unit being redesignated I/JG 130 during the course of the year when the Territorial Commands, or *Luftkreiskommandos*, gave place to *Luftwaffengruppenkommandos*. After the formation of the *Luftflotten* in the spring of 1939, the unit was again redesignated as I/JG 1, this *Gruppe* having exchanged its Bf 109D-1s for E-series fighters before participating in the Polish campaign. The Bf 109D served briefly with the I *Gruppe des Zerstörergeschwaders* 1 (formerly the I *Gruppe des schweren Jagd-*

*A Bf 109E-1 of I/JG 77 photographed during the summer of 1939. (Below) an early production Bf 109E-3 of II/JG 54 photographed immediately prior to the German offensive in the West*

geschwaders 141) at Jüterbog-Damm, before, in the late spring and early summer of 1939, the unit converted to the Bf 110, but the *Dora* enjoyed a more protracted operational life with *Zerstörergeschwadern* 2 and 26.

The I *Gruppe des Zerstörergeschwaders* 2 (formerly I/JG 231) had converted from Bf 109Bs to Bf 109D-1s during the spring of 1939 at Bernburg, and was destined to be the only *Luftwaffe* unit to take the *Dora* into action during the Polish campaign, albeit under the temporary designation of J.Gr. 102. For this campaign, J.Gr. 102 (alias I/ZG 2) was deployed at Gross Stein, south of Oppeln, in Upper Silesia, and placed under the direct command of the *Fliegerführer zur besonderen Verwendung* (Air Force Commander for Special Duties), *Generalleutnant* Wolfram von Richthofen. The Bf 109Ds of J.Gr. 102 had the primary task of providing close escort for the Junkers Ju 87Bs of I and II *Gruppen des Stukageschwaders* 77 and the Henschel Hs 123As of II (*Schlacht*)/*Lehrgeschwader* 2, but as Polish fighter opposition weakened they were increasingly employed in strafing targets of opportunity. With the completion of the Polish campaign, J.Gr. 102 relinquished its Bf 109Ds in favour of the Bf 110, the designation I/ZG 2 being restored.

The *Zerstörergeschwader* 26 "*Horst Wessel*" (formerly the *schwere Jagdgeschwader* 142) with three *Gruppen* at Dortmund, Werl, and Lippstadt, was entirely equipped with Bf 109s, the I *Gruppe* including one *Staffel* of Bf 109Ds, its other *Staffeln* operating Bf 109Bs and 109Cs, as did also the III *Gruppe*, all three *Staffeln* of the II *Gruppe* having Bf 109Ds, but no units of ZG 26 saw active service during the Polish campaign, and before the end of the year conversion to the Bf 110C-1 had been initiated.

During the first weeks of hostilities, a II *Gruppe des Jagdgeschwaders* 52 was hastily formed on the Bf 109Ds relinquished by I/ZG 1, shortly afterward converting to the Bf 109E, but although the D-series fighter had virtually disappeared from the inventories of the *Jagd-* and *Zerstörergruppen* by the end of 1939, its operational career was not over. In the summer of 1939, a night fighter *Staffel*, 10.(*Nacht*)/JG 26, had been formed to evolve suitable nocturnal interception tactics under the command of (then) *Oberleutnant* Johannes Steinhoff. This unit was initially equipped with Ar 68s and Bf 109Bs, subsequently converting to Bf 109Cs, and by the end of August a second

*(Above and below) The Bf 109 V20 (Werk-Nr. 5601), originally the Bf 109E-08, which was fitted with an engine-mounted MG FF/M 20-mm cannon for trials purposes*

*Staffel* had been formed, 10.(*Nacht*)/JG 2, also on Bf 109Cs.

In November 1939, 10.(*Nacht*)/JG 26 was based at Jever, in East Friesland, as a component of the fighter forces in the Heligoland Bight area which were under the overall command of *Oberstleutnant* Carl Schumacher, forming, with the Bf 109Es of II/JG 77, the Bf 109Cs of II/JG 186 (which was operating within JG 77 as its third *Gruppe*), the Bf 109Bs and 109Es of II/ZG 1, and the Bf 110Cs of I/ZG 76, the so-called *Jagdgeschwader* "*Schumacher*". Before the end of 1939, 10.(*Nacht*)/JG 2 had been joined by 11.(*Nacht*)/JG 2 formed on Bf 109Ds, the two *Staffeln* becoming IV/JG 2 in February 1940, and transferring to the Heligoland Bight area where 10.(*Nacht*)/JG 26

*Continued on page 64*

*The detail views (below right) illustrate (A) the Bf 109E-1 with early-type windscreen and canopy retained by initial production E-3s; (B) the 66 Imp. gal. (300 l) drop tank introduced by the E-7 and the dust/sand filter, and (C) the SC 250 bomb as carried by the E-1/B, E-4/B, E-4/N and E-7/U2*

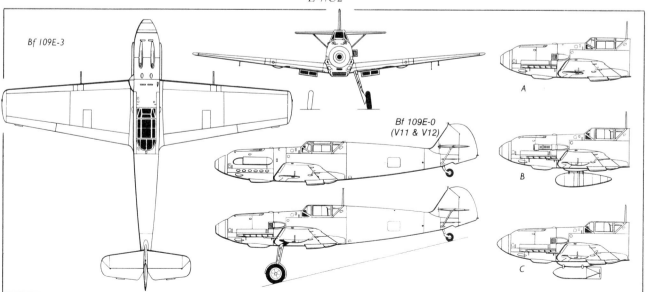

Bf 109E-3

Bf 109E-0
(V11 & V12)

A

B

C

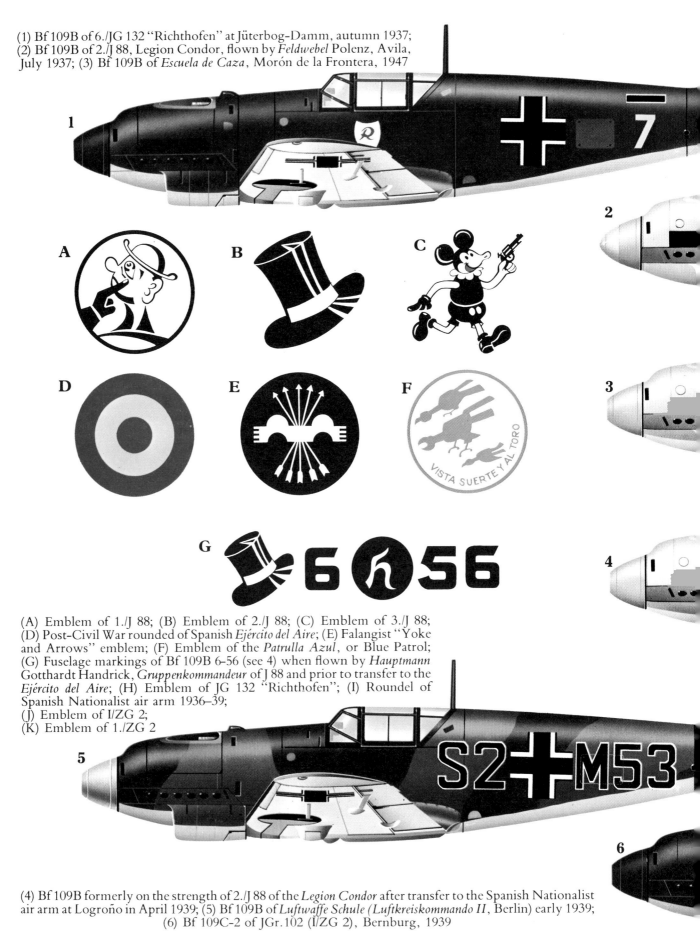

(1) Bf 109B of 6./JG 132 "Richthofen" at Jüterbog-Damm, autumn 1937;
(2) Bf 109B of 2./J 88, Legion Condor, flown by *Feldwebel* Polenz, Avila,
July 1937; (3) Bf 109B of *Escuela de Caza*, Morón de la Frontera, 1947

1

A    B    C

D    E    F

G    6 ◌ 56

2

3

4

(A) Emblem of 1./J 88; (B) Emblem of 2./J 88; (C) Emblem of 3./J 88;
(D) Post-Civil War rounded of Spanish *Ejército del Aire*; (E) Falangist "Yoke
and Arrows" emblem; (F) Emblem of the *Patrulla Azul*, or Blue Patrol;
(G) Fuselage markings of Bf 109B 6-56 (see 4) when flown by *Hauptmann*
Gotthardt Handrick, *Gruppenkommandeur* of J 88 and prior to transfer to the
*Ejército del Aire*; (H) Emblem of JG 132 "Richthofen"; (I) Roundel of
Spanish Nationalist air arm 1936–39;
(J) Emblem of I/ZG 2;
(K) Emblem of 1./ZG 2

5

6

(4) Bf 109B formerly on the strength of 2./J 88 of the *Legion Condor* after transfer to the Spanish Nationalist
air arm at Logroño in April 1939; (5) Bf 109B of *Luftwaffe Schule (Luftkreiskommando II*, Berlin) early 1939;
(6) Bf 109C-2 of JGr.102 (I/ZG 2), Bernburg, 1939

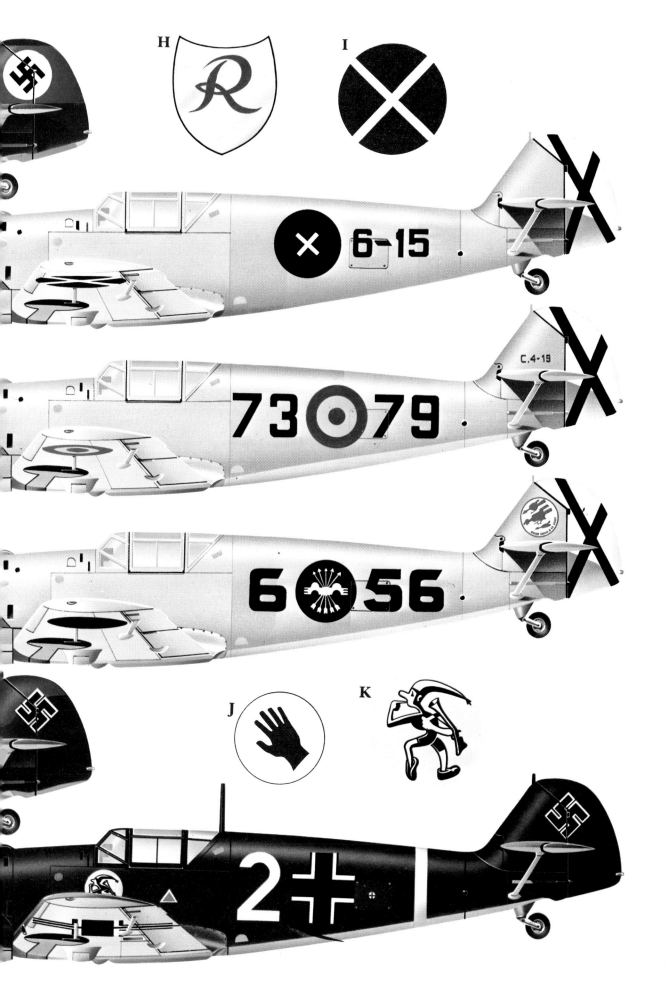

H

I

J

K

6-15

73 79

C.4-19

6 56

2

51

(1) Bf 109C-2 of *Jagdfliegerschule* 1 (JFS 1) at Werneuchen, 1940;
(2) Bf 109C-2 of 10.(N)/JG 26 at Jever, Autumn 1939

(A) Emblem of *Jagdfliegerschule* 1 at Werneuchen;
(B) Emblem of *Jagdfliegerschule* 2 at Zerbst;
(C) Emblem of Pilot School A/B 123 (Croatian)

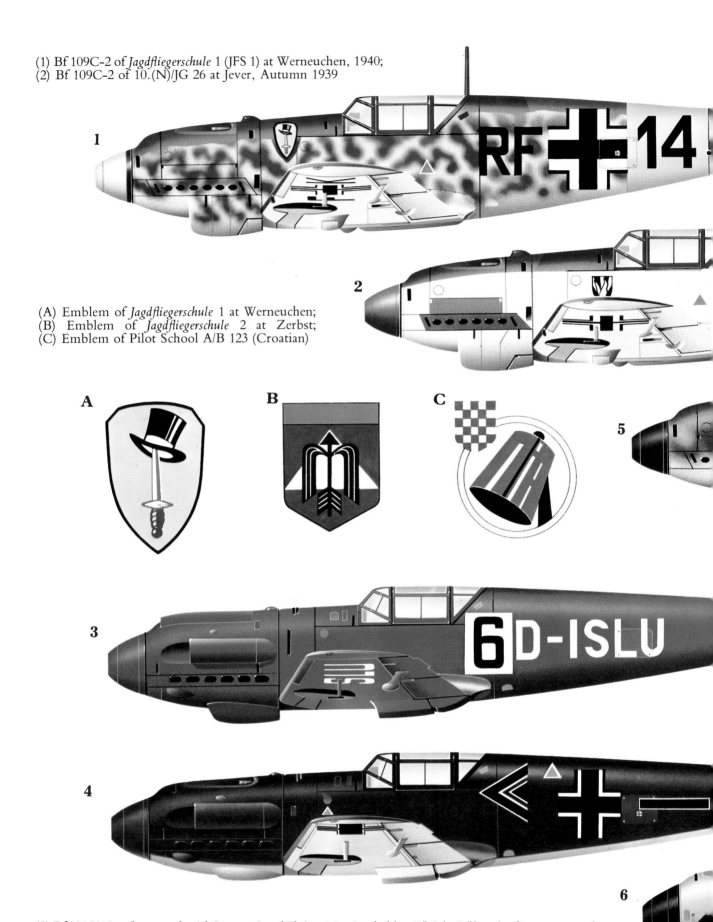

(3) Bf 109 V10 as flown at the 4th International Flying Meeting held at Zürich–Dübendorf in summer of 1937; (4) Bf 109 development aircraft, possibly V11 or V12 repainted to simulate service aircraft for propaganda photographs in 1939.

(D) and (E) Unidentified personal emblems employed by Bf 109Es during Polish campaign, September 1939; (F) Early form of *Nachtjäger* emblem; (G) Emblem of 3./ZG 26 "Horst Wessel"; (H) Emblem of 9./ZG 26 "Horst Wessel"

(5) Bf 109C–2 of Pilot School A/B 123 (Croatian) at Agram, Zagreb, March 1942; (6) Bf 109E-1 of the 25 *Grupo* of the 23 *Regimiento de Caza* of the Spanish *Ejercito del Aire*, 1952

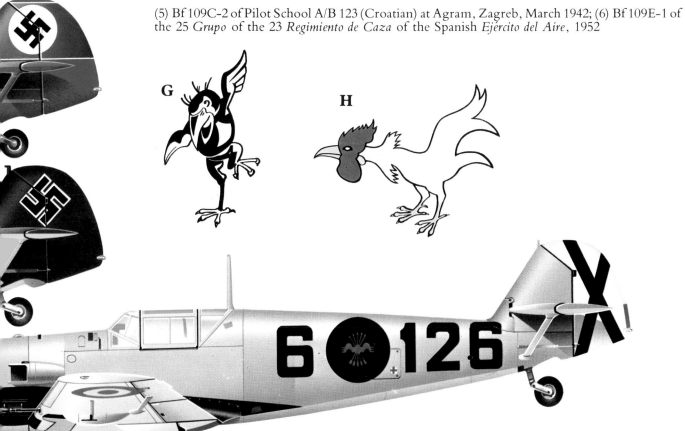

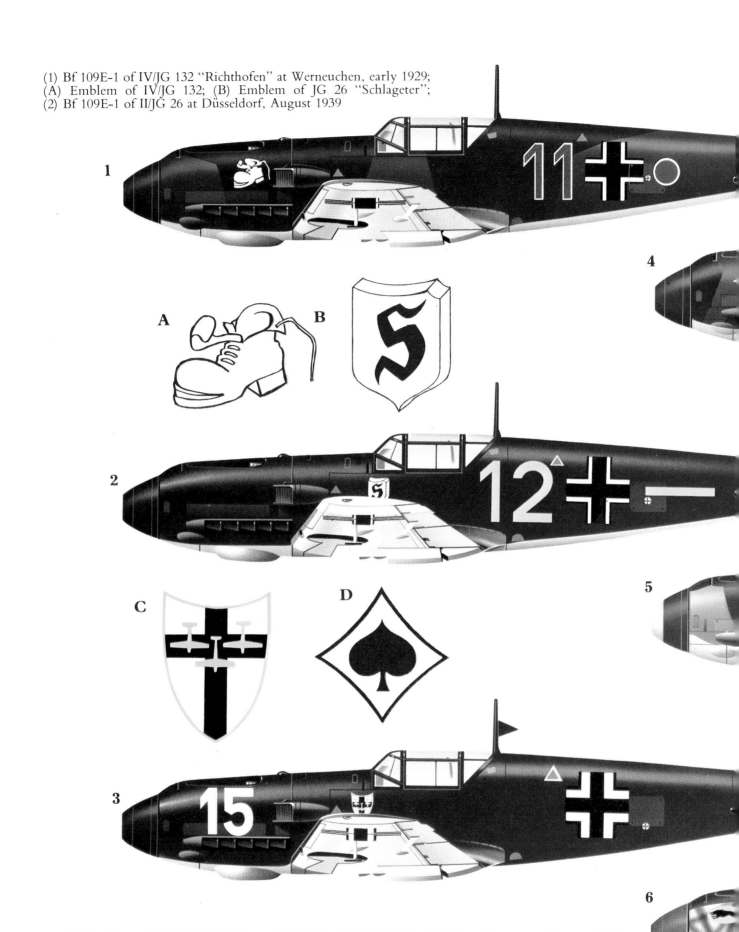

(1) Bf 109E-1 of IV/JG 132 "Richthofen" at Werneuchen, early 1929;
(A) Emblem of IV/JG 132; (B) Emblem of JG 26 "Schlageter";
(2) Bf 109E-1 of II/JG 26 at Düsseldorf, August 1939

(C) Emblem of I/JG 1; (D) Emblem of 8./JG 51; (3) Bf 109E-1 of I/JG 1 at Seerappen, August 1939;
(G) Emblem of III/JG 52; (H) Emblem of I/JG 52; (6) Bf 109E-1 of III/JG 52 at Hopstädten, August 1940.

(4) Bf 109E-1 of III/JG 51 at Bönninghardt, April 1940; (E) Emblem of 7./JG 51; (F) Emblem of 8./JG 51; (5) Bf 109E-1 of I/JG 53 "Pik-As" at Wiesbaden-Erbenheim during winter of 1939–40.

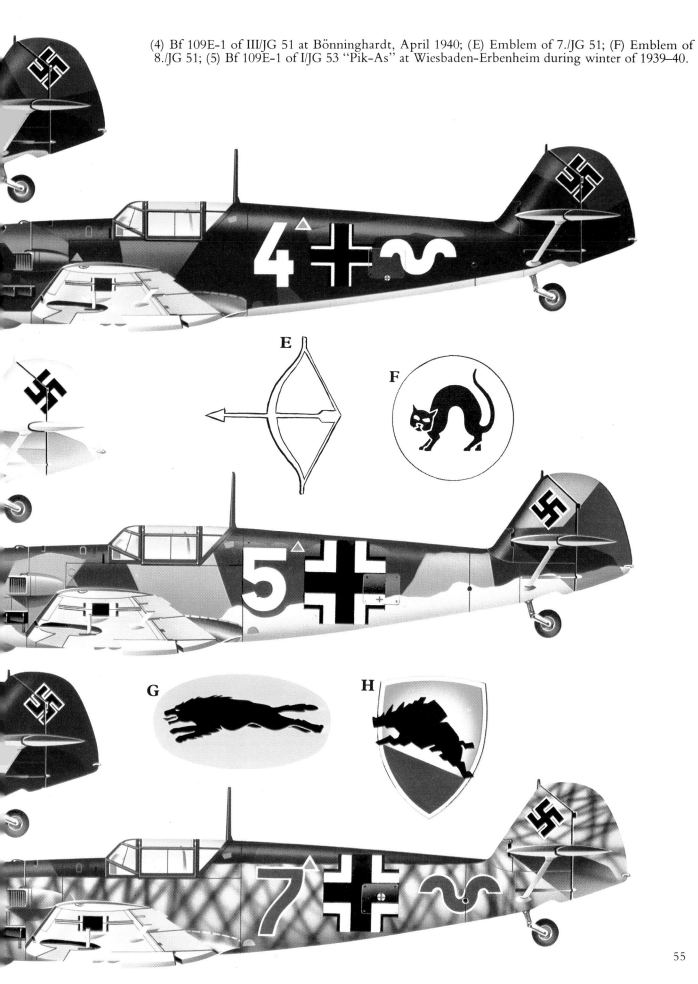

# Messerschmitt Bf 109E-4 Cutaway Drawing Key:

1 Hollow airscrew hub
2 Spinner
3 Three-blade VDM variable-pitch airscrew
4 Airscrew pitch-change mechanism
5 Spinner back plate
6 Glycol coolant header tank
7 Glycol filler cap
8 Cowling fastener
9 Chin intake
10 Coolant pipe fairing
11 Exhaust forward fairing
12 Additional (long-range) oil tank
13 Daimler-Benz DB 601A engine
14 Supplementary intakes
15 Fuselage machine gun troughs
16 Anti-vibration engine mounting pads
17 Exhaust ejector stubs
18 Coolant pipes (to underwing radiators)
19 Oil cooler intake
20 Coolant radiator
21 Radiator outlet flap

22 Cowling frame
23 Engine mounting support strut
24 Spent cartridge collector compartment
25 Ammunition boxes (starboard loading)
26 Engine supercharger
27 Supercharger air intake fairing
28 Forged magnesium alloy cantilever
   engine mounting
29 Engine mounting/forward bulkhead
   attachment
30 Ammunition feed chutes
31 Engine accessories
32 Two fuselage-mounted MG 17 machine
   guns
33 Blast tube muzzles
34 Wing skinning
35 Starboard cannon access
36 20-mm MG FF wing cannon
37 Leading-edge automatic slot
38 Slot tracks
39 Slot actuating linkage
40 Wing main spar
41 Intermediate rib station

42 Wing end rib
43 Starboard navigation light
44 Aileron outer hinge
45 Aileron metal trim tab
46 Starboard aileron
47 Aileron/flap link connection
48 Combined control linkage
49 Starboard flap frame
50 Cannon ammunition drum access
51 Fuselage machine gun cooling slots
52 Gun mounting frame
53 Firewall/bulkhead
54 Instrument panel rear face (fabric covered)
55 Oil dipstick cover
56 Control column
57 Oil filler cap (tank omitted for clarity)
58 Rudder pedal assembly
59 Aircraft identity data plate (external)
60 Main spar centre-section carry-through
61 Underfloor control linkage
62 Oxygen regulator
63 Harness adjustment lever
64 Engine priming pump
65 Circuit breaker panel
66 Hood catch
67 Starboard-hinged cockpit canopy
68 Revi gunsight (offset to starboard)
69 Windscreen panel frame
70 Canopy section frame
71 Pilot's head armour
72 Pilot's back armour
73 Seat harness
74 Pilot's seat
75 Seat adjustment lever

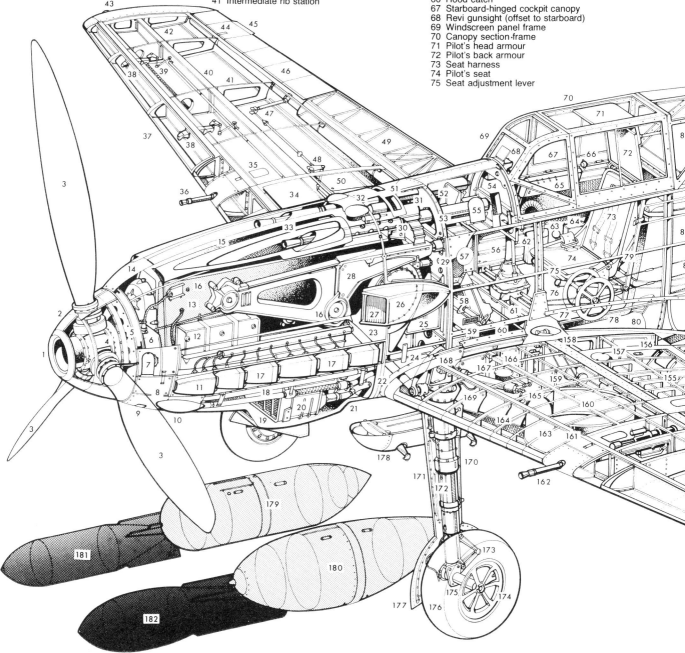

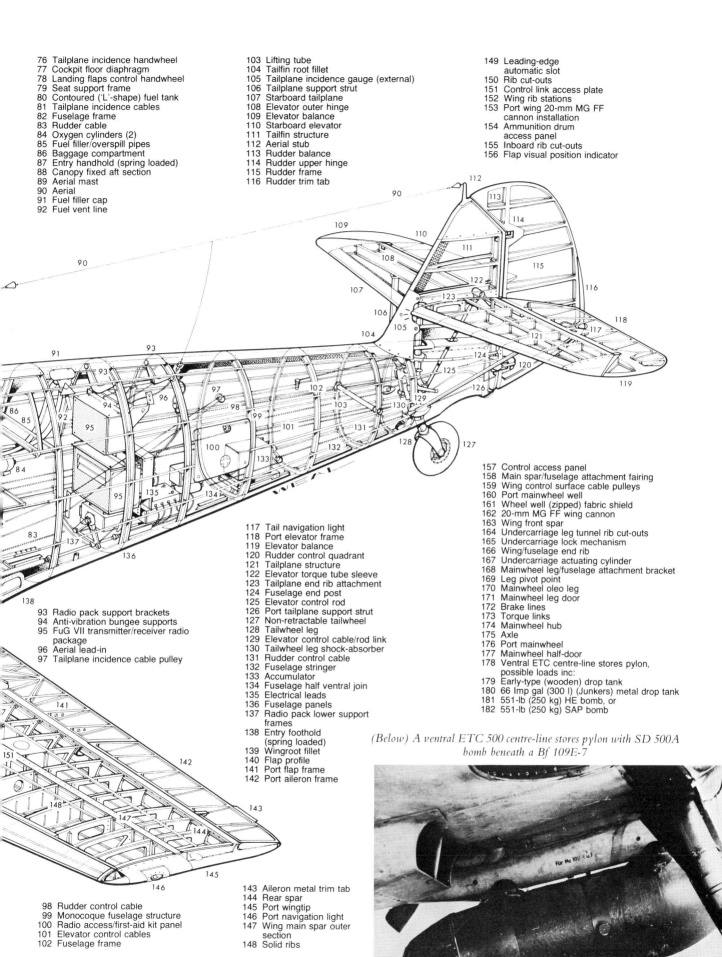

76 Tailplane incidence handwheel
77 Cockpit floor diaphragm
78 Landing flaps control handwheel
79 Seat support frame
80 Contoured ('L'-shape) fuel tank
81 Tailplane incidence cables
82 Fuselage frame
83 Rudder cable
84 Oxygen cylinders (2)
85 Fuel filler/overspill pipes
86 Baggage compartment
87 Entry handhold (spring loaded)
88 Canopy fixed aft section
89 Aerial mast
90 Aerial
91 Fuel filler cap
92 Fuel vent line

103 Lifting tube
104 Tailfin root fillet
105 Tailplane incidence gauge (external)
106 Tailplane support strut
107 Starboard tailplane
108 Elevator outer hinge
109 Elevator balance
110 Starboard elevator
111 Tailfin structure
112 Aerial stub
113 Rudder balance
114 Rudder upper hinge
115 Rudder frame
116 Rudder trim tab

149 Leading-edge
    automatic slot
150 Rib cut-outs
151 Control link access plate
152 Wing rib stations
153 Port wing 20-mm MG FF
    cannon installation
154 Ammunition drum
    access panel
155 Inboard rib cut-outs
156 Flap visual position indicator

93 Radio pack support brackets
94 Anti-vibration bungee supports
95 FuG VII transmitter/receiver radio
   package
96 Aerial lead-in
97 Tailplane incidence cable pulley

117 Tail navigation light
118 Port elevator frame
119 Elevator balance
120 Rudder control quadrant
121 Tailplane structure
122 Elevator torque tube sleeve
123 Tailplane end rib attachment
124 Fuselage end post
125 Elevator control rod
126 Port tailplane support strut
127 Non-retractable tailwheel
128 Tailwheel leg
129 Elevator control cable/rod link
130 Tailwheel leg shock-absorber
131 Rudder control cable
132 Fuselage stringer
133 Accumulator
134 Fuselage half ventral join
135 Electrical leads
136 Fuselage panels
137 Radio pack lower support
    frames
138 Entry foothold
    (spring loaded)
139 Wingroot fillet
140 Flap profile
141 Port flap frame
142 Port aileron frame

157 Control access panel
158 Main spar/fuselage attachment fairing
159 Wing control surface cable pulleys
160 Port mainwheel well
161 Wheel well (zipped) fabric shield
162 20-mm MG FF wing cannon
163 Wing front spar
164 Undercarriage leg tunnel rib cut-outs
165 Undercarriage lock mechanism
166 Wing/fuselage end rib
167 Undercarriage actuating cylinder
168 Mainwheel leg/fuselage attachment bracket
169 Leg pivot point
170 Mainwheel oleo leg
171 Mainwheel leg door
172 Brake lines
173 Torque links
174 Mainwheel hub
175 Axle
176 Port mainwheel
177 Mainwheel half-door
178 Ventral ETC centre-line stores pylon,
    possible loads inc:
179 Early-type (wooden) drop tank
180 66 Imp gal (300 l) (Junkers) metal drop tank
181 551-lb (250 kg) HE bomb, or
182 551-lb (250 kg) SAP bomb

*(Below) A ventral ETC 500 centre-line stores pylon with SD 500A
bomb beneath a Bf 109E-7*

98 Rudder control cable
99 Monocoque fuselage structure
100 Radio access/first-aid kit panel
101 Elevator control cables
102 Fuselage frame

143 Aileron metal trim tab
144 Rear spar
145 Port wingtip
146 Port navigation light
147 Wing main spar outer
    section
148 Solid ribs

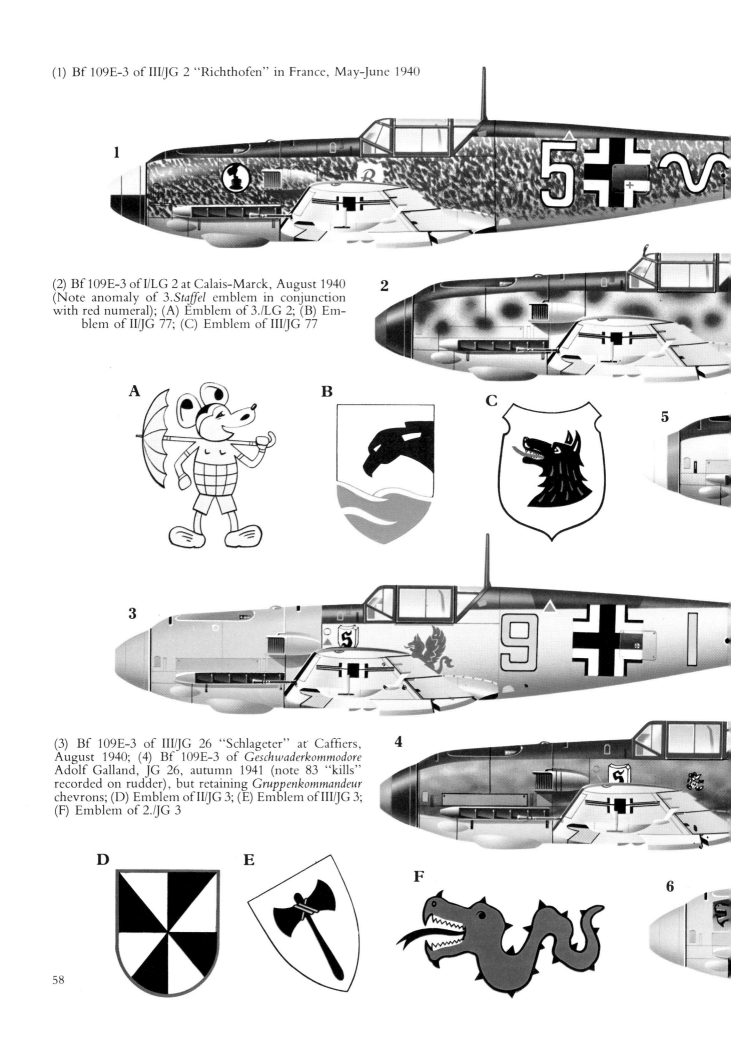

(1) Bf 109E-3 of III/JG 2 "Richthofen" in France, May–June 1940

(2) Bf 109E-3 of I/LG 2 at Calais-Marck, August 1940 (Note anomaly of 3.*Staffel* emblem in conjunction with red numeral); (A) Emblem of 3./LG 2; (B) Emblem of II/JG 77; (C) Emblem of III/JG 77

(3) Bf 109E-3 of III/JG 26 "Schlageter" at Caffiers, August 1940; (4) Bf 109E-3 of *Geschwaderkommodore* Adolf Galland, JG 26, autumn 1941 (note 83 "kills" recorded on rudder), but retaining *Gruppenkommandeur* chevrons; (D) Emblem of II/JG 3; (E) Emblem of III/JG 3; (F) Emblem of 2./JG 3

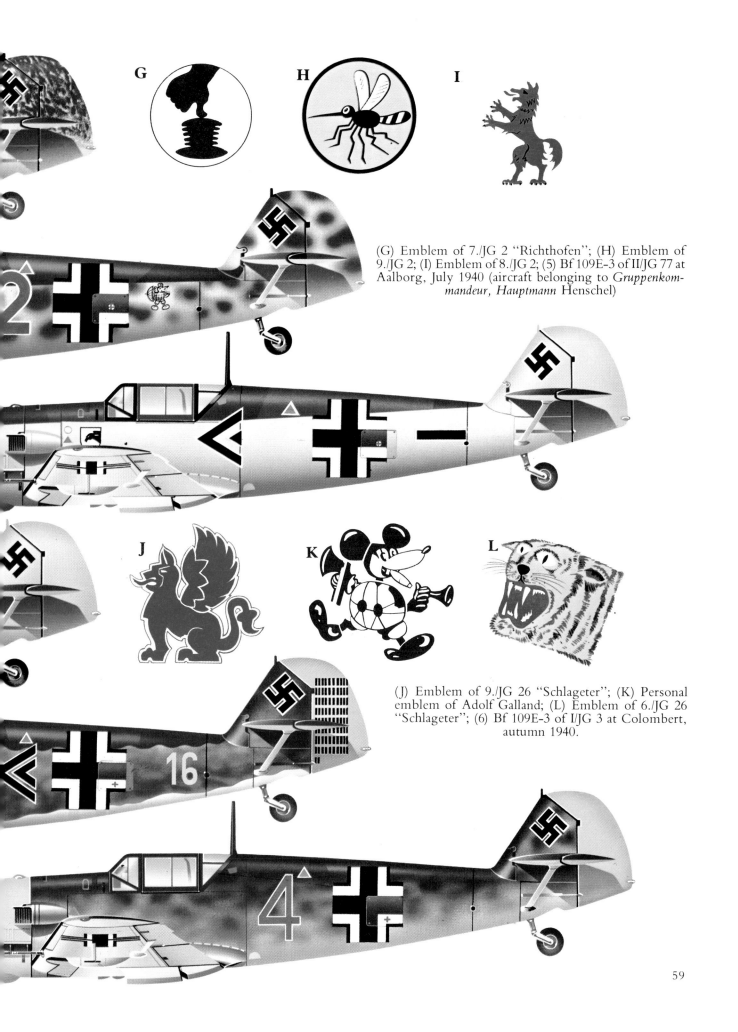

(G) Emblem of 7./JG 2 "Richthofen"; (H) Emblem of 9./JG 2; (I) Emblem of 8./JG 2; (5) Bf 109E-3 of II/JG 77 at Aalborg, July 1940 (aircraft belonging to *Gruppenkommandeur, Hauptmann* Henschel)

(J) Emblem of 9./JG 26 "Schlageter"; (K) Personal emblem of Adolf Galland; (L) Emblem of 6./JG 26 "Schlageter"; (6) Bf 109E-3 of I/JG 3 at Colombert, autumn 1940.

(1) Bf 109E-3 of *Fliegerkompagnie* 6 of the Swiss *Fliegertruppe* based at Thun, late 1939; (A) Emblem of *Fliegerkompagnie* 6; (B) Emblem of *Fliegerkompagnie* 15

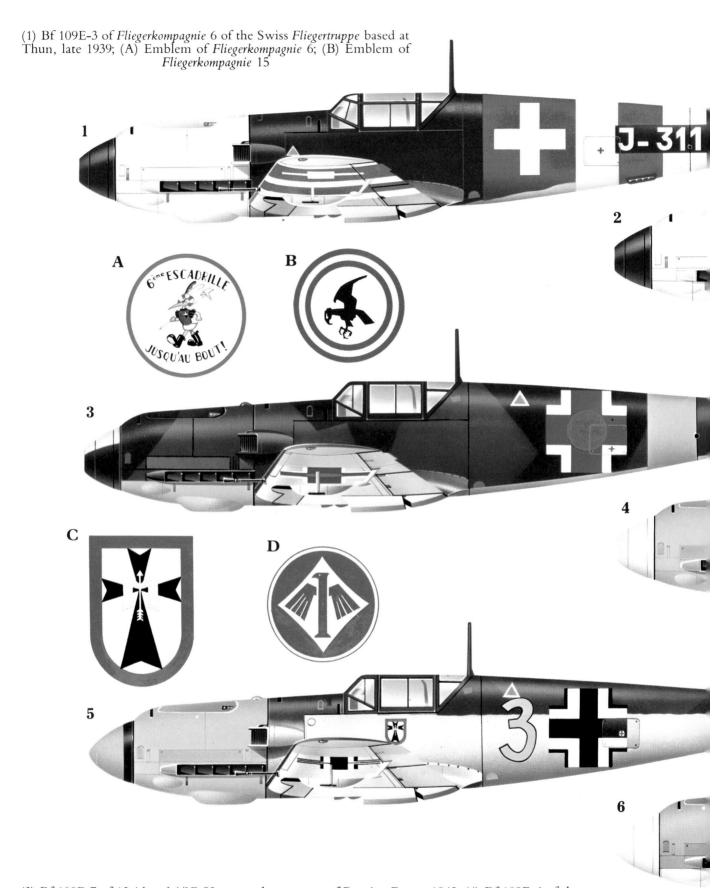

(3) Bf 109E-7 of 13.(*slowak*.)/JG 52 on southern sector of Russian Front, 1942; (4) Bf 109E-4 of the *Flotila 1 vinâtoare* of the Royal Rumanian Air Force, 1942; (C) Emblem of JG 1; (D) Later emblem of JG 1 (introduced mid-1943); (5) Bf 109E-4 of I/JG 1 at De Kooy, Netherlands, early 1941

(2) Bf 109E-3 of the Swiss *Fliegertruppe* (note that the number and width of the red-and-white neutrality stripes on the wings and fuselages of Swiss Bf 109s differed, the striping being omitted from the fuselages of some aircraft); (E) Swiss national insignia; (F) Personal emblem carried by a Bf 109E of *Fliegerkompagnie* 6 at Payerne, 1944

E

F

G

H

(G) National insignia carried by aircraft of the Slovakian Air Force; (H) National insignia carried by aircraft of the Royal Rumanian Air Force; (6) Bf 109E-4/B of III/SKG 210 at El Daba, October 1942

(1) Bf 109E-4/N Trop of I/JG 27 at Ain El Gazala, June 1941; (A) Emblem of I/JG 27; (B) Emblem of 7./JG 26 "Schlageter"; (C) Personal emblem of *Leutnant* Steindl of II/JG 54 "Grünherz"

(2) Bf 109E-7 of III/JG 26 "Schlageter" at Gela, Sicily, spring 1941; (3) Bf 109E-7/B of *Gruppenstab* III/SKG 210, Central Sector of Eastern Front, autumn 1941

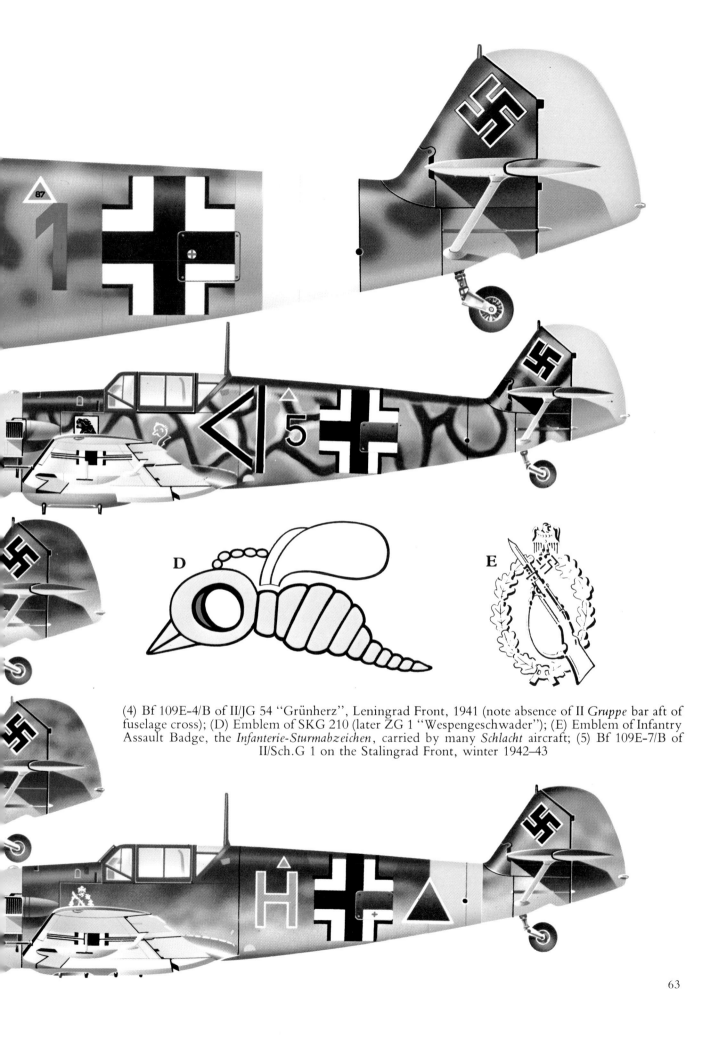

(4) Bf 109E-4/B of II/JG 54 "Grünherz", Leningrad Front, 1941 (note absence of II *Gruppe* bar aft of fuselage cross); (D) Emblem of SKG 210 (later ZG 1 "Wespengeschwader"); (E) Emblem of Infantry Assault Badge, the *Infanterie-Sturmabzeichen*, carried by many *Schlacht* aircraft; (5) Bf 109E-7/B of II/Sch.G 1 on the Stalingrad Front, winter 1942–43

*Continued from page 49*

(having meanwhile converted to Bf 109Ds) was absorbed to bring the *Gruppe* up to full three-*Staffel* strength. The Bf 109Ds were still being flown in the nocturnal defence of northern Germany by IV/JG 2 during the summer of 1940, but thereafter the Jumo-powered model of the Bf 109 was finally phased out.

Surprisingly, the conflict brought with it no immediate increase in Bf 109 production. On the contrary, the factories manufacturing this fighter were allowed to continue operating at substantially less than capacity and even on a single-shift basis, and only a further 449 Bf 109Es had been accepted by the end of the year (bringing 1939 total production to 1,540), some of these being exported to Switzerland. September saw 108 Bf 109Es roll off the assembly lines, followed by 102 in

---

### Bf 109E-3 Specification

**Power Plant:** One Daimler-Benz DB 601Aa 12-cylinder inverted-vee liquid-cooled engine rated at 1,175 h.p. for take-off, 1,000 h.p. at 12,140 ft. (3 700 m), and 775 h.p. maximum continuous.
**Performance:** (At 5,875 lb./2 665 kg) Maximum speed, 290 m.p.h. (467 km/h) at sea level, 307 m.p.h. (494 km/h) at 3,280 ft. (1 000 m), 322 m.p.h. (518 km/h) at 6,560 ft. (2 000 m), 348 m.p.h. (560 km/h) at 14,560 ft. (4 440 m), 336 m.p.h. (542 km/h) at 19,685 ft. (6 000 m); maximum continuous cruise, 300 m.p.h. (483 km/h) at 13,120 ft. (4 000 m); range cruise, 202 m.p.h. (325 km/h) at 3,280 ft. (1 000 m), 210 m.p.h. (338 km/h) at 6,560 ft. (2 000 m), 233 m.p.h. (375 km/h) at 22,965 ft. (7 000 m); maximum range, 410 mls. (660 km); initial climb rate at 5,400 lb. (2 450 kg), 3,280 ft./min. (17,83 m/sec); time to 3,280 ft. (1 000 m), 1·1 min., to 9,840 ft. (3 000 m), 3·6 min., to 19,685 ft. (6 000 m), 7·75 min.; service ceiling, 34,450 ft. (10 500 m).
**Weights:** Empty, 4,189 lb. (1 900 kg); empty equipped, 4,685 lb. (2 125 kg); loaded, 5,875 lb. (2 665 kg).
**Dimensions:** Span, 32 ft. 4½ in. (9,87 m); length, 28 ft. 4½ in. (8,64 m); height, 8 ft. 2⅓ in. (2,50 m); wing area, 174·053 sq. ft. (16,17 m²).
**Armament:** Two 20-mm (Oerlikon) MG FF cannon with 60 r.p.g. in wings and two fuselage-mounted 7,9-mm Rheinmetall Borsig MG 17 machine guns with 1,000 r.p.g.

---

*A Bf 109E-3 undergoing servicing with cowling removed to reveal DB 601Aa engine and fuselage-mounted MG 17s*

October, 117 in November, and 122 in December, the average monthly output for the year thus dropping to 128·3 machines.

### Evaluated by the Allies

The Bf 109E took little part in Operation *Weserübung*, the occupation of Denmark and Norway, but the Allies had an opportunity to evaluate the vaunted Messerschmitt fighter before the German offensive in the West began on May 10, 1940. The Allies obtained their first example of the Bf 109E on September 24, 1939, when a fighter (*Werk-Nr.* 3326) of II/JG 51 landed on Strassbourg-Neuhof airfield, but two weeks later, on October 6, after only limited flight testing, the aircraft was damaged when its French pilot made a heavy landing at Nancy. This aircraft was subsequently repaired but, on November 28, the Bf 109E was lost in a collision with an escorting Hawk 75A while being flown by (then) *Capitaine* Rozanoff who had earlier flown the Bf 109B in Spain. In the meantime, the French had acquired a further example of the Messerschmitt fighter. This, an early production Bf 109E-3 (*Werk-Nr.* 1304) of I/JG 76 (later II/JG 54), fell intact into French hands, on November 22, 1939, when the *Oberfeldwebel* flying the *Emil*, believing himself to be over German territory, landed near Woerth, Bas-Rhin, some 12 miles (20 km) on the *French* side of the border. The aircraft was promptly dismantled and transported to the *Centre d'Essais en Vol* at Orléans-Bricy, where, after re-assembly, it was flown by several test pilots. On May 4, 1940, it was flown to the Aircraft and Armament Experimental Establishment at Boscombe Down.

On May 14 the captured Bf 109E-3 was transferred to the R.A.E. at Farnborough for general handling trials (being allocated the serial number AE479 during the following month), these, together with the initial testing at Boscombe Down, confirming the already widely-held opinion that the Hurricane, even when fitted with the Rotol three-blade constant-speed airscrew, was inferior to the German fighter in virtually all performance respects apart from low-altitude manoeuvrability and turning circle at all altitudes.

In so far as the Spitfire I was concerned, when fitted with the two-pitch airscrew – and at that stage of the war virtually all Spitfires *were* fitted with such airscrews as priority in the supply of constant-speed units had been allocated to bombers – this was also bested from several aspects by the Bf 109E-3, although its inferiority was markedly reduced by the application of a constant-speed airscrew with which the average production Spitfire was only marginally slower than its German contemporary at rated altitude. It was ascertained that the Messerschmitt could out-climb the Spitfire up to 20,000 ft. (6 095 m), above which altitude the British fighter possessed an edge, but the German fighter could usually elude the Spitfire in a dive, the float carburettor of the Merlin engine of the latter placing it at a distinct disadvantage.

The general handling characteristics and fighting qualities of the Bf 109E-3 as assessed by the three pilots of the Aerodynamic Flight of the Royal Aircraft Establishment, who accumulated 35 hours on the aircraft during May and June 1940, were summarized★ as follows:
**Take-off and landing:** All the take-off tests were done with the slotted flaps set at the recommended position of 20 deg. The throttle could be opened very quickly, for as the engine was of the direct injection type it responded almost instantaneously to throttle movement without choking. The initial acceleration was very good, and there was no tendency to swing or bucket; during the ground run the aircraft rocked slightly from side to side, but this feature was not sufficiently pronounced to worry the pilot. On opening the throttle the stick had to be held hard

---

★ R.A.E. Report No. B.A.1604.

forward. The tail came up fairly quickly, and the stick could then be eased back. It was advisable for the pilot to hold the aircraft on the ground for a short while after he felt that flying speed had been gained, as if the aircraft was pulled off too soon the left wing would not lift, and on applying opposite aileron the wing came up, then fell again, with the ailerons snatching a little. If no attempt was made to pull the aircraft off quickly, the take-off was quite easy and straightforward. The take-off run was remarkably short, and the initial rate of climb was exceptionally good. In these respects the Bf 109 was definitely superior to Spitfires and Hurricanes with two-pitch airscrews.

**Approach:** The stalling speeds when gliding were 75 m.p.h. (120 km/h) with flaps and undercarriage up and 61 m.p.h. (98 km/h) with flaps and undercarriage down. Lowering the flaps made the ailerons heavier and very slightly less effective, and gave rise to a fairly large nose-down pitching moment which could, however, be readily corrected owing to the juxtaposition of the flap and tailplane adjustment operating wheels; and the attitude of the aircraft at constant airspeed changed by about 10 deg. when the flaps were lowered. Lowering the undercarriage caused only very slight nose-heaviness. If the engine was opened up when flaps were down, as for an aborted landing in which the pilot decided to go round again, the aircraft became slightly tail heavy, but could easily be held with one hand while trim was adjusted.

Approaching with flaps and undercarriage down the pilot had an impression of sinking at speeds below 80 m.p.h. (130 km/h) and of diving at speeds above 100 m.p.h. (160 km/h). The normal approach speed was about 90 m.p.h. (145 km/h).

Gliding at 90 m.p.h. (145 km/h) with flaps and undercarriage down, the glide path was fairly steep and the view was reasonably good owing to the nose-down attitude of the aircraft. Longitudinally the aircraft was markedly stable, stick free, and the elevator was heavier and more responsive at this speed than was usual on contemporary single-seat fighters, these features adding considerably to the ease of approach. Lowering the ailerons 11 deg. with the flaps detracted little from their effectiveness, but made them feel much heavier and the rudder was rather sluggish for small movements. Normal gliding turns could be made at 90 m.p.h. (145 km/h) with flaps down and without any signs of stalling or undue loss of height.

*A Bf 109E-1 of 2./JG 20 (later 8./JG 51) undergoing re-arming during 1939 exercises*

**Landing:** This was definitely more difficult than on the Hurricane or Spitfire, mainly owing to the high ground attitude of the aircraft. The Bf 109 had to be rotated through a large angle before touch down, and this required a fair amount of skill on the part of the pilot, and tempted him to do a "wheel landing". If a "wheel landing" was made there was a strong tendency for the left wing to drop just before touch-down, and when the ailerons were used quickly to bring the wing up they snatched a little, causing the pilot to over-correct. By holding off a little high the aircraft could be made to sink slowly to the ground on all three wheels, and there was then no tendency for

*(Below) The first Bf 109E acquired by the Allies (Werk-Nr: 3326 of II/JG 51) photographed shortly after falling into French hands, and (above right) the second flyable example to be obtained by the Allies (Werk-Nr. 1304 of I/JG 76). The former was destroyed in an accident on November 28, 1939, and the latter was taken to the U.K. and extensively evaluated by R.A.E. pilots at Farnborough*

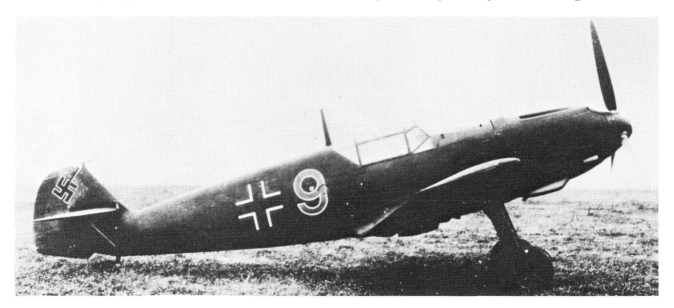

*(Above) Bf 109E-3 AE479 which had originally been Werk-Nr. 1304 in the inventory of I/JG 76. Transferred from France to the U.K. in the spring of 1940, it was eventually to be sent to the U.S.A. (see page 69) where it was written off. (Below left) The cockpit of the Bf 109E-3*

a wing to drop. A pilot quickly became accustomed to the landing technique required on this aircraft, and should have experienced no difficulty after a few practice landings.

The centre of gravity was unusually far behind the main wheels, and the brakes could be applied fully immediately after touch-down without fear of lifting the tail. The ground run was very short, and there was no tendency to swing or bucket. Owing to the large ground attitude, and the consequent high position of the nose, the view ahead during the hold-off and ground run was extremely bad, and landing at night probably presented difficulties.

**Ground handling:** Because of the large weight on the tail the Bf 109 could be taxied very fast without bouncing or bucketing, but was difficult to turn quickly. An unusually large amount of throttle was necessary in conjunction with harsh use of the differential brakes when manoeuvring in a confined space. Apart from turning performance, the ground handling qualities were good. The brakes were powerful and could be used harshly without lifting the tail. These were foot operated, but the R.A.E. pilots expressed a strong preference for the hand-operated system universal on British aircraft.

**Trim:** A small fixed tab was fitted to each aileron, these tabs being adjusted on the ground to correct any tendency to fly one wing low. No means were provided for trimming the ailerons in flight. There was no pronounced change of lateral trim with speed or throttle setting if care was taken to fly without sideslip. As no trimmer was fitted to the rudder, a small amount of sideslip was quite probable, particularly at high speeds when the rudder was fairly heavy. Owing to the large wing dihedral any such inadvertent sideslip gave rise to a pronounced rolling moment, necessitating use of the ailerons for its correction.

The absence of a rudder trimmer was a bad feature since there was a large change of directional trim with speed. A rudder angle indicator was fitted, and rudder angles necessary to fly straight and level with no sideslip were measured at various speeds when gliding and at full throttle, with flaps and undercarriage in turn up and down. It was found that when flying at full throttle there was a very rapid variation of directional trim with speed. The practical consequences were not quite so alarming as might have been expected, because the rudder was light at low speeds, and very little force was needed to hold on the 5 deg. of right rudder necessary when climbing at 150 m.p.h. (240 km/h). A French report that it was difficult to turn to the right when climbing was not confirmed, and was thought misleading. On the aeroplane tested at the R.A.E. climbing turns could be done with equal facility to both left and right.

It was at high speeds that lack of a rudder trimmer most seriously inconvenienced the pilot. At 215 m.p.h. (346 km/h) the aircraft was trimmed directionally, no rudder being required. At higher speeds left rudder had to be applied, and at 300 m.p.h. (483 km/h) about 2 deg. of left rudder were needed. The rudder was very heavy at high speeds, and a large force was necessary to apply even such a small amount. This became very tiring, and affected the pilot's ability to put on more left rudder to assist a turn to the left. Consequently at high speeds the Bf 109 turned more readily to the right than to the left.

The adjustable tailplane was controlled from a 11·7-in. (30-cm) diameter wheel on the pilot's left, 5·75 turns being required to move the tailplane through its full angular range (+3·4 deg. to −8·4 deg.), and the wheel rotation is in the natural sense (i.e., winding forward pushes the nose of the aircraft down). Tailplane angles to trim were measured at various speeds when gliding with flaps and undercarriage up, flaps up and undercarriage down, flaps and undercarriage down and at full throttle with flaps and undercarriage up. The centre of gravity was at $h = 0·302$ with undercarriage down. Raising the undercarriage had little effect on the fore-and-aft c.g. position as the wheels retracted sideways.

During the measurement of tailplane angles to trim, simultaneous readings were taken of the corresponding angles (from the stick-position indicator). The measured elevator angles were thus obtained with the tailplane setting varying, whereas, in order to obtain a picture of the stick-fixed stability of the aircraft, elevator angles to trim with the tailplane at a constant setting were necessary. By estimating the ratio of the change in tail lift per degree elevator movement to that per degree tailplane movement ($a_2a_1$) it was possible to convert the measured elevator angles to those corresponding to a fixed tailplane setting.

The nose-down change of trim due to lowering the flaps and undercarriage was large, but readily corrected. It was found that the aircraft was very stable when gliding at low speeds with flaps down, while the stability of the aircraft with flaps and undercarriage up was greater than was customary on single-seater fighters. This curtailed manoeuvrability in the looping plane, however, and contributed to the heavy "feel" of the elevator, particularly at high speeds. The aircraft was trimmed longitudinally to fly straight and level at 230 m.p.h. (370 km/h) at 10,000 ft. (3 050 m) at 2,200 r.p.m. Under these conditions the aircraft was not in trim directionally, and a slight pressure was required on the left rudder bar to keep the aircraft flying straight with no sideslip.

**High-Speed Dive:** The Bf 109 was dived at 370 m.p.h. (595 km/h) and all three controls were in turn given a slight displacement and then released. No vibration flutter or "snaking" developed. If the elevator was trimmed for level flight at full throttle, a moderately large push was necessary to hold the aircraft in the dive, and there was a temptation to wind the trimmer forward. If this was done, recovery was very difficult unless the trimmer was first wound back again, owing to the excessive heaviness of the elevator at high speeds. At 370 m.p.h. (595 km/h) a considerable amount of pressure was needed on the left rudder bar to hold the aircraft straight, and if the rudder was displaced in either direction and released, the aircraft eventually banked and turned to the right. Small rudder displacements sufficient to yaw the nose about 10 deg. gave rise to no appreciable nose-down pitching moment. Large rudder displacements did cause the nose to pitch down, but as the rudder was very heavy at 370 m.p.h. (595 km/h) they were not normally used.

**Flying Controls:** At low speeds the aileron control was very good, being similar to that of the Curtiss Hawk 75A. There was positive "feel", there being a definite resistance to stick movement, and response was brisk. In these respects the Bf 109 ailerons were better than those of the Spitfire, which became so light at low speeds that they lost all "feel". As the speed was increased the ailerons gradually became heavier, but response remained excellent. They were at their best between 150 m.p.h. (240 km/h) and 200 m.p.h. (320 km/h), and were described as "an ideal control" over this speed range. Above 200 m.p.h. (320 km/h) they became unpleasantly heavy, and at 300 m.p.h. (483 km/h) were far too heavy for comfortable manoeuvring. Between 300 m.p.h. (483 km/h) and 400 m.p.h. (644 km/h), a pilot, exerting all his strength, could not apply more than about fifth-aileron.

More detailed aileron tests (measurement of stick forces and time to bank) were made. These tests showed that, although the Bf 109 ailerons felt much heavier than those of the Spitfire at speeds between 300 m.p.h. (483 km/h) and 400 m.p.h. (644 km/h), the aircraft could be made to bank at about the same rate as the Spitfire at these high airspeeds. The more "solid" feel of the Bf 109 ailerons at high airspeeds was attributed to smaller stick travel (±4 in. compared with ±8 in. on the Spitfire), fairly rigid control circuit, and partly to the awkward seating position of the pilot. Throttling back the engine

did not alter the effectiveness of the ailerons at any speed. Lowering the flaps at low speeds (the ailerons came down 11 deg. with the flaps) made the ailerons considerably heavier and slightly reduced their effectiveness, although response was still entirely adequate.

Apart from their excessive heaviness at high speeds, the most serious defect of the Bf 109 ailerons was a tendency to snatch as the wing slots opened. This was particularly noticeable when manoeuvring. For example, if the stick was pulled back in a tight turn, putting additional $g$ on the aircraft, the slots opened at quite a high airspeed. As they opened the stick suddenly snatched laterally through several inches either way and sufficiently to upset a pilot's aim in a dog fight. The snatch appeared to be associated with the opening of the slots, for once they were fully open a steady turn could be done with no aileron vibration until the stall was approached. Some aileron snatching also occurred when gliding near the stall with flaps up and slots open but disappeared on lowering the flaps fully, and therefore did not worry the pilot during the approach glide.

The elevator was an exceptionally good control at low speeds. It was fairly heavy and not over sensitive during the approach glide, while response was excellent. Throughout the speed range the elevator was heavier than that of the Hurricane or Spitfire, but up to 250 m.p.h. (400 km/h) this was not objected to, since it was very responsive. Above 250 m.p.h. (400 km/h) the elevator became definitely too heavy for comfort, and between 300 m.p.h. (483 km/h) and 400 m.p.h. (644 km/h) was so heavy that manoeuvrability in the looping plane was seriously restricted. When diving at 400 m.p.h. (644 km/h) a pilot, pulling with all his strength, could not put on enough $g$ to black himself out if trimmed in the dive. At low speeds the elevator was slightly lighter when the engine was throttled back, and was very slightly less responsive. The elevator control was unaffected by lowering the flaps.

The rudder was light but rather sluggish at low speeds, and large displacements were required for quick response. As the speed was increased the range of sluggishness decreased, and at 200 m.p.h. (320 km/h) had disappeared, the rudder now being effective for small displacements and still quite light. Between 200 m.p.h. (320 km/h) and 300 m.p.h. (483 km/h) the rudder was the lightest of the controls for small movements, assisting

*Another view of AE479 (see opposite page) while undergoing trials in the United Kingdom*

*This Bf 109E (DG200) was basically Werk-Nr. 4101 of 2./JG 51 which made a wheels-up landing at Manston on November 27, 1940. It was restored to airworthy condition by the use of components (one wing, fin and rudder, upper enging cowling, etc) from other crashed aircraft*

directional aim for gunnery, but at 300 m.p.h. (483 km/h) the absence of a directional trimmer was severely felt, as a small amount of left rudder was necessary to fly without sideslip, and the force required, although not excessive, became very tiring. As the speed was increased to 400 m.p.h. (644 km/h) the rudder became extremely heavy, and only small displacements could be made, while the force required to hold the aircraft straight was considerable.

Throttling back the engine at low speeds made the rudder a little more sluggish, and lowering the flaps further reduced the rudder effectiveness, although response was still adequate when large displacements were used. If the speed was increased when gliding with flaps down, the rudder began juddering slightly at 100 m.p.h. (160 km/h); this juddering increasing rapidly as the speed was increased, and at 120 m.p.h. (193 km/h) was so pronounced that any further increase of speed was inadvisable. As the normal approach speed with flaps down was 90 m.p.h. (150 km/h) this rudder vibration was not normally noticed, and was of little practical importance.

The controls were fairly well harmonized between 150 m.p.h. (240 km/h) and 250 m.p.h. (400 km/h) although the elevator was somewhat heavy compared with the ailerons and rudder. At low speeds harmony was spoiled by the sluggishness of the rudder, while at high speeds harmony was poor because of the excessive heaviness of the ailerons. Features particularly liked by the pilots were the positive "feel" of the ailerons and elevator at low speeds, and the excellent response characteristics of all three controls at medium speeds. The control characteristics which were particularly complained of, and which were considered to spoil the aircraft as a fighter, were the undue stiffening up of the controls, particularly the ailerons, at high speeds; the aileron snatching caused by the slots opening during manoeuvres, and the absence of a rudder trimmer.

**Aerobatics:** Aerobatics were not easy on the Bf 109. Loops had to be started from about 280 m.p.h. (450 km/h), when the elevator was unduly heavy; there was a marked tendency for the slots to open near the top of the loop, resulting in aileron snatching and loss of direction, and in consequence accurate looping was almost impossible. At speeds below 250 m.p.h.

(400 km/h) when the ailerons were light and very effective, the aircraft could be rolled very quickly, but there was a strong tendency for the nose to fall in the final stages of the roll, and the stick had to be moved well back in order to keep the nose up. Upward rolls were difficult; the elevator was so heavy at high speed that only a gentle pull-out from the preliminary dive was possible, and a considerable loss of speed was thus inevitable before the upward rolls could be started.

**Fighting Qualities of the Bf 109E:** Mock fights were staged between the Bf 109 and a Spitfire, both flown by pilots of the R.A.E. In addition, a number of fighter pilots, all of whom had recent experience of operational flying, visited the R.A.E. with their Spitfires and Hurricanes in order to practise combat with the Bf 109. During these fights the Bf 109 was flown by an R.A.E. pilot who had completed the handling tests described earlier, and was thus thoroughly familiar with the aircraft and could be expected to get the best out of it.

The arrangements were for the aircraft to take off singly and meet at about 6,000 ft. (1 830 m). The Bf 109 then went ahead and commenced to turn as tightly as possible to see if it would out-turn the British aircraft. After doing three or four tight turns in both directions the Bf 109 was put into a dive, followed by a steep climb. The aircraft then changed position and repeated the above programme, after which the pilots engaged in a short general fight.

When doing tight turns with the Bf 109 leading at speeds between 90 m.p.h. (145 km/h) and 220 m.p.h. (354 km/h), the Spitfires and Hurricanes had little difficulty in keeping on the tail of the Bf 109. During these turns the amount of normal $g$ recorded on the Bf 109 was between 2½ and 4 $g$. The aircraft stalled if the turn was tightened to give more than 4 $g$ at speeds below about 200 m.p.h. (320 km/h). The slots opened at about ½ $g$ before the stall, and whilst opening caused the ailerons to snatch. This upset the pilot's sighting immediately and caused him to lose ground. When the slots were fully open the aircraft could be turned quite steadily until very near the stall. If the stick was then pulled back a little more the aircraft suddenly shuddered, and either tended to come out of the turn or dropped its wing further, oscillating meanwhile in pitch and roll and rapidly losing height. The aircraft immediately unstalled if the stick was eased forward. Even in a very tight turn the stall was quite gentle, with no tendency for the aircraft to suddenly flick over on to its back and spin. The Spitfires and Hurricanes could follow the Bf 109 round during the stalled turns without themselves showing any signs of stalling.

After these turns the Bf 109 was put into a steep dive at full throttle with the airscrew pitch coarsened to keep the r.p.m. down. It was found that both the Hurricane and the Spitfire could keep up with the Bf 109 in the dive, aircraft with constant speed airscrews being able to do so more readily than those with two-pitch airscrews. The ailerons and elevator of the Bf 109 became so heavy in the dive that rapid manoeuvring was impossible, while banked turns could be done more readily to the right than to the left because of the absence of rudder bias. The Bf 109 was then pulled out of the dive and climbed at a very low airspeed at an unusually steep attitude. The aircraft was under perfect control during the climb, and could be turned with equal facility in either direction. Under these conditions it outclimbed the British aircraft in most cases since most pilots climbed at a higher airspeed and a flatter angle, keeping below the Bf 109 and waiting for it to come out of the climb. However, other pilots who chose to climb at very low airspeeds, mainly those whose aircraft had constant-speed airscrews, succeeded in keeping on the tail of the Bf 109, although the Bf 109 pilot thought they would have difficulty in keeping their sights on him steadily, as he was at a steeper attitude than their sights could "line".

In most cases this steep climb at low airspeed was the only manoeuvre whereby the Bf 109 pilot could keep away from the Hurricane or Spitfire. During the general fighting which followed the set programme, one other feature of advantage to the Bf 109 emerged. If a negative $g$ was put on the aircraft for a short time, the engine did not cut as it was of the direct injection type, whereas on the Spitfire or Hurricane the engine immediately spluttered and stopped when negative $g$ was applied because the carburettor quickly ceased to deliver petrol under these conditions. Hence the Bf 109 pilot found that a useful manoeuvre when being chased was to push the stick forward suddenly and do a semi-bunt. If the British fighters followed him their engines cut giving the Bf 109 a chance to get away. This was particularly useful against the Hurricane, as its top level speed was less than that of the Bf 109 so that once the Bf 109 had escaped in this way it could avoid combat. The Spitfire, on the other hand, soon caught the Bf 109 after this manoeuvre.

When the Bf 109 was following the Hurricane or Spitfire, it was found that the British aircraft turned inside the Bf 109 without difficulty when flown by determined pilots who were not afraid to pull their aircraft round hard in a tight turn. In a surprisingly large number of cases, however, the Bf 109 suc-ceeded in keeping on the tail of the Spitfire or Hurricane during these turning tests, merely because pilots would not tighten up the turn sufficiently from fear of stalling and spinning.

During the general fighting, with the Bf 109 chasing a Spitfire or Hurricane, some pilots escaped by doing a flick half-roll and then quickly pulling up out of the subsequent dive. The Bf 109 pilot found this particularly difficult to counter, for when the Bf 109 rolled after its opponent, the speed built up quickly in the steep dive which followed the half roll, and the elevator became so heavy that a quick pull out was impossible. In addition, care had to be taken not to pull out quickly when the speed had decreased, because the aircraft stalled so readily under $g$. As a result 2,000–3,000 ft. (600–900 m) could be lost in the manoeuvre, and if a Bf 109 pilot could be tempted to do this at low altitude a crash was almost inevitable. In several cases a Bf 109 had, in fact, been observed to crash in this way without a shot being fired.

The Bf 109 pilot summed up his general impressions of the aircraft as a fighter in the following manner. "From all this dog-fighting I am certain that if the pilot of a Hurricane or Spitfire finds himself attacked by a Bf 109 he can easily out-turn it, and can lose it straight away by doing any violent man-oeuvre. The Bf 109 just cannot be made to do a really quick manoeuvre because at high speeds the controls are much too heavy, and at low speeds the slots come out, causing the ailerons to snatch, followed by the aircraft stalling if the manoeuvre is done more rapidly."

Aileron control at high speed was of considerable interest. At 400 m.p.h. (644 km/h) the Bf 109 pilot, pushing sideways with all his strength, could only apply about 1/5 aileron, thereby banking 45 deg. in about 4 secs.; on the Spitfire also, only 1/5 aileron could be applied at this speed, and again the time to 45 deg. bank was about 4 secs. Both aircraft thus had their rolling manoeuvrability at high speeds seriously curtailed by aileron heaviness. The Spitfire ailerons did not feel as "solid" at 400 m.p.h. (644 km/h) as those of the Bf 109 because there was rather more stretch in the aileron control circuit of the Spitfire. An interesting point was that the maximum sideways force a pilot could exert on the stick was about 60 lb. (27 kg) on the Spitfire, but only about 40 lb. (18 kg) on the Bf 109. The reason for this difference was that the cockpit of the Bf 109 was so cramped that a pilot could not bring his arm round into the position most favourable for applying a large side force to the stick.

*The Bf 109E-3 Werk-Nr. 1304, alias AE479, as delivered in 1942 to Wright Field with the tail assembly of another Bf 109E (Werk-Nr. 1980) that had been fitted in Britain as a result of damage suffered in a crash landing*

*Bf 109E-1s of 8./JG 2 at an advanced airfield in France late in May 1940. Together with the other components of Gruppe, this Staffel was pulled back to rest and recoup after the French campaign, re-equipping with Bf 109E-4s*

To show the effect on aileron heaviness of the geometry of the installation (aileron size, stick gearing, etc.), quite apart from aileron balance, the variation of stick force with stick displacement was calculated for the Bf 109 and Spitfire, assuming that the ailerons of both aircraft had exactly the same value. Because of their smaller size the Bf 109 ailerons should have been only about half as heavy as those of the Spitfire, other things being equal; but this was largely offset, especially for small aileron displacements, by the smaller stick travel of the Bf 109, ±4 in. compared with ±8 in. on the Spitfire. During the dog-fights against the Hurricane and Spitfire, it became apparent that the British fighters could out-turn the Bf 109 with ease when flown by determined pilots. Since the minimum radius of turn without height loss depended largely on stalling speed, and hence on wing loading, the poor turning performance of the Bf 109 could be ascribed to its high wing loading, 32·2 lb./sq. ft. (157,2 kg/m²) compared with 24·8 lb./sq. ft. (121,08 kg/m²) on the Spitfire. It was thought of interest to go into the matter a little more deeply, and to calculate the relative performances of these aircraft in circling flight, so that the sacrifice of turning performance entailed by the Bf 109's high wing loading could be assessed qualitatively.

The minimum radius of turn without height loss was obtained by flying as near the stall as possible at a comparatively small $g$. The advantage of the Spitfire over the Bf 109 at once became apparent, the minimum radius of turn without loss of height being about 696 ft. (212 m) on the Spitfire as against 885 ft. (270 m) on the Bf 109. In the view of the R.A.E. pilots, the Bf 109E's fighting qualities, good and bad, were as follows:

Good points
(i)   High top speed and excellent rate of climb.
(ii)  Good control at low speeds.
(iii) Gentle stall, even under $g$.
(iv)  Engine did not cut immediately under negative $g$.

Bad points
(i)   Controls, particularly the ailerons, far too heavy at high speeds.
(ii)  Owing to high wing loading, the aeroplane stalled readily under $g$ and had a poor turning circle.

(iii) Aileron snatching occurred as the slots opened.
(iv)  Quick manoeuvres were difficult at high speed because of (i) and at low speed because of (ii) and (iii).
(v)   Absence of a rudder trimmer, curtailing ability to bank left at high speeds.
(vi)  Cockpit too cramped for comfort when fighting.

The gentle stall and good control under $g$ were of some importance, as they enabled the pilot to get the most out of the aircraft in a circling dog-fight by flying very near the stall. The Bf 109 pilot succeeded in keeping on the tail of the Spitfire in many cases, despite the latter aircraft's superior turning performance, because a number of the Spitfire pilots failed to tighten up the turn sufficiently. If the stick was pulled back too far on the Spitfire in a tight turn, the aircraft tended to stall rather violently, flick over on to its back, and spin. Knowledge of this undoubtedly deterred pilots from tightening their turn when being chased, particularly if they were not very experienced. The most serious defect of the Bf 109 was its inability to roll fast in a high-speed dive because of its heavy ailerons. British fighters were by no means free from this defect, and in this respect the Spitfire was about as bad as the Bf 109.

This particular Bf 109E-3 was transferred to the Air Fighting Development Unit at Northolt on September 20, 1940, and suffered a crash-landing on January 5, 1941, repairs including replacement of the tail assembly by that of another Bf 109E (*Werk-Nr.* 1980). This much-flown *Emil* was transferred to No. 1426 (Enemy Aircraft) Flight at Duxford on December 11, 1941, and was eventually to be shipped to the U.S.A. on April 7, 1942, for evaluation at Wright Field. More than a year earlier Britain was to acquire another airworthy example of the Bf 109E, this being assembled from components of several machines and flown for the first time on February 25, 1941, with the serial number DG200, subsequently being used by Rolls-Royce for performance calibration trials against Spitfires and Hurricanes.

## The Eagle attacks

For the assault in the West virtually the entire *Jagdflieger* were gathered to the six *Fliegerkorps* – comprising *Luftflotten* 2 and 3, which, with the end of the Phoney War on May 10, 1940, had at their disposal 1,016 Bf 109 fighters from the total *Luftwaffe* Bf 109 strength of 1,346 (1,076 serviceable) machines. During the first eight months of the conflict the fighters of the opposing sides had found little opportunity to come to grips, and the French appraisal of the capabilities of the Bf 109E by which their *Groupes de Chasse* were opposed was unrealistic.

The severe weather of the winter of 1939–40 had greatly restricted fighter activity on the western front, which, in any case, had been confined largely to routine patrols and the escort of tactical reconnaissance aircraft on shallow penetrations of enemy territory. Nevertheless, the shortcomings of the *Armée de l'Air*'s principal fighter equipment should have been rendered obvious by the limited combat that it *had* seen against the Bf 109E and certainly by the reports of the test pilots that had flown the captured *Emil* at Orléans-Bricy. Yet the German offensive found the French still cherishing the beliefs that the manoeuvrability of the M.S. 406 gave it an advantage over the Messerschmitt, and that the Hawk 75A, if perhaps inferior in firepower to its German adversary, was its equal in other respects.

These beliefs undoubtedly owed much to somewhat exaggerated claims made, probably in good faith, by *Armée de l'Air* fighter pilots after skirmishes with Bf 109s during the Phoney War, but were not borne out in fact, and technical inferiority was quickly revealed to be such that even the skill and valour of the pilots flying the M.S. 406s and Hawk 75As proved of little avail.

The offensive in the West was, in so far as the *Luftwaffengeneralstab* was concerned, as much a calculated risk as had been the Polish campaign. Reserves of fighters, fuel and ammunition were insufficient for a sustained campaign. Production of the Bf 109E fighter had risen little during the early months of 1940. Indeed, average monthly production for the year was to be only 155·65 aircraft, an increase of little more than 12 per cent over that of the previous year, although admittedly this was in part due to the mistaken belief that, with the successful termination of the French campaign, the war was virtually over, some aircraft factories being allowed to diversify, manufacturing such items as aluminium prefabricated huts and extending ladders, and it was not until Erhard Milch took over from Ernst Udet as *Generalluftzeugmeister* that a realistic production programme was initiated, and raw materials carefully conserved.

Apart from IV/JG 2 operating in the night fighter role in northern Germany with Bf 109Ds, all *Jagdgruppen* were by now operating the Bf 109E-1 and E-3, and few were held in reserve when the attack on France and the Low Countries was unleashed, *Gruppen* of JG 1, JG 2, JG 3, JG 21, JG 26, JG 27, JG 51, JG 52, JG 53 and JG 54 establishing aerial superiority from the outset; superiority that was never to be seriously challenged. The *Armée de l'Air* and British Air Component fighters were constantly in action against the *Luftwaffe*, but the rapidity of the German Army's advance, which necessitated repeated abandonment of airfields as they were overrun, disorganized repair and maintenance. Logistic support was disrupted by constant attacks on road and rail communications by the *Stuka* and *Kampfgruppen*, and the serviceable strengths of the French and British fighter units fell rapidly. More Allied fighters were, in fact, lost on their bases in strafing attacks, or simply abandoned through lack of fuel or unserviceability, than were lost in combat.

As the *Jagdstaffeln* moved forward behind the advancing *Wehrmacht*, combat attrition took its toll. Actual combat losses were not particularly heavy, 147 Bf 109s being lost during May (this figure including losses in Norway), a further 88 sustaining more than 10 per cent damage. June saw the loss of only 88 Bf 109s in combat with 37 damaged, but despite prodigious efforts on the part of the ground crews in refuelling, re-arming, and performing minor repairs on the fighters, the number of serviceable Bf 109Es steadily dwindled, and the lack of adequate reserves began to make itself felt. Fortunately for the *Luftwaffe*, the forces opposing it had been thrown into complete disarray, enabling it to maintain its aerial superiority.

As supply lines lengthened with the fighting in northern France approaching Dunkirk, the situation of some *Jagdgruppen*

*(Above right and below) Bf 109E-1 fighters of 7./JG 52 photographed on a Dutch airfield in the summer of 1940. The temporary yellow nose, wingtip and (on some aircraft) rudder are noteworthy, and the dappled camouflage finish makes interesting comparison with the aircraft of this Jagdgeschwader's III Gruppe illustrated on page 55*

*Bf 109E-7s of II(Schlacht)/LG 2 at Calais-Marck in September 1940, these operating primarily in the fighter-bomber role*

became increasingly critical, and at times serviceable Bf 109Es were grounded through lack of fuel. Forced to operate at ever-increasing distances from their bases, the battle-weary *Jagdflieger* now began to encounter for the first time Spitfires flying from bases across the Channel, gaining their first experience of combat with the fighter that was to provide the Bf 109E with its principal opponent in the months ahead. The *Luftwaffe*'s failure to fulfil its designated task at Dunkirk, the prevention of the evacuation by sea of British and French troops, was due in no small part to the inability of the *Jagdstaffeln*, sapped of much of their strength and lacking advanced airfields, to provide adequate protection for the bombers and dive bombers which thus suffered a severe mauling from home-based British fighters.

The final phase of the western campaign, which began on June 5, 1940, and ended less than three weeks later with an Armistice, presented the *Jagdgruppen* with no insuperable problems, and units were progressively withdrawn from the line to rest and recoup. Attrition, although lower than had been anticipated by the *Luftwaffengeneralstab*, had been serious enough. Virtually all the *Jagdgruppen* were well below statutory strength, and although there was no shortage of pilots, insufficient Bf 109E fighters were immediately available to replace the losses that had been sustained.

A proportion of Bf 109E-3 production was still being taken up by export orders, the fulfilment of which was considered vital in order to obtain much-needed strategic materials. Forty Bf 109Es ordered for 1940 delivery by the Hungarian government were *not* delivered, it is true, perhaps because of German anxiety to avoid antagonizing Rumania, but five Bf 109E-3s that had been ordered in 1939 by a Soviet Technical Purchasing Commission in exchange for raw materials *were* delivered during 1940, and deliveries continued during the early part of the year to Yugoslavia and Switzerland.

The *Luftwaffe* was in no condition to mount an immediate assault against Britain, although preparations for such an assault were begun as soon as the French campaign terminated, the necessary ground organization being built up in France. The three *Gruppen des Jagdgeschwaders* 51 were virtually the only Bf 109E units facing Britain across the Straits of Dover during the month following the Franco-German Armistice, most other units having been pulled out of the line for rest and re-equipment. On July 12, JG 51 was joined by III/JG 3, this modest force being supplemented during the last week of the

month by JG 26, JG 27 and JG 52, and the build-up for *Adlerangriff* (Attack of the Eagles), as the forthcoming assault on Britain had been dubbed, began to gain tempo. According to the Quartermaster-General's strength return for July 20, a total of 809 Bf 109 fighters was available to *Luftflotten* 2 and 3. Of these 656 were serviceable and of a further 84 on the strength of *Luftflotte* 5, 69 were serviceable.

*Bf 109E-3 of 9./JG 26 based at Caffiers in August 1940*

In the meantime, the lessons taught by the French campaign were being incorporated in the Bf 109E. A cockpit canopy of revised design and embodying heavier framing had been introduced on the Bf 109E-3, together with some protection in the form of 8-mm armour for the pilot, seat armour weighing 53 lb. (24 kg) and a further 28·6 lb. (13 kg) being added by a curved plate attached to the hinged canopy over the pilot's head. Wing-mounted MG FF cannon of improved fire rate had resulted in the appearance of the Bf 109E-4 which rapidly replaced the E-3 during the summer and autumn of 1940. The Ikaria-Werke at Velten was working on a belt-feed for the MG FF cannon, although, in the event, this development was not ready for testing until early 1941 (on a Bf 109E-7) and was discarded.

*Bf 109E-3 of 5./JG 51 based at Desvres in August 1940*

The shortcomings in the range of the Bf 109E, which had proved something of an embarrassment to the *Jagdstaffeln* during the final phases of the French campaign, had been foreseen by the *Luftwaffenführungsstab*, and a jettisonable 66 Imp. gal. (300 l) fuel tank for use by the fighter had been developed and, in fact, manufactured in some numbers prior to the offensive in the West. Produced from moulded plywood, it was found to leak badly after exposure to the elements for any length of time. Furthermore, the fighter pilots considered it to possess an incendiary proclivity, and it therefore saw no service use when the suitably-equipped Bf 109E-7 began to arrive late in August 1940.

*Bf 109E-3 of 9./JG 2 based at Le Havre in August 1940*

With the approach of *Adlerangriff* further thought was given to the problem of increasing the endurance of the Bf 109E so that the fighter could supplement the protection expected to be afforded the *Kampfgruppen* by the Bf 110 in operations over Britain. One scheme that reached the test stage during the summer of 1940 was the idea of bombers towing their own fighter escort which would cast off from their tugs on approaching the British coastline. Trials were performed at Augsburg by a Messerschmitt test pilot, Karl Baur, with an

*Emil* equipped with a fully-feathering airscrew and an attachment point for a towline in the hollow airscrew spinner. The Bf 109E was attached to a Bf 110C by a towline, both aircraft taking-off under their own power, and after cruise altitude was attained the engine of the Bf 109E was cut and the airscrew feathered. Although the tests were considered successful the scheme was not adopted.

It was also during the French campaign that the possibility of employing the Bf 109E as a *Jagdbomber* (fighter-bomber), or *Jabo*, was first considered. Tests were conducted with single bombs ranging in weight from 110 to 551 lb. (50 to 250 kg) which were hung from a rudimentary rack beneath the fuselage and provided with an electric release gear. To evaluate the *Jabo* under operational conditions, an experimental unit, *Erprobungsgruppe* 210, was formed with Bf 109Es and Bf 110Cs adapted to carry bombs. Under the command of *Hauptmann* Walter Rubensdörffer, this unit began operations against shipping in the Channel during July 1940, 1. and 2.*Staffeln* with the Bf 110 and 3.*Staffel* with the Bf 109.

*Two outstanding Bf 109E pilots of the "Battle of Britain": Helmut Wick (left) who gained his 40th "kill" on October 6, 1940, and (right) Hans Hahn who scored 68 "kills" on the Channel Front*

The pilots received only rudimentary instruction in bombing techniques and, initially, were provided with no aid to bombing accuracy, but it was soon discovered that the *Revi* reflector sight could be utilized in diving attack, the angle of dive for bombing being indicated graphically by a red line painted on each side of the cockpit canopy at 45 degrees to the horizon. For bombing from low and medium altitudes the recommended diving speed was 373 m.p.h. (600 km/h), while for bombing from high altitudes the recommended diving speed was 403 m.p.h. (650 km/h). Such was the success of the Bf 109E *Jabo* that the *Oberbefehlshaber* issued an order that a *Jabo Staffel* should be formed within every *Jagdgeschwader*, and a number of Bf 109E-1 fighters were retroactively modified for the *Jabo* role under the designation Bf 109E-1/B, these usually carrying a single 110-lb. (50-kg) SC 50 bomb, while some Bf 109E-4 fighters on the assembly line were completed as Bf 109E-4/B fighter-bombers with a fuselage rack capable of lifting either four 110-lb (50-kg) bombs or a single 551-lb. (250-kg) bomb.

Produced in parallel with the Bf 109E-4 was the basically similar Bf 109E-5 reconnaissance fighter from which the wing-mounted cannon were removed and a single vertical Rb 21/18 camera mounted in the fuselage aft of the cockpit. Another Tac-R version of the *Emil* was the Bf 109E-6 which retained the wing-mounted cannon and carried an Rb 50/30 camera.

Yet a further variant of the E-series fighter that had reached service evaluation before the *Luftwaffe* and the R.A.F. joined combat in earnest in the "Battle of Britain" was the Bf

*Adolf Galland (above) became one of the leading exponents of the Bf 109's combat capabilities. Appointed Kommodore of JG 26 on August 22, 1940, he eventually became General der Jagdflieger*

109E-4/N which differed from the standard E-4 in having the DB 601Aa engine supplanted by a DB 601N. The latter power plant had flattened instead of concave piston heads, the compression ratio being increased from 6·9 to 8·2, and, using 96 octane C3 fuel in place of 87 octane B4, provided 1,200 h.p. for take-off at 2,600 r.p.m. with full boost for one minute, and a maximum emergency output of 1,270 h.p. for a similar period at 16,400 ft. (5 000 m).

## A battle of attrition

While, during the summer of 1940, much effort was being expended in improving the capabilities of the basic Bf 109, the fighter was being committed to what was to be its sternest trial and undoubtedly the most decisive aerial battle of W.W. II, the "Battle of Britain". The opening phase of the "Battle" consisted primarily of probing and coastal skirmishing which began early in July while the *Jagdflieger* were still largely preoccupied with making good attrition suffered during the invasion of France and the Low Countries. When the assault in the West had begun on May 10, *Luftflotten* 2 and 3 included 1,016 Bf 109 fighters in the forces at their disposal, but by the time fighting finally terminated in France virtually all *Jagdgruppen* were far below establishment, and the number of serviceable fighters included in the strength returns was lower than at any time during W.W. II.

By July 20, 10 weeks after the opening of the western offensive, *Luftflotte* 2, based in the Netherlands, Belgium and

*Werner Mölders, seen below describing a combat to JG 51 personnel during the "Battle of Britain", was the first General der Jagdflieger*

*(Above and below) A Bf 109E-3 Werk-Nr. 1361 serving as a prototype for the Bf 109E-7 and E-8 and seen above with a 551-lb bomb and below with a 1,101-lb bomb*

northern France, and *Luftflotte* 3, based in France, had had their single-seat fighter strength restored to 80 per cent of that with which they had begun the campaign, possessing 809 Bf 109Es of which 656 were serviceable. By August 10, three days before what *Reichsmarschall* Göring had designated *Adlertag* (Day of Eagles) which was to mark the opening of the "Battle of Britain" proper, 934 Bf 109Es were available to these *Luftflotten* (against an establishment of 1,011), of which 805 were service-

*Hans Philipp, Staffelkapitän of 4./JG 54 during the "Battle", was the second Luftwaffe pilot to gain 200 "kills"*

able, despite the loss of some 70 fighters during the previous month on operations and through normal service attrition.

On *Adlertag* the *Emil*-equipped element of *Luftflotte* 2 (apart from the Bf 109E-1/B and E-4/B fighter-bombers of 3./*Erprobungsgruppe* 210), was provided by the *Stab* and three *Gruppen* of each of *Jagdgeschwadern* 3, 26, 51 and 52, and the *Stab* and I *Gruppe* of JG 54 under the *Jagdfliegerführer* (*Jafü*) 2, while *Luftflotte* 3 included the *Stab* and three *Gruppen* of each of *Jagdgeschwadern* 2, 27 and 53 under *Jafü* 3. These *Luftflotten*, equipped and trained as a tactical air force, now embarked on what was to be a three-month strategic battle with the knowledge that the *Emil* on which so much reliance was placed possessed sufficient endurance for a mere 20 minutes actual combat over Britain, and that London represented the effective limit of its tactical radius.

The *Oberbefehlshaber* himself, Hermann Göring, and his staff undoubtedly underrated the effectiveness of the British fighters opposing the *Luftflotten* committed to *Adlerangriff*, but their most serious error of judgement was to be their appreciation of the British aircraft industry's ability to make good R.A.F. Fighter Command's attrition. At the outset the Bf 109E was assigned the task of engaging the opposing British fighters in open combat, a role for which it was ideally suited, but when the vulnerability of the twin-engined Bf 110 became obvious, the single-seat fighter had also to provide close escort for the bombers, and the fewer than 700 serviceable Bf 109Es available to *Luftflotten* 2 and 3 were inadequate for the dual role.

In the initial phases of the "Battle" the Bf 109E-equipped *Jagdgruppen* were able to take full advantage of the superior climbing and diving capabilities that their fighters enjoyed over those of their opponents, and their excellent tactics evolved during the Spanish Civil War enabled them to play havoc with the out-dated tactics retained by R.A.F. Fighter Command. The latter flew in compact formations based on tight three-plane elements which, if aesthetically attractive, were totally impracticable as only the formation leader was in a position to appraise the tactical situation, his companions being forced to concentrate on keeping station, with the result that, during the first weeks of the "Battle", many R.A.F. fighter formations were "bounced" by Bf 109Es. Furthermore, the R.A.F. formations utilized one of five standard attack procedures at the discretion of the formation leader once the enemy was sighted, these procedures being known as "Fighting Area Attacks". Such inflexible tactics were disastrous, and eventually the R.A.F. began to imitate its opponent.

Despite subsequent dramatization of this epic battle which, in Britain at least, tended to create an impression of studied nonchalance on the part of R.A.F. fighter pilots, and total disrespect for their fighter opponents other than for their numbers, the British pilot's attitude was anything *but* nonchalant, and he had every reason to treat the Bf 109E with the *greatest* respect. Indeed, most of the 1,172 aircraft lost by R.A.F. Fighter Command during July–October 1940 fell to the guns of the Messerschmitt single-seater.

The Bf 109E was highly effective and the master of both the Spitfire and the Hurricane in several performance respects, although lacking certain qualities inherent in the British fighters. The pair of wing-mounted 20-mm MG FF cannon carried by most Bf 109Es engaged in the "Battle" provided, with the twin 7·9-mm MG 17 machine guns, a formidable armament. Although having a very much lower rate of fire than the Browning machine guns of the British fighters, the MG FF's explosive shells could do infinitely more damage. Unfortunately for the *Jagdgruppen*, by September they had largely lost their freedom of action, being assigned to the close escort of bombers and seriously handicapped in being no longer permitted to pursue the tactics best suited to the *Emil*.

By the beginning of September, the Bf 109E elements of *Luftflotten* 2 and 3 had been reorganized to cater for the changing tactics enforced on them. Under *Luftflotte* 2, the *Jagdfliegerführer* (*Jafü*) 1 (which had been formed during the previous month) had the Bf 109Es of the *Stab* and II *Gruppe des Jagdgeschwaders* 76, and *Jafü* 2 comprised the *Stab* and three *Gruppen* of JG 53, the *Stab* of JG 51, and was in process of taking on strength the *Stab* and I and II *Gruppen* of JG 3 which were being transferred from *Luftflotte* 3. One *Schwarm* from each of III/JG 3 and I/JG 52 was attached to *Luftgaukommando* VI; *Stab*/JG 1, II/JG 51 and II/JG 52 were attached to *Luftgaukommando* XI; one *Schwarm* from each of the three *Gruppen* of JG 54 and one *Schwarm* from II/JG 51 were attached to *Luftgaukommando Holland*, and the fighter-bombers of *Erprobungsgruppe* 210 had been joined by the Bf 109E-7s of I(*Jagd*)/*Lehrgeschwader* 2 and the Bf 109E-4/Bs of II(*Schlacht*)/LG 2. The *Emil*-equipped elements of *Luftflotte* 3 now consisted of the *Stab* and three *Gruppen* of JG 2 (which at times operated under *Luftflotte* 2 control), and the *Stab* and three *Gruppen* of JG 27 which, for administrative purposes, came under VIII *Fliegerkorps*, itself in process of transfer to *Luftflotte* 2.

In the close escort role the Bf 109E could no longer use its speed to advantage, and the fact that it could be out-turned by both the Spitfire and the Hurricane now proved a serious disadvantage. The operational attrition of the *Jagdgruppen* steadily escalated in consequence, and the difficulties of the *Emil*-equipped units were aggravated by the *Oberbefehlshaber*, who, infuriated by the losses suffered by the *Kampfgruppen*, ordered them to stay still closer to their charges. The "Battle" dragged on until October 31 without the *Luftwaffe* having achieved anything of strategic significance, and the emasculated *Jagdflieger* were withdrawn from the assault, suffering, like their British counterparts, from physical and nervous strain. Neither side had been defeated; both were battered and weary.

The *Luftwaffe* had lost 1,792 aircraft on operations, 610 of these, or slightly more than one third, being Bf 109Es. With the 235 Bf 110Cs lost by the *Zerstörergruppen*, the *Luftwaffe* had lost 845 fighters on operations during July–October 1940, while R.A.F. Fighter Command lost 1,172 (631 Hurricanes, 403 Spitfires, 115 Blenheims and 23 Defiants), relatively few of these having fallen victim to the *Kampfgruppen* whose bombers were indifferently armed and could rarely bring more than one small-calibre weapon to bear on an attacking fighter.

One result of the "Battle" was its salutary effect on the tempo of Bf 109 evolution, which included the rapid development and service introduction of the F-series fighter. This, from the aerodynamic viewpoint and from the aspect of handling characteristics, was to carry the basic Messerschmitt single-seat fighter design to the peak of its development. There was, of course, no immediate transition from E- to F-series on the assembly lines, and more than a year was to elapse before the last examples of the earlier sub-type were to leave the factories.

The need to raise the output of Bf 109 fighters was by this time fully appreciated by the *Generalluftzeugmeister-Amt*, and production, which had fallen steadily during 1940, and was a mere trickle by January 1941 (in which month only 79 fighters resulted from the combined efforts of Messerschmitt, Arado, Erla, Fieseler and WNF), began to rise rapidly from February 1941, in which month the AGO Flugzeugwerke at Oschersleben began to augment the output of the Bf 109-manufacturing complex. Acceptances, which rose to 128 in February, attained 362 in April, although admittedly the last-mentioned figure was markedly higher than the output of any other single month in 1941, and was not, in fact, to be attained again until February 1943.

*Bf 109E-3s of JG 2 "Richthofen". All three Gruppen of this Jagdgeschwader were active during the "Battle of Britain", these being assigned to Luftflotte 3 but sometimes operating under Luftflotte 2 control*

*(Above) The Bf 109E-3 of Major Helmut Wick of I/JG 2 who was shot down on November 28, 1940, and (below) Bf 109E-4s of III/JG 27 at Carquebut, Northern France, summer 1940*

# The Eagle seeks fresh prey

The *Jagdgruppen* had meanwhile enjoyed little time to recuperate from the "Battle of Britain" before having to initiate preparations for the Balkan campaign, or Operation *Marita*, and the assault on the Soviet Union by which it was to be followed. Rumania had become a signatory to the Axis Tripartite Pact on November 23, 1940, being joined on March 1, 1941, by Bulgaria, and towards the end of March, when *Luftwaffe* units began moving into Rumanian and Bulgarian bases in strength, several of the *Jagdgruppen* were engaged in working up on the

Bf 109F or were in process of converting to the later fighter from the Bf 109E.

Most units that had not begun conversion were deployed for the support of Balkan operations, the Bf 109Es of the *Stab* and II and III *Gruppen* of JG 27, I (*Jagd*)/LG 2 and II(*Schlacht*)/LG 2 being the first to reach bases in Rumania and Bulgaria, being closely followed by I/JG 27 and the *Stab* and II and III *Gruppen* of JG 77. The I *Gruppe* of JG 27 was, in fact, only in transit to Sicily where, by the beginning of April, its aircraft were being tropicalized for operations in North Africa. This involved the introduction of a dust filter over the supercharger air intake, and the provision of emergency desert survival equipment which included a carbine, and with its fighter and fighter-reconnaissance aircraft designated Bf 109E-4/Trop and E-5/Trop respectively, I/JG 27 arrived in North Africa on April 20, 1941.

Two weeks earlier, on April 6, the *Luftwaffe* had launched its assault on Greece and Yugoslavia, the latter having repudiated the Axis Tripartite Pact after the overthrow of Prince Paul's regime, and the strange situation had arisen in which the *Jagdgruppen* found themselves opposed by the same type of fighter as that on which they were mounted.

On April 6, 1941, when the *Wehrmacht* assault against Yugoslavia began with an air attack on Belgrade, the 6th Fighter Regiment, which was responsible for the defence of the Yugoslav capital, comprised two Fighter Groups each with two squadrons, these being the 32nd Fighter Group (32. *Lovačka grupa*) with 22 serviceable Bf 109Es at the Prnjavor airfield, near Krušedol, about 30 miles (48 km) from Belgrade, and the 51st Fighter Group (51.*Lovačka grupa*) with 10 serviceable Bf 109Es on the strength of one of its squadrons which was

*(Below) Pilots of the Yugoslav Royal Air Force's 6th Fighter Regiment at the unit's peacetime Zemun base, and (above) Yugoslav Bf 109Es dispersed and camouflaged photographed shortly before the Wehrmacht invasion of the country. The base is believed to be Prnjavor airfield some 30 miles from Belgrade*

based at Zemun together with the other squadron which possessed an inventory of only six IK-Z fighters. The 2nd Fighter Regiment, to which some of the Bf 109Es had been handed earlier in the year and had been assigned the task of defending the most important industrial targets, consisted of the 31st Fighter Group with 11 Bf 109Es based at Sušičko polje, near Kragujevac, and the 52nd Fighter Group with 18 Hurricanes based at Knić airfield. There were also three Bf 109Es based at Mostar as part of the Independent Squadron of the Fighter Training unit (*Samostalna eskadrilja lovaćke škole*). Thus, only 46 of the Messerschmitt fighters were immediately available when the *Wehrmacht* attacked.

The Bf 109Es of the 32nd and 51st Fighter Groups were among the first JKRV aircraft to oppose the *Luftwaffe*, joining the IK-Zs of the 51st Fighter Group, which had taken-off minutes earlier, in attacking the first wave of *Luftwaffe* bombers over Belgrade. They succeeded in destroying some 10 of the intruders, but, by the end of the day, had suffered the loss of 15 fighters – 13 Bf 109Es and two IK-Zs – more than 40 per cent of the total strength of the 6th Fighter Regiment. Despite being officially forbidden to join the mêlée over Belgrade as their assigned task was the defence of the Serbian industrial towns, two Bf 109Es from the 2nd Fighter Regiment joined the Belgrade defenders and shot down two Ju 87Bs, one of the JKRV Messerschmitts being lost in the process. Ammunition presented a major problem from an early stage in the fighting as no incendiary bullets for the MG 17 machine guns of the Bf 109Es had been delivered from Germany. Thus, all ammunition from *Luftwaffe* aircraft brought down was carefully salvaged and delivered to the Messerschmitt-equipped squadrons.

On the second day of the German invasion, the JKRV Bf 109Es found that they had to run the gauntlet of their own anti-aircraft fire – the order to fire only on Bf 109Es with *yellow* noses had little effect on the understandably nervous Yugoslav batteries which had suffered their share of strafing and consequently fired at anything with wings that came within range. Although fewer *Luftwaffe* aircraft appeared over Belgrade during April 7, the 6th Fighter Regiment was again engaged in heavy fighting, losing a further 12 Bf 109Es and another IK-Z, while the Bf 109Es of the 2nd Fighter Regiment confined its activities to the skies over East Serbia. During the evening of April 8, the surviving Bf 109Es of the 6th Regiment – four from the 32nd Group and three from the 51st Group – were transferred to the Veliki Radinci airfield, near Ruma. Inclement weather prevented any operations on the following day, but on April 10, the day on which Zagreb fell, the Bf 109Es took-off several times to engage the *Luftwaffe* in minor skirmishes. By now, however, the Yugoslav High Command was paralysed and communications were chaotic, and in the belief that Paul von Kleist's *Panzers* would arrive at its base at any moment, the 2nd Fighter Regiment burned its aircraft assuming that it was thus preventing them falling into the hands of the enemy. A similar fate overtook the remaining Bf 109Es of the 6th Fighter Regiment on the following day as a German armoured thrust approached the Veliki Radinci airfield.

Another foreign recipient of the Messerschmitt fighter, the Swiss *Fliegertruppe*, had employed its Bf 109s in combat situations meanwhile. Three additional *Fliegerkompagnien*, Nos. 7, 8 and 9 had converted to the Bf 109E-3 by February 1940, and when, after May 10, *Luftwaffe* aircraft began regularly violating Swiss airspace in returning to South German bases after attacking French targets, the *Fliegertruppe* was ordered to take sterner measures to stop these intrusions and the Swiss-flown Messerschmitt fighters began to fire their guns in earnest. In fact, on the day that this order was issued, a Ju 88A flying towards Basle from the direction of Belfort was intercepted by a Swiss Bf 109E during a border surveillance flight. Warning shots across

*Bf 109E-3s of the Swiss Fliegertruppe displaying the red-and-white identification striping applied during W.W. II. These aircraft saw a considerable amount of combat in countering intrusions of Swiss airspace*

the nose of the *Luftwaffe* aircraft brought answering fire from the Ju 88A and so the Swiss pilot attacked the intruder which then turned back towards the border. Within hours, another Swiss Messerschmitt knocked out an engine of an intruding He 111 which then turned and left Swiss air space near Altenrhein.

A week later, an He 111 was actually shot down by Swiss Messerschmitts near Lignieres, and encounters between the fighters of the *Fliegertruppe* and the *Luftwaffe* became increasingly frequent, the Bf 109s taking-off to turn back formations of He 111s time and time again, the *Luftwaffe* crews invariably opening fire on sighting the Swiss fighters, and before the end of May, these encounters had resulted in the destruction of two more He 111s, one crashing near Ursins and the other near Lutter. These incidents provoked violent reaction from *Reichsmarschall* Göring, who, his threats ignored, attempted to teach the Swiss a sharp lesson, and on June 4, 1940, formations of He 111s again penetrated Swiss air space but now accompanied by an escort of Bf 110 fighters! There was little doubt that the intention of the intrusion was to entice the Swiss fighters into the air, and a series of battles ensued. The Swiss fighters were invariably outnumbered, but two Bf 110s and one He 111 were shot down, only one Swiss fighter being lost, a Bf 109D from *Fliegerkompagnie* 15.

On June 8, 32 Bf 110s were reported circling at various altitudes above the Jura mountains, their intention obviously being to challenge the Swiss fighters, and another formation of Bf 110s attacked and destroyed a patrolling *Fliegertruppe* C-35 biplane. Three *Fliegerkompagnien*, Nos. 6, 15 and 21, were at a state of readiness and two Bf 109Es of *Fliegerkompagnie* 15 were the first to intercept the intruders. One of the Bf 109Es was immediately shot down and the surviving Swiss fighter succeeded in shooting out the engine of a Bf 110 before, outnumbered by more than 30 to one, its pilot concluded that discretion was the better part of valour and disengaged with several of the Bf 110s in hot pursuit. He succeeded in making good his escape by flying into the Taubenlochschlucht, a mountain ravine into which he knew that none but a Swiss pilot would dare to follow. After landing, he learned that the Bf 110 that he had attacked had come down near Laufen and its crew had been interned.

Meanwhile, 12 more Swiss Bf 109Es had put in an appearance over the Jura and during the hectic mêlée that followed, three more Bf 110s were brought down, one crashing at Oberkirch, one at Triengen and the third at Rechesy, the Swiss fighters suffering no casualties.

A few days later, with the collapse of French resistance, *Luftwaffe* intrusions into Swiss air space came to an end and some time was to elapse before Switzerland was to find itself at the crossroads of the routes of Allied day and night bombers operating against German-controlled industry. The *Flieger-kompagnien* equipped with Bf 109E-3s were to continue border surveillance tasks and training exercises in the meantime, their strength being unexpectedly augmented on July 25, 1942, when two *Luftwaffe* Bf 109F fighters were to be interned after landing at Belp as a result of a navigational error during a flight from Le Bourget to Freiburg. In the event, these two aircraft were not assigned to a *Fliegerkompagnie* owing to the spares problem that they would undoubtedly have incurred had they been placed in service. In consequence, they remained in a hangar at Belp throughout the war★.

The *Fliegertruppe* fighter element was to be confronted with a new problem from August 1943, when U.S.A.A.F. B-17 Fortresses and B-24 Liberators began to intrude on Swiss air space in their efforts to avoid pursuing *Luftwaffe* fighters. The

---

★ The two Bf 109F-4/Z fighters were presented to Switzerland by the Allies after W.W. II and received the *Fliegertruppe* serials J-715 and J-716. A test flight was carried out with each machine and the two aircraft were subsequently flown to Emmen and, as the *Fliegertruppe* had no interest in them, were handed over to the Eidg. Flugzeugwerk which scrapped them at the beginning of 1947.

bombers were normally escorted to the nearest airfield by a *Doppelpatrouille* of four fighters, two guiding the bomber in and two bringing up the rear in case its pilot should, at the last moment, elect to head for home in preference to internment. Usually, such operations presented no undue difficulties, but exceptions were inevitable, one such occurring on September 5, 1944. On this occasion, four Bf 109E-3s of *Fliegerkompagnie* 7 were convoying a B-24 Liberator to Dübendorf airfield, when, some 10 miles (16 km) from the airfield, the pilot of the Messerschmitt flying to the rear and starboard of the bomber saw his companion on the portside suddenly fall in flames. Almost simultaneously his own fighter was hit by machine gun fire which started a small phosphorous fire in the cockpit, the engine starting to vibrate strongly before cutting. He then saw a U.S.A.A.F. P-51D Mustang turning to make another firing pass at his crippled fighter, the American pilot presumably being under the impression that he was attacking a *Luftwaffe* aircraft. The Mustang made four firing passes at the Swiss Bf 109E which crash-landed on Dübendorf airfield. The R/T employed by the Swiss Bf 109Es was prone to malfunction and the entire incident had passed unnoticed by the pilots of the two fighters leading the Liberator!

By general consensus, the Bf 109E-3 was to be considered the most effective combat aircraft employed by the *Fliegertruppe* during the war years. The *Fliegerkompagnien* equipped with this type of course suffered normal attrition as well as combat losses – *Fliegerkompagnie* 7 re-equipping with the Bf 109G-6 in the early summer of 1944, as recounted later (see page 120) – but were to continue to fly the Bf 109E-3 well into the postwar years. Indeed, the survivors were to be augmented *after* World War II by one additional aircraft which was assembled from spares and a further eight which utilized spare DB 601Aa engines and had airframes licence-built by the Dornier-Werke at Altenrhein, which also built four pairs of wings and seven extra fuselages for application to damaged aircraft. The example assembled from spares and the eight licence-built aircraft were all fitted with an Escher-Wyss EW-V6 controllable-pitch airscrew in place of the standard VDM unit – this having earlier been flight tested by the 37th Bf 109E-3 supplied by the parent company – and could be identified by their pointed spinners which supplanted the cropped spinner incorporating a cooling

*(Above left and below) The last of a batch of eight Bf 109E-3s assembled partly from spares by the Dornier-Werke at Altenrhein after W.W. II and fitted with Escher-Wyss EW-V6 airscrews, Saurer fuel injection nozzles and pump, and Hasler twin-ignition equipment. This aircraft, J-399, was delivered on March 19, 1946*

*A rotte of Bf 109E-4/N Trop fighters of I/JG 27 flying over the desert during operations from Ain El Gazala in the summer of 1941. (Foot of page) Bf 109E-7/Trop fighters of 7./JG 26 at Gazala, summer 1941*

intake. The DB 601Aa engines installed in the eight Dornier-built examples were modified to incorporate some Swiss accessories, including a Saurer fuel injection pump and nozzles, Hazler twin-ignition equipment and PEM spark plugs. The Dornier-Werke licence programme was completed with the delivery of the last aircraft on March 19, 1946, and the Bf 109Es were to soldier on in Swiss service for nearly four more years, being progressively replaced by Mustangs and Vampires, and the last Messerschmitt being withdrawn from service on December 28, 1949.

Fighter cover for the assault on Crete which began on May 20, 1941, was provided by the Bf 109Es of the *Stab* and the II and III *Gruppen* of JG 77, to which the Bf 109Es of I(*Jagd*)/LG 2 were subordinated as a third *Gruppe*, these units operating from Molai in the Peloponnese, but the bulk of the *Jagdgruppen* were by this time in process of being redeployed for Operation *Barbarossa*, the invasion of the Soviet Union, the opening months of which were to see the last really extensive use of the *Emil* by the *Luftwaffe*, although it was to linger on in service for at least a further two years.

Production of the Bf 109E-4/N had given place to the similarly-powered Bf 109E-7, which had made its appearance during the "Battle of Britain", and which differed solely in having provision for either a 66 Imp. gal. (300 l) drop tank or a 551-lb. (250-kg) SC 250 bomb, a tropicalized version being delivered to I/JG 27 in North Africa as the Bf 109E-7/Trop. Further variants were the Bf 109E-7/U2, which had 5-mm armour bolted beneath the oil cooler, radiators and fuel pump to reduce its susceptibility to groundfire in the close-support role, and the Bf 109E-7/Z which was a particularly significant development in that, for the first time, a nitrous oxide (GM 1) power boosting system was employed. Injected into the super-charger above the rated altitude of the engine, the nitrous oxide was retained under pressure in liquid form in a heavily-lagged cylindrical container aft of the cockpit, compressed air forcing the liquid to the engine for which it provided additional oxygen, also acting as an anti-detonant.

Although the system proved itself effective, and was to be utilized by numerous later sub-types of the Bf 109, it initiated the weight spiral which was to result in a progressive deterioration of the fighter's flying characteristics. The aft movement of the c.g. resulting from the introduction of the GM 1 container led to a yawing tendency when the fighter was pulled out of a steep dive. If the yaw was not immediately corrected the Bf 109E-7/Z usually stalled and spun, but this stability problem

*A Bf 109E-7 of JG 5 flying over the Northern Sector of the Eastern Front in 1942. This example was fitted with the dust/sand filter standardized for tropicalized versions*

*(Above) A Bf 109E-7 of 13.(slowak)/JG 52, a Slovak-manned Staffel attached to Jagdgeschwader 52 and operating over the southern sector of the Russian Front*

was considered too marginal to warrant modifications which, it was believed, would penalize the fighter in other ways.

Long before the last E-series fighters left the assembly lines early in 1942, two further sub-types had made their début, these, the Bf 109E-8 and E-9, having appeared during the autumn of 1940. The principal innovation was provided by the power plant, the DB 601E, which, with maximum permissible revolutions again increased, improved supercharging and other modifications, offered 1,350 h.p. for take-off at 2,700 r.p.m. Apart from the power plant and improved back armour for the pilot, the Bf 109E-8 was essentially similar to the Bf 109E-7, and the Bf 109E-9 was a photo–reconnaissance equivalent, lacking wing armament, and having an Rb 50/30 camera installed in the rear fuselage.

The Bf 109E was being phased out of *Luftwaffe* service in the pure fighter role by mid-1941, but the following year saw its introduction by other air arms. The Imperial Japanese Army had ordered three Bf 109E-4s for evaluation. These reached Japan in June–July 1941, and were flown in comparative trials with the Kawasaki Ki. 61 *Hien* (Swallow) and other indigenous Japanese fighters, but no further examples were acquired. Rumania, on the other hand, obtained 69 Bf 109E-4s early in 1942, these equipping the three squadrons of the 1st Fighter Group (*Grupul 1 Vinatoare*) of the Royal Rumanian Air Forces.

*(Above left) A Bf 109E-7 of the Bulgarian Air Force in the markings adopted temporarily after September 9, 1944, when the service began fighting alongside the Soviet Air Force, and (below) two Bf 109E-4s of the 1st Fighter Group of the Royal Rumanian Air Forces flying in formation with a similar aircraft of the Luftwaffe*

Bulgaria, too, was a recipient of the Bf 109E-4 in 1942, 19 examples being delivered and incorporated in the 6th Royal Bulgarian Fighter Regiment.

Early in 1942, the Slovak Air Force was to receive 14 Bf 109E-7s which equipped a *Staffel* manned by Slovakian volunteers, this unit being attached to *Jagdgeschwader* 52 as 13.(*slowak*.)/JG 52, and operated on the southern sector of the Russian Front alongside the similarly-equipped Croatian 15.(*kroat*.)/JG 52. As Croatia was not at war with the Soviet Union, the Croat personnel were considered as a "foreign legion", as were also the Spanish personnel of the *Escuadron Azul* which began operations on Bf 109E-7s under the VIII *Fliegerkorps* on the Russian Front as 15.(*span*.)/JG 27 until replaced in March 1942 by 15.(*span*.)/JG 51, also on Bf 109E-7s which remained in service with the Spanish volunteers on the central sector until they gave place to Bf 109Fs in October 1942. A second Slovakian squadron, 11.*stíhací letka*, converted to the Bf 109E-7 from the Avia B.534 late in 1942 but remained in Slovakia at Piestany.

Bf 109Es participated in numerous experimental programmes, and among several unconventional proposals for increasing the ferry range of the fighter that reached the test stage was the provision of a pair of 66 Imp. gal. (300 l) capacity over-wing slipper-type tanks which could be jettisoned when their contents were expended. Trials with a Bf 109E-4 fitted with the over-wing tanks were conducted by the *Forschungs-anstalt Graf Zeppelin* under the appellation *Wurzelsepp*, and it was ascertained that there were no appreciable changes in the flying characteristics of the fighter with consumption of the contents of the over-wing tanks, and that these could be jettisoned safely.

From these tests at Stuttgart-Ruit in 1942, Dipl.-Ing. Isermann, who had conceived the scheme, evolved the idea of adapting the over-wing tanks as personnel containers for use by Bf 109s and other aircraft, such containers being suitable for low-level agent dropping, casualty evacuation, etc. The design of a container capable of accommodating a man lying prone, together with his parachute pack presented some aerodynamic problems, but these were eventually overcome, and, fitted to the Bf 109E-4 previously employed for the over-wing fuel tank tests, the containers were tested in flight during the summer of 1943, trials, indicating that they reduced normal cruising speed by only 13 m.p.h. (21 km/h). Tests were later continued with a Bf 109G-12 and other aircraft.

*A Bf 109E participating in a series of pick-a-back trials in 1942 during which it was attached to a super-structure mounted above a DFS 230 transport glider*

A Junkers test pilot, Siegfried Holzbauer, undoubtedly influenced by the successful pre-war trials with the Short Mayo S.20/S.21 composite, suggested the application of the Bf 109 as a means of guiding a time-expired Junkers Ju 88 fitted with a large hollow-charge warhead which, he foresaw, could be used for attacking ships or heavily-fortified targets. It was proposed that the Bf 109 be attached to a superstructure mounted above the pilotless Ju 88, the pilot of the fighter guiding the two aircraft to the vicinity of the target and then, before detaching his Bf 109 from the superstructure, setting the controls of the pilotless lower component so that it would approach the selected target in a shallow glide. The proposal was dismissed by the *Technischen Amt* as too unorthodox to have any practical application, but, in 1942, Fritz Stamer of the *Deutschen Forschungsinstitut für Segelflug* initiated a series of *Huckepack* (Pick-a-back) trials with the primary aim of testing the feasibility of this arrangement for transport gliders. For these tests both a Klemm Kl 35 and a Focke-Wulf Fw 56 were mounted above a DFS 230 transport glider, and, subsequently a Bf 109E was also tested as the upper *Huckepack* component. The success achieved prompted the revival of Holzbauer's proposals and, early in 1943, instructions from the *Technische Amt* to proceed with a prototype conversion of a Bf 109/Ju 88 composite (see page 91).

Another interesting experimental programme was conducted with a Bf 109E-1 fitted with a fixed ski (*Schneekufen*) undercarriage, the undercarriage wells being faired over. A series of trials were undertaken in January 1941 in which the aircraft took-off both on skis and with the aid of a jettisonable three-wheel trolley, but as few difficulties were encountered in the operation of fighters from hard-packed snow runways the scheme was not adopted. The experimental ski-equipped aircraft made 80 test flights before crashing.

*One of the many interesting experiments conducted with the Emil was this Bf 109E-1 equipped with fixed skiis. Seen taking-off, this aircraft had its wheel wells faired over and completed 80 test flights before crashing*

# A seagoing Eagle

During the late 'thirties, the aircraft carrier had a major role in the planning of the *Oberkommando der Marine*, and in February 1939, when *Admiral* Erich Raeder, the *Oberbefehlshaber der Kriegsmarine*, proposed his "Plan Z" which, it was hoped, would enable the German Navy to seriously challenge British sea power by 1944, two carriers, the *Graf Zeppelin* and the *Peter Strasser*, had been laid down, and the nucleus of a *Trägergruppe* (Carrier Group) had been formed with Bf 109B fighters and Ju 87A dive bombers at Kiel-Holtenau. Messerschmitt's Augsburg design office had been instructed to develop a specialized shipboard variant of the Bf 109E fighter, and Junkers at Dessau was engaged in the design of a carrier-based variant of the Ju 87B dive bomber. It was envisaged that these aircraft would eventually equip *Trägergruppe* 186 and the additional *Trägergruppen* that were to follow it.

Messerschmitt's proposals for a shipboard fighter, designated Bf 109T (the suffix letter indicating *Träger*), were submitted early in 1939, and consisted of an essentially simple adaptation of the basic Bf 109E-1 in which the gross wing area was increased by the extension of each outer panel by 21¼ in. (54 cm), the leading-edge slots being lengthened commensurately, flap travel being increased and the interconnected ailerons being extended.

Catapult points were introduced between the fifth and sixth fuselage mainframes, and an arrester hook was attached immediately aft of the seventh mainframe, the local structure being strengthened to absorb the stresses. A break point was incorporated in the wing spar immediately outboard of the gun bays to permit manual folding of the outer panels, reducing overall width to 15 ft. 0¾ in. (4,59 m), although this was complicated by the need to detach the flaps prior to folding. Armament comprised two fuselage-mounted 7,9-mm MG 17 machine guns coupled with alternative wing-mounted weapons which could be either two additional MG 17s or two 20-mm MG FF cannon. The Bf 109T was accepted, and the entire project was transferred to Fieseler for detail design, and for the conversion of 10 Bf 109E-1 airframes already on the assembly line as pre-production Bf 109T-0 fighters. Simultaneously, Fieseler received a contract for the manufacture of 60 Bf 109T-1s.

The Bf 109T-0 was powered by the DB 601A engine, had retractable spoilers on the upper surfaces of the wing at one-third chord to steepen the angle of glide, and had more robust oleo legs to cater for the higher descent rates. After trials at the *Erprobungsstelle* at Travemünde during the winter of 1939–40, it had been intended that the Bf 109T-0s should be passed to II/JG 186 (the nucleus of which had been provided by 5. and 6. *Trägerjagdstaffeln* 186) for operational evaluation. However, work on the *Graf Zeppelin* had been largely suspended in October 1939, and, in the belief that the operation of a single carrier within range of enemy land bases was impracticable, was halted entirely in May 1940. The II/JG 186 had, meanwhile, operated as the third *Gruppe* of JG 77 with Bf 109E-1s in the Low Countries and France, and in June 1940, was transferred to Trondheim in Norway, being redesignated III/JG 77 on the 6th of the following month.

Assembly of the 60 Bf 109T-1 shipboard fighters by the Gerhard Fieseler Werke had been halted simultaneously with the decision to stop further work on the *Graf Zeppelin*, but the successes of British carrier aircraft against the Italian Navy in the Mediterranean late in 1940 rekindled interest in this type of warship, and although no decision to resume work on the *Graf Zeppelin* was taken immediately (this decision was not, in fact, to be taken until May 13, 1942), Fieseler was instructed to complete the 60 Bf 109T-1s but to remove what carrier equipment had already been fitted, and deliver the aircraft as land-based fighter-bombers suitable for operation from short strips.

Stripped of catapult points and arrester hook, and fitted with a ventral rack for a 66 Imp. gal. (300 l) drop tank, four 110-lb. (50-kg) bombs or a single 551-lb. (250-kg) bomb, the fighter was redesignated Bf 109T-2, and began to leave the assembly line in the early spring of 1941. It was decided that the Bf 109T-2 would be ideally suited for operation from small, exposed airfields, such as several of those from which the *Jagdflieger* were forced to operate in Norway. The III/JG 77 had been transferred southwards for Operation *Marita*, having been succeeded in Norway by I/JG 77 operating primarily from Stavanger-Sola, and after delivery to Aalborg, Denmark, the Bf 109T-2s were ferried from there to Sola by I/JG 77 pilots. Conversion from the Bf 109E-3 to the Bf 109T-2 began in June 1941, all three *Staffeln* converting in the following weeks, a *Schwarm* being detached to Trondheim (eventually becoming the *Einsatzstaffel Drontheim*, or "Trondheim Operational Squadron").

Powered by a DB 601N engine using 96 octane C3 fuel, the Bf 109T-2 was found to possess a performance closely comparable with that of the Bf 109E-4/N, despite its larger wing, which, together with the tailwheel locking device, increased the suitability of the fighter for operation from short, windswept strips. After the arrival of the Bf 109T-2s at Sola, the wing spoilers were found to be unnecessary and were deactivated. At its clean loaded weight of 6,173 lb. (2 800 kg), the Bf 109T-2 could take-off and clear a 82-ft. (25,00-m) obstacle within 550 yards (500 m), unstick speed being 74·5 m.p.h. (120

---

## Bf 109T-2 Specification

**Power Plant:** One Daimler-Benz DB 601N 12-cylinder inverted-vee liquid-cooled engine rated at 1,200 h.p. for take-off and 1,270 h.p. for one minute at 16,400 ft. (5 000 m).

**Performance:** (At 6,173 lb./2 800 kg) Maximum speed (at full throttle), 295 m.p.h. (475 km/h) at sea level, 307 m.p.h. (495 km/h) at 3,280 ft. (1 000 m), 320 m.p.h. (515 km/h) at 6,560 ft. (2 000 m), 332 m.p.h. (535 km/h) at 9,840 ft. (3 000 m), 345 m.p.h. (555 km/h) at 13,120 ft. (4 000 m), 354 m.p.h. (570 km/h) at 16,400 ft. (5 000 m), 357 m.p.h. (575 km/h) at 19,685 ft. (6 000 m), (at emergency power, 304 m.p.h. (490 km/h) at sea level, 317 m.p.h. (510 km/h) at 3,280 ft. (1 000 m), 328 m.p.h. (528 km/h) at 6,560 ft. (2 000 m), 339 m.p.h. (546 km/h) at 9,840 ft. (3 000 m), 351 m.p.h. (565 km/h) at 13,120 ft. (4 000 m); maximum cruise, 275 m.p.h. (443 km/h) at sea level, 289 m.p.h. (465 km/h) at 3,280 ft. (1 000 m), 303 m.p.h. (488 km/h) at 6,560 ft. (2 000 m), 317 m.p.h. (510 km/h) at 9,840 ft. (3 000 m), 330 m.p.h. (532 km/h) at 13,120 ft. (4 000 m), 343 m.p.h. (552 km/h) at 16,400 ft. (5 000 m); maximum range with 66 Imp. gal. (300 l) drop tank, 568 mls. (915 km) at 199 m.p.h. (320 km/h) at sea level, 460 mls. (740 km) at 220 m.p.h. (355 km/h) at 16,400 ft. (5 000 m), 454 mls. (730 km) at 283 m.p.h. (455 km/h) at 29,530 ft. (9 000 m); initial climb rate at 6,173 lb. (2 800 kg), 3,346 ft./min. (17,00 m/sec); time to 9,840 ft. (3 000 m), 3 min., to 19,685 ft. (6 000 m), 6·4 min., to 26,250 ft. (8 000 m), 10 min.; service ceiling, 34,450 ft. (10 500 m).

**Weights:** Empty, 4,409 lb. (2 000 kg); empty equipped, 4,905–4,967 lb. (2 225–2 264 kg); loaded (clean), 6,173 lb. (2 800 kg); maximum overload, 6,786 lb. (3 078 kg).

**Dimensions:** Span, 36 ft. 4¼ in. (11,08 m); length, 28 ft. 9 in. (8,76 m); height, 8 ft. 6½ in. (2,60 m); wing area, 188,368 sq. ft. (17,5 m²).

**Armament:** Two 20-mm (Oerlikon) MG FF cannon with 60 r.p.g. in wings and two fuselage-mounted 7,9-mm Rheinmetall Borsig MG 17 machine guns with 1,000 r.p.g., plus one 551-lb. (250-kg) or four 110-lb. (50-kg) bombs.

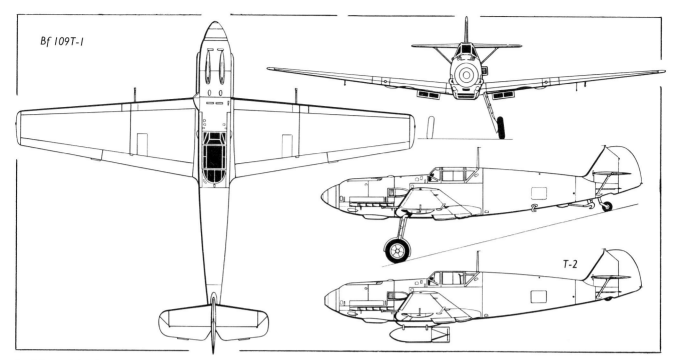

Bf 109T-1

T-2

km/h), and landing distance from 82 ft. (25,00 m) without application of brakes was 765 yards (700 m), landing speed being 80 m.p.h. (130 km/h).

On January 24, 1942, I/JG 77, still equipped with the Bf 109T-2, was redesignated I/JG 5, and shortly afterwards the 3.*Staffel* was transferred to the island of Herdla, near Bergen, where the dimensions of the wooden-planked strip were barely larger than those of a carrier deck. In March 1942, a British carrier air strike drove the battleship *Tirpitz* away from two Allied convoys on the Murmansk run, bringing the issue of carriers for the *Kriegsmarine* to the fore once again, *Admiral* Raeder demanding the completion of the *Graf Zeppelin* for the escort of Germany's commerce raiders. Instructions for work to be resumed on the carrier were issued on May 13, but by this time the Bf 109T was considered obsolescent for shipboard operation and the Bf 109T-2s remained in service with I/JG 5 under *Luftflotte* 5 (*West*) until re-equipment of the *Gruppe* with the Fw 190A-3 during the summer of 1942.

The short-field performance of the Bf 109T-2 led to the

surviving fighters of this type being issued to the so-called *Jagdstaffel Helgoland* when this unit was formed on April 10, 1943, for operation from the tiny fortified island of Heligoland. The *Staffel* was redesignated 11./JG 11 in the following November, and again redesignated as 8./JG 4. A new 11./JG 11 was formed from the previous 8./JG 11 but the dwindling numbers of Bf 109T-2s remained under *Luftflotte Reich* until the summer of 1944 when the survivors were transferred to IV/JG 5 under *Luftflotte* 5 (*West*), continuing on operations alongside Bf 109Gs and Fw 190s until the end of the year when the T-series of the Bf 109 finally disappeared from the inventory.

*The long-span Bf 109T-2 (above and below) was a shore-based adaptation of the shipboard Bf 109T-1, and was operated by I/JG 77 from Stavanger-Sola from mid-1941, a Schwarm being detached to Trondheim. Later the 3.Staffel operated the Bf 109T-2 from the island of Herdla, near Bergen*

83

# A rejuvenated Eagle

A vital attribute of any successful combat aircraft design is a capacity for development, for, without such, it cannot hope to keep pace for long with the changing demands and fluctuations of aerial warfare. Such a quality, provided it demands no extensive redesign of fundamental components with consequent major retooling, can be of incalculable value. That Messerschmitt's Bf 109 possessed this attribute was to be seen in the spring of 1941, when the F-series fighter made its operational début.

In Britain the highest priority had been allocated to redressing the superiority in certain aspects of performance enjoyed by the Bf 109E over the Spitfire, and with the availability of the Merlin 45 series of two-stage engines, the early months of 1941 saw the operational début of the Spitfire V. But the Augsburg design office had not rested on its laurels, and enabled the *Luftwaffe* to counter the more potent Spitfire with an even more effective version of the standard Messerschmitt single-seater which the R.A.F. began to encounter over the Channel coast during March and April of 1941 when *Jagdgeschwader* 2 and 26 introduced the Bf 109F.

*(Above) The Bf 109 V23, the first F-series prototype to be fitted with the definitive wing*

Early in 1940, the Augsburg design office had instituted a programme of aerodynamic refinement of the basic Bf 109 design to take full advantage of the increases in power promised by developed versions of the DB 601 engine, and the result, the Bf 109F, was to carry the fighter to the crest of its evolution. Subsequent development, dictated by the exigencies of the air war, was to result in progressive increases in weight without commensurate increases in power and lift, and, from the pilot's viewpoint, a steady deterioration in handling characteristics and powers of manoeuvre.

The wing of the Bf 109 had remained essentially unchanged from prototype until the initiation of the aerodynamic improvement programme, and even now no changes were made to the profile, taper or basic structure. However, one of the major sources of drag was the underwing radiator, and in order to use the sharply divergent entry passages necessary to recess the radiator further into the wing, a boundary layer bypass system was evolved. This collected the turbulent air on the lower wing surface immediately ahead of the radiator bath, led this air over the radiator and discharged it through a duct in the upper portion of the inboard flap, which was split lengthwise to form a double flap. When both portions acted in unison with the outer plain flaps these served simply as wing flaps, but when the upper and lower portions moved in opposite directions under the control of a thermostat placed between the glycol header tank and the radiator, the lower portion fulfilled the function of a radiator flap.

The wing leading-edge slots were reduced in span, as were also the ailerons, but the latter, which were no longer interconnected with the flaps, were increased in chord so that their area remained unaltered, and they were changed from slotted to Frise type. These changes were accompanied by a reduction in wing span. A slightly deeper, more symmetrical engine cowling was designed, the airscrew spinner being markedly enlarged, and the supercharger air intake was moved further out from the side of the fuselage to obtain a greater ram effect. Simultaneously, the airscrew diameter was reduced from 10 ft. 2 in. (3,10 m) to 9 ft. 8½ in. (2,96 m), and a novel airscrew constant speed unit introduced, this being controlled by the throttle lever, although it could be overridden by the pilot and the airscrew pitch controlled in the same way as on the Bf 109E.

The rudder area was reduced from 8·1 to 7·5 sq. ft. (752 to 697 cm²), and the symmetrical fin section gave place to a cambered section to reduce the amount of rudder needed on the

*(Above left and below) The Bf 109 V24 was the fourth F-series prototype but was not fitted with the definitive wing featured by the Bf 109 V23. It introduced a redesigned supercharger air intake and deeper oil cooler*

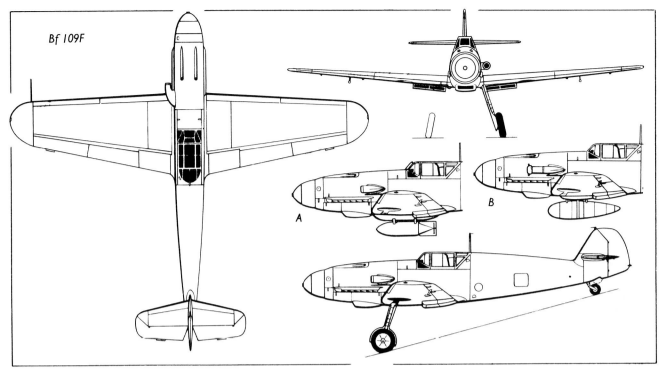

Bf 109F

*The general arrangement drawing represents all the basic F sub-series. Detail A illustrates the Bf 109F-4/B with SC 250 bomb, and detail B shows the optional 66 Imp. gal. (300 l) drop tank and dust/sand filter*

climb. The struts bracing the horizontal tail surfaces that had been so characteristic of all early variants of the Bf 109 were deleted, and a cantilever tailplane placed slightly below and forward of the original position. The tailwheel was made semi-retractable and, some six degrees more rake were applied to the main undercarriage legs.

The new model was intended to receive the DB 601E engine affording 1,350 h.p. for take-off at 2,700 r.p.m. and during the late spring of 1940, work began on four F-series prototypes and 10 pre-production Bf 109F-0 fighters. The first F-series prototype, the Bf 109 V21 (*Werk-Nr.* 5602), retained the earlier DB 601Aa engine but embodied all the previously listed aerodynamic refinements, together with a 2-ft. (61-cm) reduc-

tion in overall wing span, and the second prototype, the Bf 109 V22 (*Werk-Nr.* 1800), was similar but received a pre-production DB 601E engine, subsequently being used primarily for power plant development tasks. The third and fourth F-series prototypes, the Bf 109 V23 (*Werk-Nr.* 5603 CE + BP) and the Bf 109 V24 (*Werk-Nr.* 5604 VK + AB), were both DB 601E-powered but differed in several respects.

As the reduced wing span featured by the V21 and V22 had had a detrimental effect on the characteristics of the aircraft, the V23 was fitted with new, detachable semi-elliptical wing-tips which restored all but 11·6 sq. in. (75 cm²) of the wing area. Flight test proved the wingtips efficacious, and these were adopted as standard although not applied to the V24 which, completed in parallel with the V23, featured a redesigned supercharger air intake of the form eventually to be standardized, and a deeper oil cooler bath beneath the engine cowling.

From the outset it had been envisaged that, while the fuselage-mounted MG 17 machine guns would be retained in the armament of the Bf 109F, the wing-mounted 20-mm MG FF weapons would be discarded in favour of a single engine-mounted Mauser MG 151 firing through the hollow airscrew shaft. This weapon had a markedly superior muzzle velocity and fire rate to the MG FF, and was being developed in both 15-mm and 20-mm versions. The concentration of all armament in the fuselage had a beneficial effect on manoeuvrability, and, in the view of most experienced fighter pilots, the single MG 151 coupled with the twin MG 17s offered a more potent combination than the quartette of weapons previously mounted by the Bf 109. However, neither MG 151 cannon nor DB 601E engine was available for installation when the Bf 109F-0 pre-production fighters began to leave the assembly line in the late autumn of 1940, and the power plant was not, in fact, to be available for a further year.

Service evaluation of the Bf 109F-0, powered by a DB 601N engine mounting an MG FF/M cannon, resulted in extremely favourable reports. Manoeuvrability was decidedly better in all respects than that of the similarly-powered Bf 109E-4/N. A

## Bf 109F-2 Specification

**Power Plant:** One Daimler-Benz DB 601N 12-cylinder inverted-vee liquid-cooled engine rated at 1,200 h.p. for take-off and 1,270 h.p. for one minute at 16,400 ft. (5 000 m).

**Performance:** (At 6,173 lb./2 800 kg) Maximum speed at emergency power, 321 m.p.h. (517 km/h) at sea level, 358 m.p.h. (576 km/h) at 9,840 ft. (3 000 m), 373 m.p.h. (600 km/h) at 19,685 ft. (6 000 m); maximum cruise, 290 m.p.h. (467 km/h) at sea level, 328 m.p.h. (528 km/h) at 9,840 ft. (3 000 m), 348 m.p.h. (560 km/h) at 16,400 ft. (5 000 m); range with 66 Imp. gal. (300 l) drop tank, 547 mls. (880 km) at 220 m.p.h. (354 km/h) at sea level, 470 mls. (756 km) at 305 m.p.h. (490 km/h) at 27,890 ft. (8 500 m); initial climb rate, 3,860 ft./min. (20,48 m/sec); time to 3,280 ft. (1 000 m), 0·9 min., to 9,840 ft. (3 000 m), 2·55 min., to 16,400 ft. (5 000 m), 5·2 min.; service ceiling, 36,090 ft. (11 000 m).

**Weights:** Empty equipped, 5,188 lb. (2 353 kg); normal loaded, 6,173 lb. (2 800 kg); maximum overload, 6,760 lb. (3 066 kg).

**Dimensions:** Span, 32 ft. 6½ in. (9,92 m); length, 29 ft. 3⅞ in. (8,94 m); height 8 ft. 6⅓ in. (2,60 m); wing area, 173·299 sq. ft. (16,1 m²).

**Armament:** One 15-mm Mauser MG 151/15 engine-mounted cannon with 200 rounds and two 7,9-mm Rheinmetall Borsig MG 17 fuselage-mounted machine guns with 500 r.p.g.

(Above and below left) Bf 109F-4s of 10./JG 2 at Caen-Carpiquet. Aircraft illustrated below is that of the Staffelkapitän, Oberleutnant Liesendahl, who was shot down on July 17, 1942, off Brixham, Devon

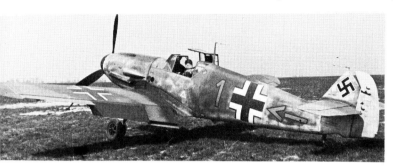

360° turn at 3,280 ft. (1 000 m) could be effected within 18 seconds as compared with the 25 seconds of the earlier fighter, and from the same altitude 2,900 ft. (855 m) could be gained in a combat turn as compared with 1,970 ft. (600 m). Initial climb rate was increased from 3,420 to 3,730 ft./min. (17,37 to 19,40 m/sec), and an altitude of 16,400 ft. (5 000 m) was reached in 5·2 min. as compared with 6·1 min. Some criticism was voiced concerning the substantial reduction of weight of fire with only the single MG FF/M cannon installed, but the general handling characteristics received nothing but praise.

The first production Bf 109F-1 fighters left the assembly lines during November 1940, and were essentially similar to the pre-production aircraft that had preceded them, apart from the supercharger air intake which, of rectangular section on the Bf 109F-0, was of round section on the production model, and similar in design to that tested by the Bf 109 V24.

Shortly after the first Bf 109F-1s were delivered to service evaluation units, three aircraft were lost in what were temporarily inexplicable circumstances. In two cases the pilot had signalled that the engine was vibrating violently before his aircraft crashed out of control, and all Bf 109F-1s were temporarily grounded pending an investigation. The engine itself was initially suspect but no comparable accidents had been reported with the similarly-powered Bf 109E-4/N and as no

other cause for the accidents could be discovered, flying was resumed. Shortly afterwards another Bf 109F-1 crashed, and as the engine suffered only minor damage, suspicion was directed towards the tail assembly when it was discovered that all the rivets in the skin plating were broken, loose, or missing completely.

In the further investigation that followed it was ascertained that, with the removal of the bracing struts, the proportion of the rigidity to the strength of the tail assembly had changed, and that at certain r.p.m. a high-frequency oscillation set up in the tailplane spar was overlapped by the engine, and the sympathetic vibrations resulted in a structural failure. This problem was overcome by the application of external stiffening plates which were screwed on to the rear fuselage, and service deliveries were resumed, the first recipients including JG 2 "Richthofen" and JG 26 "Schlageter" on the Channel coast which, in March and April 1941, had begun to take the Bf 109F-1 and F-2 on strength, the latter having a 15-mm MG 151 in place of the engine-mounted MG FF/M.

All three Gruppen of JG 2 converted to the Bf 109F-1 and F-2, together with I and III Gruppen of JG 26, the II Gruppe retaining its Bf 109E-7s until conversion to the Fw 190A-1 began in July 1941. The arrival of the Bf 109F on the Channel coast prevented the Spitfire V gaining the ascendancy that it would have enjoyed had it been opposed only by the Bf 109E. The Bf 109F still lacked the turning circle of the Spitfire V, but it could outclimb and outdive the new model of the British fighter.

On July 10, 1941, the R.A.F. had an opportunity to examine a Bf 109F-1 when Hauptmann Rolf Pingel, the Gruppenkommandeur of I/JG 26, was shot down in combat over St. Margaret's Bay, near Dover. Apart from superficial damage to the radiators and airscrew, the Bf 109F-1 was intact, and (with the serial number ES906) was flown at Farnborough on September 19, 1941. Three weeks later it was flown to Duxford for comparative trials with British fighters, but on October 20 the pilot

The Bf 109F-1 flown by Hauptmann Rolf Pingel, the Gruppenkommandeur of I/JG 26, when he was shot down in combat over St. Margaret's Bay, near Dover. This aircraft was subsequently repaired and flown as ES906

was overcome by carbon monoxide fumes while testing the captured fighter, and the Bf 109F-1 crashed and was destroyed at Fowlmere, Cambridgeshire.

## The Eagle in Russian skies

Most of the *Jagdstaffeln* not participating in Operation *Marita*, the Balkans campaign, had, meanwhile, begun conversion to the Bf 109F in preparation for Operation *Barbarossa*, the invasion of the Soviet Union, launched on June 22, 1941. When this event took place, almost two-thirds of the participating *Jagdgruppen* had converted or partly converted to the Bf 109F from the Bf 109E. More than 60 per cent of the *Luftwaffe's* first-line strength was committed to *Barbarossa*, and almost half of the *Jagdgruppen* involved were attached to *Luftflotte* 2, these being, I, II and III/JG 53 on Bf 109Fs, I, II, III and IV/JG 51 (under II *Fliegerkorps*) also on Bf 109Fs, and II and III/JG 27 (VIII *Fliegerkorps*) on Bf 109Es. These *Gruppen* were deployed over the Central Sector. To the south, *Luftflotte* 4 included I and II/JG 52 on Bf 109Es, I, II and III/JG 3 (V Fliegerkorps) on Bf 109Fs, and II and III/JG 77 and I (*Jagd*)/LG 2 (IV *Fliegerkorps*) on Bf 109Es, while to the north, *Luftflotte* I included I, II and III/JG 54 on Bf 109Fs.

A total of 440 serviceable Bf 109s was available to the *Jagdgruppen* engaged in *Barbarossa*, and these were responsible for the majority of the 322 Soviet aircraft claimed destroyed in aerial combat and by *Flak* during the first day of operations. This claim was in no way exaggerated as official Soviet sources subsequently admitted the loss by midday of June 22 of no fewer than 1,200 aircraft of which slightly more than 800 had been destroyed on the ground. Some 60 per cent of these losses were suffered by the Soviet Air Forces on the Western Front (South Lithuania, Byelo-Russia and part of northern Ukraine) where 528 aircraft were knocked out on the ground and 210 were lost in aerial combat, a further 277 aircraft being lost on the South-West Front (Ukraine). But despite their appreciably lower performances, the Soviet I-153 and I-16 fighters posed the Bf 109Es and 109Fs several problems and demanded some revision of tactics.

Possessing more manoeuvrable if slower fighters than their German opponents, the higher skilled among the Soviet pilots adopted tactics which the *Jagdflieger* found extremely frustrating, waiting until the German fighter pilots were about to fire, and then, at the last possible moment, using their exceptional powers of manoeuvre to slip out of their sights. A pilot of the *Stabsschwarm* of JG 53, *Leutnant* Schiess, commented that the Soviet pilots frequently judged to a nicety the point at which their opponents were about to open fire, then pulled their fighters round in a tight 180° turn to attack head on.

Great as were the successes of the *Jagdgruppen* on the Eastern Front, the wastage in fighters outpaced the rate of replacement, and unit strengths declined alarmingly as the weeks passed. Production of the Bf 109E had been largely phased out by the late spring of 1941, its place having been taken by the Bf 109F, but despite increased impetus placed behind single-seat fighter production, and the rapid rise in monthly output during the first few months of the year, total acceptances of Bf 109 fighters during the course of 1941 were, at 2,628 aircraft, barely 40 per cent higher than the previous year.

This limited increase in the year's output was due in part to the phasing in of the Fw 190 production, Arado switching to the Focke-Wulf fighter in November and AGO following suit in December. Fieseler had been phased out of the Bf 109 programme in July, and during the last quarter of the year, Messerschmitt's Regensburg assembly line had delivered only four machines, the principal manufacturers having been Erla and WNF which delivered 683 and 836 respectively.

The development pattern of the Bf 109F had, meanwhile,

*(Above) A Bf 109F-2 of JG 2 on the Channel coast, and (below) four of JG 2's most successful pilots (left to right) Egon Mayer, Rudolf Pflanz, Walter Oesau, and Erich Leie*

followed broadly that already established by the E-series fighter. The installation of a nitrous oxide (GM 1) power boosting system in the Bf 109F-2 had resulted in the Bf 109F-2/Z, and the Bf 109F-2/Trop, a tropicalized version of the standard production model, had reached Libya with II/JG 27 in September 1941, and had begun to replace the Bf 109E-7/Trop in service with I/JG 27. By the beginning of 1942, the availability of the DB 601E resulted in the Bf 109F-3, this power plant using 87 octane B4 fuel in place of the 96 octane C3 necessitated by the DB 601N of the Bf 109F-1 and -2. Clean loaded weight had steadily escalated, the 5,754 lb. (2 610 kg) of the Bf 109F-1 having risen to 6,184 lb. (2 805 kg) with the Bf 109F-3, and despite some evidence of weight consciousness on the part of the manufacturers, the upward spiral continued with the Bf 109F-4.

Produced almost simultaneously with the Bf 109F-3, the -4 differed primarily in that the calibre of its engine-mounted MG 151 was increased from 15-mm to 20-mm, ammunition capacity being reduced from 200 to 150 rounds. Improved self-sealing was applied to the fuel tank, and pilot protection was revised, this comprising the usual armour-glass windscreen, an armour-glass rear headshield below which was a 6-mm rectangular armour plate to protect the pilot's neck and shoulders, a rectangular 5-mm plate also being mounted above the armour-glass shield at an angle of approximately 45 degrees to protect the top of the pilot's head. The usual FuG 7a R/T was installed, a *Revi* C/12D reflector sight was fitted, and fire-selection equipment permitted the machine guns and cannon to be fired independently or in unison.

The Bf 109F-4 and F-4/Trop rapidly replaced earlier F-series

*(Above) A factory-fresh Bf 109F-4 prior to delivery to the Luftwaffe late in 1941*

*(Above) A Bf 109F-4 of III/JG 26 on the Channel coast early 1942, and (below) the Bf 109F-4/B fighter-bomber*

fighters with the *Jagdgruppen* from late 1941, although by this time the Focke-Wulf Fw 190A was being phased into service in steadily increasing numbers, and during the first weeks of 1942 a fighter-bomber version, the Bf 109F-4/B, attained service status, this appearing on the Channel coast shortly afterwards. The two *Jagdgeschwader* facing Britain under *Luftflotte* 3 were, by this time, equipped almost entirely with the Fw 190A-2 and -3, although III/JG 26 had relinquished its Fw 190A-2s in favour of Bf 190F-4s pending delivery of the more powerful Bf 109G. The single fighter-bomber *Staffel* of each *Jagdgeschwader*, 10.(*Jabo*)/JG 2 and 10.(*Jabo*)/JG 26, had continued to operate the Bf 109E-4/B until the availability of the Bf 109F-4/B with which both had re-equipped by April 1942.

The Bf 109F-4/B differed little from the standard fighter, apart from having a bomb-fusing battery box installed in the fuselage and a ventral ETC 250 bomb carrier for a single 551-lb. (250-kg) SC 250 bomb, and 10.(*Jabo*)/JG 2, operating primarily from Beaumont le Roger, and 10.(*Jabo*)/ 26, based on Poix, further to the north, flying at low altitude across the Channel to escape radar detection, used their new equipment with considerable effect in pinpoint attacks on shipping and coastal targets. In view of the fact that at no time did the combined strength of the *Staffeln* exceed 30 aircraft, British defences over a wide area were taxed out of all proportion to the smallness of the German effort.

Considerable disagreement existed among leading German fighter pilots regarding the adequacy of the Bf 109F-4's armament. Werner Mölders favoured the existing light armament of one 20-mm and two 7·9-mm weapons, but Adolf Galland had always considered the reduction in the number of weapons that had accompanied the introduction of the F-series to be a retrogressive step, and the first of a series of *Rüstsätze* (Field Conversion Sets) evolved for application to the Bf 109F comprised a supplementary pair of 20-mm MG 151 cannon mounted in underwing gondolas with 120 r.p.g., and so fitted, the fighter became the Bf 109F-4/R1.

Although the additional armament increased the fighter's potency as a bomber destroyer, it had an adverse effect on the handling qualities, reducing its competence in fighter-versus-fighter combat, and accentuating the tendency of the fighter to swing pendulum-fashion in flight. This movement had to be counteracted by use of the rudder, and necessitated particular attention being paid to the trimming of the ailerons and rudder as the "feel" of the aircraft was otherwise lost.

Several other *Rüstsätze* were tested on the Bf 109F-4 with varying degrees of success, but as the F-series had already been overtaken on the assembly lines by the G-series, few were actually applied in service. However, some aircraft were fitted

*(Left and below) Bf 109G-2s of II and III Gruppen of JG 54 on the Northern Sector of the Eastern Front in the summer of 1942, that illustrated above being photographed at Siverskaya and belonging to 4./JG 54*

*(Above) a Bf 109E-4/B of II/JG 54 flown by Leutnant Steindl over the Leningrad Sector of the Eastern Front in 1942.*

with an ETC 250 fuselage rack capable of lifting a 551-lb. (250-kg) SC 250 bomb, a 66 Imp. gal. (300 l) drop tank, or, by means of an ER 4 adapter, four 110-lb. (50-kg) SC 50 bombs, and with this the fighter was designated Bf 109F-4/R6.

Other derivatives of the basic Bf 109F-4 included the Bf 109F-4/Z with nitrous oxide (GM 1) injection, and two tactical reconnaissance models, the Bf 109F-5 with the engine-mounted cannon removed, a single camera mounted vertically in the aft fuselage, and provision for a 66 Imp. gal. (300 l) drop tank, and the Bf 109F-6 with all armament removed and a special camera bay introduced to permit interchangeability of Rb 20/30, Rb 50/30 or Rb 75/30 cameras.

The production life of the Bf 109F was relatively short, however, as by the end of 1941, the G-series had reached the assembly lines, and although substantially more than 2,000 F-series fighters had been manufactured, within a year only some 16 per cent of the Bf 109s in the first-line inventory were Bf 109Fs, the remainder being Bf 109Gs.

A number of ex-*Luftwaffe* Bf 109Fs soldiered on in the service of Germany's allies after the sub-type had virtually disappeared from the *Jagdgruppen*. For example, 15 ex-JG 26 Bf 109F-4s were delivered to Spain in 1942 for service with the 25 Grupo of the 23 Regimiento. The Bf 109F fighters were used primarily at Alcalá de Henares for the conversion of Spanish pilots bound for Russia, and in October 1942, the *Escuadron Azul*, or 15.(span.)/JG 51, converted from Bf 109E-7s to Bf 109F-4s while operational on the Eastern Front, flying these until July 1943.

In October 1942, the 1./1 *vadasz század* (Fighter Squadron) of the Royal Hungarian Air Force, the *Magyar Királyi Légierö*, which was operating under German command on the Russian Front as the *ungarische Jagdstaffel*, began conversion from the Re 2000 to the Bf 109F-4, and by the beginning of 1943 two *Gruppi* of Italy's *Regia Aeronautica* had begun conversion to the Bf 109F-4/R1 and the Bf 109F-4/B, these being the 3° *Gruppo*

### Bf 109F-4 Specification

**Power Plant:** One Daimler-Benz DB 601E 12-cylinder inverted-vee liquid-cooled engine rated at 1,350 h.p. for take-off and 1,300 h.p. at 18,045 ft. (5 500 m).

**Performance:** (At 6,393 lb./2 900 kg) Maximum speed, 334 m.p.h. (538 km/h) at sea level, 346 m.p.h. (557 km/h) at 9,840 ft. (3 000 m), 388 m.p.h. (624 km/h) at 21,325 ft. (6 500 m); maximum cruise, 310 m.p.h. (499 km/h) at sea level, 332 m.p.h. (534 km/h) at 9,840 ft. (3 000 m), 355 m.p.h. (571 km/h) at 16,400 ft. (5 000 m); range with 66 Imp. gal. (300 l) drop tank, 528 mls. (850 km) at 298 m.p.h. (480 km/h) at sea level, 442 mls. (710 km) at 314 m.p.h. (505 km/h) at 16,400 ft. (5 000 m); initial climb rate, 4,290 ft./min. (22,1 m/sec); time to 3,280 ft. (1 000 m), 0·85 min, to 9,840 ft. (3 000 m), 2·6 min.; service ceiling 39,370 ft. (12 000 m).

**Weights:** Empty equipped, 5,269 lb. (2 590 kg); normal loaded, 6,393 lb. (2 900 kg); maximum overload, 6,872 lb. (3 117 kg).

**Dimensions:** Span, 32 ft. 6½ in. (9,92 m); length, 29 ft. 2⅓ in. (8,90 m); height, 8 ft. 6⅓ in. (2,60 m); wing area, 173·299 sq. ft. (16,1 m²).

**Armament:** One 20-mm Mauser MG 151/20 engine-mounted cannon with 150 rounds and two 7,9-mm Rheinmetall Borsig MG 17 fuselage-mounted machine guns with 500 r.p.g.

*Bf 109F-2s of III/JG 54 operating in the Leningrad sector in the late autumn of 1941*

*A Bf 109F-4/R1 landing in Tunisia in the spring of 1943 after ferrying from Sicily. The Bf 109F-4/R1 was intended primarily for anti-bomber operations. (Foot of page) Bf 109G-2/Trop fighters of I/JG 53 operating from a Sicilian base in 1943*

(154ª and 155ª *Squadriglie*) *Caccia Terrestre* and the 150° *Gruppo* (363ª and 364ª *Squadriglie*) *Caccia Terrestre*.

Many F-series airframes were allocated to experimental programmes. One Bf 109F-2 (*Werk-Nr.* 9246) was tested with four EG 65 launchers for 73-mm Rheinmetall-Borsig RZ 65 rocket missiles which it was intended to launch in salvoes against both ground targets and bomber formations, but the complexity of the installation and the adverse effect on performance imposed by its drag led to the discontinuation of development. Interest in the potentialities of V-type or "butterfly" tail assemblies led to the application of such a tail to a Bf 109F-4 (*Werk-Nr.* 14003 VJ + WC), the initial flight test being performed by Karl Baur on January 21, 1943, subsequent testing being shared with *Flugkapitän* Fritz Wendel. The V-type tail proved to offer no marked advantage over the orthodox tail assembly, and disadvantages included a deterioration of longitudinal stability, a strengthening of the Bf 109's tendency to swing to port during landing, and some lateral oscillation under turbulent conditions.

One of the F-series prototypes, the Bf 109 V24 (*Werk-Nr.* 5604), was used at Göttingen for tunnel testing the ventral radiator bath of the Me 309, and was subsequently utilized by Caudron-Renault for the development of a flap-blowing system, the testing of which was undertaken in the wind tunnel at Chalais-Meudon, while another, the Bf 109 V23 (*Werk-Nr.* 5603), was modified to test a fixed tricycle undercarriage as part of the Me 309 development programme. Other F-series airframes utilized in the Me 309 experimental programme were a Bf 109F-1 (*Werk-Nr.* 5642), which, as the Bf 109 V31, flew with a broad-track, inward-retracting undercarriage and a semi-retractable radiator bath, and two other Bf 109F-1s (*Werk-Nummern* 5716 and 5717) which, as the Bf 109 V30 and V30a, flight tested the Me 309 cabin pressurization and air-conditioning systems. Another Bf 109F airframe was adapted to take a BMW 801 air-cooled radial engine, but extreme turbulence in the vicinity of the tail necessitated the abandoning of trials, and yet another was flown with a Jumo 213 with an annular radiator.

# An unorthodox role

While the Bf 109F participated in several unusual experiments, the most unorthodox operational role that it was called upon to play was that of a guidance system for a crude but highly original missile produced by attaching a hollow-charge warhead to a time-expired Junkers Ju 88 bomber. This development, known by the code name *Beethoven*, was prompted by the success enjoyed by a series of *Huckepack* (Pick-a-back) trials in which a Bf 109E had been mounted above a DFS 230 transport glider (see page 81), the idea being to attach the fighter to a converted bomber, the pilot of the former guiding the latter to a suitable target.

The design of a superstructure on which the Bf 109 was to be mounted was undertaken by the DFS, drawing upon the Institute's earlier experience with *Huckepack* Bf 109E/DFS 230 combination. This consisted of two steel-tube struts attached to the Ju 88 wing mainspars on each side of the fuselage, the forward strut being vertical and the aft strut being inclined forward, these attaching at their tips to the arms of a V-strut connected to a fuselage mainframe, thus forming two inclined tripods. The apices of the tripods were intended to marry up with connections on the mainspar of the Bf 109 forming the upper component. A single strut supported the tail of the fighter, this being spring-operated and, when disengaged by the Bf 109's pilot, sprung back to be caught by a yoke on the rear fuselage of the lower component. This yoke incorporated an electrical contact which released the main attachment points at the apices of the tripods immediately the tail-support strut sprang back, and also prevented the strut rebounding to strike the tail of the Bf 109.

The prototype conversion consisted of a Bf 109F-4 and a Ju 88A-4, the lower component being referred to as a *Mistel* (Mistletoe), the connection between this parasitic evergreen and the lower component of the *Huckepack* combination being obvious. The combination was also referred to unofficially as the "*Vater und Sohn*" (Father and Son) after a popular German strip cartoon, but *Mistel* was to become a generic term for the lower component of all such combinations, irrespective of the type of aircraft involved.

In July 1943, instructions were given to Junkers to proceed with the conversion of 15 Ju 88A airframes for *Mistel* use. Prototype trials proved successful, and the *Beethoven* programme was transferred to Nordhausen where, during the spring of 1944, pilots of the *Einsatz-Staffel* of IV/KG 101

received conversion training on the Bf 109F upper component from Junkers test pilots.

The initial model was known as the *Mistel* 1 and, like the prototype, comprised a Bf 109F-4 and a Ju 88A-4, the first few conversions being completed as *Mistel* S 1 trainers, the "S" indicating *Schulung* (Training). All *Misteln* were initially flown and tested with the standard Ju 88 nose section, the cockpit being stripped to its bare essentials and providing accommodation for a crew of two. This nose section could be detached by means of quick-release bolts and replaced by an 8,380-lb (3 800-kg) hollow-charge warhead which used the same attachment points.

Large hollow-charge warheads had been tested with considerable success against the obsolete French battleship *l'Ocean* during the later part of 1943, and other experiments were performed in which the warhead was tested against reinforced concrete, the one-ton steel core bursting through concrete some 60 ft. (18,20 m) thick. The final warhead tests were performed at Peenemünde in April and May of 1944, and in the following month the *Einsatz-Staffel* of IV/KG 101 arrived

*(Above right) The prototype Mistel conversion comprising a Bf 109F-4 and a Ju 88 A-4, and (below) fully operational Mistel 1 composites of II/KG 200 on a Danish airfield late in 1944. The II Gruppe was to have attacked the British Fleet in Scapa Flow in December 1944 but this operation was eventually abandoned*

at St. Dizier and *Mistel* 1s to attack Allied invasion forces.

The *Mistel* 1 was basically similar to the original prototype conversion, apart from somewhat sturdier bracing struts, and two methods of operation were proposed. The first of these called for take-off and flight to the target area on the power of the lower component alone, the airscrew of the Bf 109F being feathered and its pilot only starting the engine during the final phase of the approach to the target. The second method of operation was to employ the engines of both components from take-off, the latter being generally adopted, the BF 109F drawing fuel from the tanks of the lower component until the two parted company. When the objective was reached, the pilot of the Messerschmitt set the controls to approach the target in a shallow glide, and at the appropriate distance detached his aircraft and climbed away, the pilotless lower component continuing on its set course.

The *Einsatz-Staffel* of IV/KG 101, commanded by *Hauptmann* Horst Rudat, had five *Mistel* 1s on strength when it arrived at St. Dizier, and performed its first operational sortie with one of these on the night of June 24, 1944. This proved abortive as the lower component had to be released prematurely when a Mosquito night fighter suddenly appeared. Shortly afterwards, the unit's four remaining *Misteln* were used for a nocturnal attack on Allied shipping in the Seine Bay, this time escorted by Bf 109G fighters. Flares were dropped and the attack pressed home, but results could not be observed owing to the smoke screen emitted by the target vessels. Reconnaissance undertaken on the following day revealed that all the *Misteln* had found their targets but none of the vessels hit had been sunk.

Considerable trouble was experienced with these early *Misteln* as the maximum overload weight of the Ju 88 was normally restricted to the order of 30,865 lb. (14 000 kg), this being exceeded with full fuel load and the Bf 109F-4 in position, and take-offs from rough runways proved extremely hazard-

ous as shocks frequently burst the tyres of the undercarriage. As a result of losing a number of *Misteln* in take-off accidents resulting from burst tyres, a jettisonable third mainwheel was later added beneath the fuselage of the *Mistel* 3 series which replaced the Bf 109F-4 with a Focke-Wulf Fw 190A-8.

On October 10, 1944, the *Einsatz-Staffel* of IV/KG 101 became the nucleus of the *Einsatz-Gruppe* III/KG 66, intended solely for *Mistel* operations, but 10 days later, before operations could be joined, III/KG 66 became II/KG 200. By this time, it had been agreed that available *Misteln* should be reserved for one decisive blow, and among several plans formulated was an attack on the British Fleet in Scapa Flow which was to take place in December 1944. For this operation some 60 *Misteln* were gathered on Danish airfields, and it was intended that this force should be accompanied by 5./KG 200, a *Beleuchter* (Illuminator) *Staffel* which was to illuminate the target with flares. Constant bad weather delayed the launching of the operation, and when this finally improved, a full moon rendered the possibility of success marginal as the *Misteln* were incapable of exceeding 235 m.p.h. (380 km/h) at 14,765 ft. (4 500 m) and, unable to manoeuvre and lacking any form of defence, they would have proved easy targets for interceptors.

In January 1945, inclement weather again delayed the launching of the attack by II/KG 200, and an alternative proposal was then considered, this being *Unternehmen Eisenhammer* (Operation Iron Hammer), a scheme to deal a decisive blow against the Soviet armament industry which had for long been a fond plan of the High Command. The operation was not scheduled to take place until March 1945, owing to delays in the availability of sufficient *Misteln* and the training of adequate numbers of pilots, *Eisenhammer* called for II/KG 200 to have no fewer than 100 *Misteln* on strength. Some time before this, however, the Bf 109F-4 had given place to the Fw 190A in the *Beethoven* programme, and, in the event, *Eisenhammer* was destined never to be launched.

*A Mistel 1 as ferried to the Einsatz-Staffel of IV/KG 101. The upper component is a Bf 109F-4 and the standard nose employed for ferrying and training is seen fitted, this being replaced by a large hollow-charge warhead for operations*

# An Eagle known as Gustav

Although not immediately obvious to the Allies, each phase of the air war reflected the lack of long-term planning on the part of the leaders of the Third Reich. At the time Operation *Barbarossa* was launched against the Soviet Union in mid-1941, the aircraft manufacturing programme was noteworthy for nothing more than the modesty of the increase in single-seat fighter production, and in view of the high attrition soon being suffered in the campaign to which the *Jagdflieger* had been committed, the ineptness of Göring, Udet, and the *Reichsluftfahrtministerium* was soon manifest.

An equally serious example of this ineptness that was to affect the *Jagdflieger* was failure to ensure availability of an acceptable production successor for the Bf 109 before the peak of its development was past and the end of its heyday in sight. In 1941 the Bf 109 was still undeniably a very effective warplane but tooling should have begun for a successor. The highly promising Fw 190 had barely reached the threshold of its service career and was still beset by numerous teething troubles, and there was no recourse but to develop further the now-ageing Messerschmitt fighter. Thus, while the *Jagdflieger* were engaged in the opening phases of the war against the Soviet Union, the Augsburg design office of Messerschmitt was embarking on the development of yet another version of the Bf 109 which, resulting from force of circumstances, was to become numerically the most important of all models of the fighter.

Whereas previously the demand for maximum possible speed had been mitigated to some extent by the importance attached to qualities of manoeuvre and handling, high power and weight loadings were now considered acceptable in order to increase emphasis on speed. In consequence, many service pilots understandably considered the Bf 109G, or *Gustav* as it was soon to be widely but unofficially known, to be a retrogressive step when it was first issued to the *Jagdstaffeln* early in 1942. Although differing little externally from the Bf 109F which it succeeded, and, initially at least, carrying the same armament, it signified a further stage in weight escalation that had already begun to have a detrimental effect on the handling characteristics and manoeuvrability of the fighter.

Changes in the nature of the air war had dictated provision for cockpit pressurization, the only external signs of which were to be seen in the heavier canopy framing and the deletion of the lower quarter-lights. The introduction of the more powerful and heavier DB 605 engine had demanded some local structural strengthening with, in consequence, a further increment in weight. This, in turn, necessitated heavier and more robust undercarriage legs. However, the deterioration in flying characteristics suffered by the G-series fighter was considered an acceptable penalty to be paid for the higher speeds attainable.

The DB 605A engine differed from the DB 601E primarily in having a redesigned cylinder block in which maximum possible bore had been obtained while retaining the original cylinder centres. The increased cylinder capacity, the raising of the compression ratio (to 7·3 for the port cylinder block and 7·5 for the starboard block) and an increase in maximum permissible r.p.m. to 2,800 resulted in virtually unchanged overall dimensions but a take-off output of 1,475 h.p. with 1,355 h.p. being available at 18,700 ft. (5 700 m), 1,310 and 1,250 h.p. being delivered for climb and combat at sea level and 19,290 ft. (5 880 m) respectively.

The pressure cabin was of the "cold wall" type, and merely represented a modification of the normal Bf 109 cockpit. The fireproof bulkhead, floor and sidewalls were sealed, while a sloping plate behind the pilot's seat completed the enclosure,

also forming rear armouring. The windscreen was of sandwich type, air between the glazed panels being maintained in dry condition by a calcium chloride capsule; the sliding glazed panels in the canopy sides were also of sandwich construction and were held securely against the canopy framing by internal pressure; rubber packing pieces sealed the joints around the canopy, and to reduce the risk of leakage, the main controls had rotary movement at their points of egress from the cabin. The enclosure was designed to provide for a pressure differential of 4·4 lb./sq. ft. with a safety factor of 1·8. Installation of the DB 605A engine was accompanied by an enlarged carburettor air intake, the oil cooler beneath the cowling was enlarged and additional small intakes were added aft of the spinner.

The construction of a pre-production batch of Bf 109G-0 fighters was begun in the late summer of 1941, but non-availability of the DB 605A engine led to the decision to retain the DB 601E for the pre-production *Gustav*, the first example of which, *Werk-Nr.* 14 0001 VJ + WA, was completed in October. Apart from the power plant, which was housed by a DB 605A-type cowling complete with larger oil cooler, the Bf 109G-0 was similar to the initial production G-series variant,

*(Below) The first Bf 109G-0 Werk-Nr. 14 0001 which retained the DB 601E but had a DB 605A cowling*

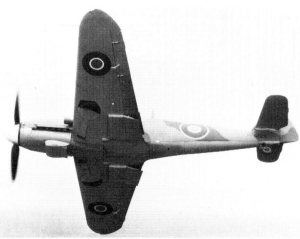

(Above and below left) A Bf 109G-2 Werk-Nr. 10 639 captured in Sicily, freighted to Britain and taken on charge in February 1944 by No. 1426 Flight, subsequently being allocated the serial RN228

the Bf 109G-1, which began to leave the assembly lines during the early spring of 1942.

With a DB 605A-1 engine and carrying an armament of one 20-mm MG 151 and two 7,9-mm MG 17s, the BF 109G-1 had provision for nitrous oxide (GM 1) injection as standard, the insulated cylindrical tank for the GM 1 being mounted on the fifth rear fuselage frame with the necessary liquid oxygen bottles aft. Although the addition of the GM 1 installation increased loaded weight to 7,055 lb. (3 200 kg), the complete equipment plus 25 Imp. gal. (115 l) of nitrous oxide weighing more than 400 lb. (180 kg), it had a phenomenal effect on altitude performance, boosting power output to 1,250 h.p. at 27,890 ft. (8 500 m) when injected at the "normal" rate of 7.95 lb./min. (3,3 kg/min).

Produced simultaneously with the Bf 109G-1 was the Bf 109G-2 which was identical to the parallel model apart from having cabin pressurization equipment deleted, and the latter was, in fact, the first version to attain service status, although the Bf 109G-3 and G-4 were delivered at virtually the same time, these differing from the Bf 109G-1 and G-2 in having wider tyres on non-spoked wheels necessitating blister fairings in the upper wing surface, a larger, wider-tyred tailwheel and FuG 16z R/T in place of the FuG 7a. The G-4 was a photo-recce variant.

Late in April 1942, the *Stab* and I *Gruppe* of JG 2 based at Beaumont le Roger, Liegescourt and Triqueville under *Jagdfliegerführer* 3 began conversion from the Fw 190A to the Bf 109G-2, and almost simultaneously the III *Gruppe* of JG 26 at Wevelghem under *Jagdfliegerführer* 2 began conversion from the Bf 109F to the Bf 109G-3. The *Gustav* was first encountered by the R.A.F. during the following month, and it is of interest to recall the comments of Pierre Clostermann, D.F.C., concerning combat between the Spitfire V and the German fighter.

"Before the introduction of negative-*g* carburettors in our Spitfires, it was rather a tough job to keep within range [of the Bf 109G]. Not being as manoeuvrable laterally as the Fw 190 and so unable to flick on its back quickly enough before diving, the pilot of the Bf 109G would push his stick forward as if to start an outside loop. The Spitfire V following could not do the same because the engine would cut straight away, so, to maintain a continuous flow of petrol to the carburettor, it had to perform a complicated succession of barrel rolls around the 109's trajectory. Usually the Spitfire V could not catch the Bf 109G, but if the German pilot thought that the Spitfire was gaining he would use GM 1 and leave his opponent standing."

Both the Bf 109G-2 and G-4 could be employed in the

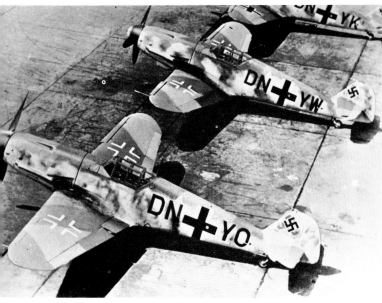

*(Immediately below) An early production Bf 109G-1. This model introduced the DB 605A engine and was produced in parallel with the Bf 109G-2 seen (bottom) awaiting ferrying to operational units in the summer of 1942*

reconnaissance role as the G-2/R2 and G-4/R2, with MG 151 cannon and GM 1 system removed and a single camera installed in the rear fuselage, and some experiments were undertaken with a photographic Bf 109G-2 fitted with a WT (*Waffentropfen* or "Weapon Drop") 17 beneath the fuselage, this enclosing two aft-firing MG 17 machine guns together with their ammunition. However, the weight and drag of the installation mitigated against its service adoption. Six Bf 109G-2s were fitted experimentally with Messerschmitt Me P6 variable pitch airscrews as Bf 109G-2/U1s.

An unusual experiment conducted with a Bf 109G-2 resulted from an attempt to evolve a *Jagdbomber mit vergrösserter Reichweit* (extended-range fighter-bomber), or *Jabo-Rei*, capable of delivering a single 1,102-lb. (500 kg) SC 500 bomb. The principal problem was the provision of adequate clearance for the bomb during take-off, and this problem was turned over to the Gerhard Fieseler design office for solution. Fieseler designed an auxiliary undercarriage member which, with a single low-pressure tyre and small-diameter wheel, featured a long-travel oleo leg inserted in the fuselage immediately aft of the fuel tank. The cylindrical jacket of the oleo leg was attached to the first aft fuselage mainframe by explosive bolts which could be activated by the pilot, the auxiliary leg being lowered to the ground by parachute after take-off had been effected.

Strong points were introduced in the wing immediately inboard of the leading-edge slots, and shackles were provided for two 66 Imp. gal. (300 l) drop tanks. The modification of a Bf 109G-2 to the Fieseler designs was entrusted to the Skoda Werke near Prague, and completed under the designation FiSk 199. Tests were conducted as the Bf 109G-2/R1 at overload weights in excess of 9,000 lb. (4 080 kg), but although trials were successful, and the separation of the auxiliary undercarriage member from the aircraft in flight presented no difficulties, no further development of the Bf 109G-2/R1 *Jabo-Rei* was undertaken.

Meanwhile, operations of the Bf 109F in North Africa had been accompanied by cooling difficulties with the engine-mounted MG 151 cannon, causing frequent malfunction. As weight of fire without the cannon was totally inadequate, the tropicalized version of the Bf 109G-1 differed in armament from examples of the fighter intended for operation in more temperate climes. The 20-mm cannon was retained by the Bf 109-G1/Trop but the two 7,9-mm MG 17 machine guns with 500 r.p.g. gave place to two 13-mm MG 131 machine guns with 300 r.p.g., the muzzle troughs of which were located further aft on the cowling. The breech blocks of these larger weapons were enclosed by fairings which marred the upper

## Bf 109G-2 Specification

**Power Plant:** One Daimler-Benz DB 605A 12-cylinder inverted-vee liquid-cooled engine rated at 1,475 h.p. for take-off, 1,355 h.p. at 18,700 ft. (5 700 m), and 1,250 h.p. at 27,890 ft. (8 500 m) with GM 1 (nitrous oxide) injection.

**Performance:** (At 6,834 lb./3 100 kg) Maximum speed, 317 m.p.h. (510 km/h) at sea level, 331 m.p.h. (533 km/h) at 3,280 ft. (1 000 m), 350 m.p.h. (563 km/h) at 6,560 ft. (2 000 m), 365 m.p.h. (587 km/h) at 9,840 ft. (3 000 m), 369 m.p.h. (594 km/h) at 16,400 ft. (5 000 m), 398 m.p.h. (640 km/h) at 20,670 ft. (6 300 m), 383 m.p.h. (616 km/h) at 28,540 ft. (8 700 m); range, 340 mls. (547 km) at 322 m.p.h. (518 km/h) at 19,030 ft. (5 800 m), with 66 Imp. gal. (300 l) drop tank, 528 mls. (850 km) at 311 m.p.h. (500 km/h) at 18,045 ft. (5 500 m); initial climb rate (at 6,724 lb./3 050 kg), 4,590 ft./min. (24,6 m/sec); time to 6,560 ft. (2 000 m), 1·5 min., to 13,120 ft. (4 000 m), 3·2 min., to 19,685 ft. (6 000 m), 5·1 min. to 26,250 ft. (8 000 m), 7·6 min., to 32,810 ft. (10 000 m), 12 min.; service ceiling, 39,370 ft. (12 000 m).

**Weights:** Empty, 4,968 lb. (2 253 kg); empty equipped, 5,687 lb. (2 580 kg); normal loaded, 6,834 lb. (3 100 kg); maximum overload, 7,055 lb. (3 200 kg).

**Dimensions:** Span, 32 ft. 6½ in. (9,92 m); length, 29 ft. 7½ in. (9,03 m); height, 8 ft. 2½ in. (2,50 m); wing area, 173·299 sq. ft. (16,1 m²).

**Armament:** One 20-mm Mauser MG 151/20 engine-mounted cannon with 150 rounds and two 7,9-mm Rheinmetall Borsig MG 17 fuselage-mounted machine guns with 500 r.p.g.

*(Below) A Bf 109G-5 of 7./JG 27 flying over the Eastern Mediterranean late in 1943. At this time 7./JG 27 was operating over the Mediterranean as semi-independent Schwärme. (Above right) A Bf 109G-6/R6 serving with II/JG 26 operating from French bases in the autumn of 1942*

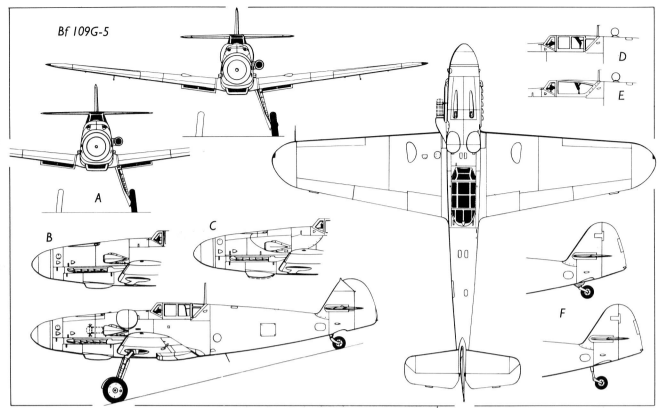

Bf 109G-5

*The general arrangement drawing depicts the Bf 109G-5 with tropical filter shown by dotted line. The scrap views depicts (A) narrow wheels (which permitted upper wing bulges to be dispensed with) of G-1 and G-2; (B) Nose of MG 17-armed G-1 to G-4; (C) overall fairing covering MG 131 breeches and supercharger of late (DB 605AS-powered) G-6 and G-14; (D) short mast and D/F loop of late G-6; (E) clear-vision canopy standard on G-10 and G-14 (retrofitted to G-6); (F) wooden fin-and-rudder of G-6/U2 and G-14/U2, and lengthened (fixed) tailwheel leg on (some) G-6 and G-10*

contour of the forward fuselage, and the Bf 109G-1/Trop was, in consequence, promptly christened the "*Beule*" ("Bump") by its pilots.

Difficulties were also experienced in providing the super-charger air intake with an efficient dust filter. The intake was a simple, circular-section elbow set at a shallow angle of attack for optimum relationship with the slipstream and other flow conditions, and after testing numerous filters of German design, a filter of Italian type was standardized, and used in North Africa, the Mediterranean, and on the South Russian Front where dust conditions were also severe.

The DB 605 engine adopted for the *Gustav* proved reliable in service, although some difficulties resulted from low oil pressures at all altitudes. Messerschmitt maintained that the hydraulic supercharger coupling resulted in a tendency to trap small air bubbles in the oil regardless of the tank design, while Daimler-Benz insisted that the design of the horseshoe-shaped

*(Above right and below) Bf 109G-6/R2 "formation destroyers" each equipped with a pair of Wfr.Gr. 21 mortars beneath the wings. The 21-cm mortar shells were intended to break up the defensive boxes adopted by the U.S. 8th Air Force*

tank was at fault, pointing out that no similar problem had been experienced with any installation other than that of the Bf 109G. Daimler-Benz eventually evolved a de-aerator which was supposed to separate entrapped air, and this was introduced on the Bf 109G assembly line, but when it was ascertained that the full oil pressure requirements still could not be met the fighter reverted to the original oil system, and the problem was never fully resolved.

Nitrous oxide (GM 1) injection was generally considered less effective than additional supercharging, and the next G-series production model, the Bf 109G-5 (which, like all subsequent variants, standardized on the twin fuselage-mounted MG 131 machine guns), was delivered with both the DB 605A engine and GM 1, and with the DB 605AS engine which used the larger supercharger of the DB 603. The increased height and width of this supercharger resulted in a rather untidy installation on the port side of the engine, but this modification afforded a maximum output of 1,200 h.p. at 26,250 ft. (8 000 m), 1,150 h.p. being available for climb and combat at 25,600 ft. (7 800 m).

An interesting modification first introduced on the Bf 109G-5 was a wooden tailplane, with this change the aircraft being designated Bf 109G-5/U2. The detail calculations for this wooden tailplane were undertaken by a group of Latvian engineers at the Riga subsidiary of the Espenlaub Werke, and heavier than the standard metal tailplane, the wooden component necessitated a counterweight being bolted to the oil-tank bracket.

Whereas provision for cabin pressurization was retained by the Bf 109G-5, this feature was deleted from subsequent production models, having been found to be of dubious operational value, and the Bf 109G-6, which reached the assembly lines in the late autumn of 1942, was the first "standard" model intended from the outset to accept various *Rüstsätze* (Field Conversion Sets) to increase its suitability for specific operational tasks as the tactical situation dictated. Furthermore, the Bf 109G-6 could accept several versions of the DB 605A engine (from the spring of 1944 the DB 605D was also installed as an *Umrüst-Motor*, or "Conversion Engine"), and the insulated cylindrical 25 Imp. gal. (115 l) tank behind the cockpit could be used for either GM 1 or methanol-water (MW 50), the latter being injected into the supercharger below the rated altitude of the engine.

Boost pressure from the supercharger was utilized to apply pressure to the tank, forcing the MW 50 along a pipe to an injection nozzle in the eye of the supercharger. The flow of methanol-water mixture was controlled by a solenoid valve activated by an automatic throttle switch and a master switch in the cockpit, and a four per cent increase in power could be obtained even at constant boost pressure. The increased power could be used for a maximum of 10 minutes at a time, but at least five minutes had to elapse between successive periods of operation.

The DB 605AM in the Bf 109G-6 consumed fuel at 106 Imp. gal. (482 l) per hour at take-off, but when using MW 50 with higher boost pressure, consumption was increased to 141 Imp. gal. (641 l) per hour. Thus, any extensive use of methanol-water markedly reduced endurance and also had a deleterious effect on the life of the sparking plugs which had to the changed every 15–20 hours. On the other hand, MW 50 boosted take-off power from 1,475 to 1,800 h.p., and made 1,700 h.p. available at 13,450 ft. (4 100 m). Some Bf 109G-6s received the DB 605ASCM engine which switched from 87 octane B4 fuel to 96 octane C3, affording special emergency power of 2,000 h.p. at sea level and 2,030 h.p. at 1,640 ft. (500 m), with 1,800 h.p. available at 16,400 ft. (5 000 m). This "AS" engine, as previously mentioned in connection with the G-5, possessed a larger

supercharger that could not be easily accommodated within the existing cowling, and rather than add yet another unsightly and drag-inducing bulge to the forward fuselage, a subtly-contoured overall fairing was applied that extended from the gun troughs to the windscreen arch. This effectively enclosed both the supercharger and the gun breeches, thus eliminating the "*Beule*" of the standard G-5 and G-6. This fairing characterized all subsequent variants with the DB 605AS or DB 605D engines and these were fitted with broader-bladed propellers.

Apart from the previously-mentioned changes, the Bf 109G-6 was the first G-series variant to introduce the 30-mm MK 108 engine-mounted cannon firing through the airscrew hub, a highly lethal weapon evolved by Rheinmetall-Borsig and of which production averaged 120 per month during 1942, with deliveries destined to reach a peak of 10,000 per month in September–October 1944. This cannon was provided with 60 rounds of belt-fed ammunition, and one hit from its 30-mm shell was usually sufficient to destroy an opposing fighter, but inadequate supplies dictated the retention of the 20-mm MG 151 by a proportion of Bf 109G-6s.

## The Gustavs multiply

Production of the Bf 109 fighter during 1942, which was devoted almost exclusively to the *Gustav*, rose steadily under Milch's aegis, a growing complex of sub contractors feeding the Messerschmitt, Erla, and WNF assembly lines. From 122 in January 1942, when Bf 109 acceptances were almost at their lowest ebb of the war years, the monthly output rose gradually to attain 306 acceptances in December, bringing the year's total production of the Bf 109 to 2,664. This was only 36 more aircraft than had been delivered in 1941, but it should be borne in mind that, whereas only 224 Fw 190 fighters had been accepted in 1941, no fewer than 1,878 were delivered in 1942, bringing the year's output of single-seat fighters to 4,542, representing an increase of almost 60 per cent.

By the late summer of 1942, of the approximately 900 Bf 109 fighters on the strength of the first-line *Jagdgruppen*, two-thirds were G-series aircraft, the bulk of the remainder being F-series machines. On September 20, 1942, of the formations comprising *Luftflotte* 3 in France and the Low Countries only 11./JG 2 and 11./JG 26 (these *Staffeln* having been formed earlier

*Continued page 112*

---

### Bf 109G-6 Specification

**Power Plant:** One Daimler-Benz DB 605AM 12-cylinder inverted-vee liquid-cooled engine rated at 1,475 h.p. for take-off and 1,355 h.p. at 18,700 ft. (5 700 m), or 1,800 h.p. for take-off and 1,700 h.p. at 13,450 ft. (4 100 m) with MW 50 (methanol-water) injection.

**Performance:** (At 6,940 lb./3 148 kg) Maximum speed with MW 50 injection, 340 m.p.h. (547 km/h) at sea level, 366 m.p.h. (590 km/h) at 6,560 ft. (2 000 m), 372 m.p.h. (600 km/h) at 9,840 ft. (3 000 m), 380 m.p.h. (611 km/h) at 13,120 ft. (4 000 m), 386 m.p.h. (621 km/h) at 22,640 ft. (6 900 m); range, 350 mls. (563 km) at 330 m.p.h. (530 km/h) at 19,030 ft. (5 800 m), with 66 Imp. gal. (300 l) drop tank, 620 mls. (998 km) at 317 m.p.h. (510 km/h) at 19,865 ft. (6 000 m); initial climb rate at 6,940 lb. (3 148 kg), 3,346 ft./min. (17,00 m/sec); time to 9,840 ft. (3 000 m), 2·9 min., to 18,700 ft. (5 700 m), 6 min.; service ceiling, 37,890 ft. (11 550 m).

**Weights:** Empty equipped, 5,893 lb. (2 673 kg); normal loaded, 6,940 lb. (3 148 kg); maximum overload, 7,496 lb. (3 400 kg).

**Dimensions:** Span, 32 ft. 6½ in. (9,92 m); length, 29 ft. 7½ in. (9,03 m); height, 8 ft. 2½ in. (2,50 m); wing area, 173·299 sq. ft. (16,1 m²).

**Armament:** One 30-mm Rheinmetall Borsig MK 108 engine-mounted cannon with 60 rounds or 20-mm Mauser MG 151/20 cannon with 150 rounds, and two 13-mm Rheinmetall Borsig MG 131 fuselage-mounted machine guns with 300 r.p.g.

(1) Bf 109F-2 of III/JG 54 "Grünherz" on the Leningrad Front, winter
1941–42; (A) Emblem of III/JG 54 "Grünherz"; (B) Emblem of 9./JG 54;
(2) Bf 109F-2/Trop of I/JG 77 at Comiso, Sicily, summer 1942

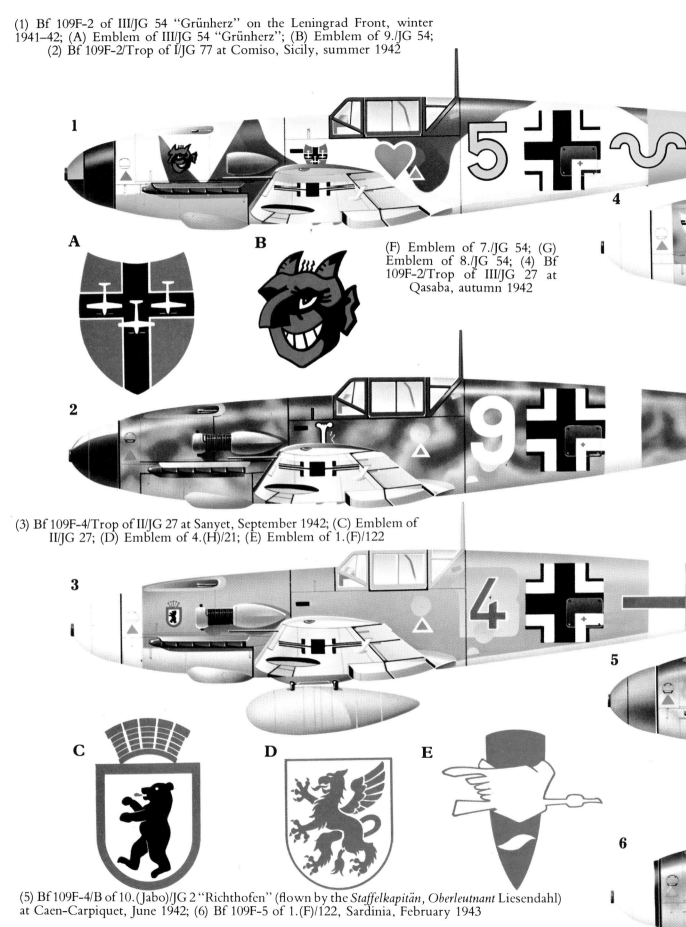

(F) Emblem of 7./JG 54; (G)
Emblem of 8./JG 54; (4) Bf
109F-2/Trop of III/JG 27 at
Qasaba, autumn 1942

(3) Bf 109F-4/Trop of II/JG 27 at Sanyet, September 1942; (C) Emblem of
II/JG 27; (D) Emblem of 4.(H)/21; (E) Emblem of 1.(F)/122

(5) Bf 109F-4/B of 10.(Jabo)/JG 2 "Richthofen" (flown by the *Staffelkapitän, Oberleutnant* Liesendahl)
at Caen-Carpiquet, June 1942; (6) Bf 109F-5 of 1.(F)/122, Sardinia, February 1943

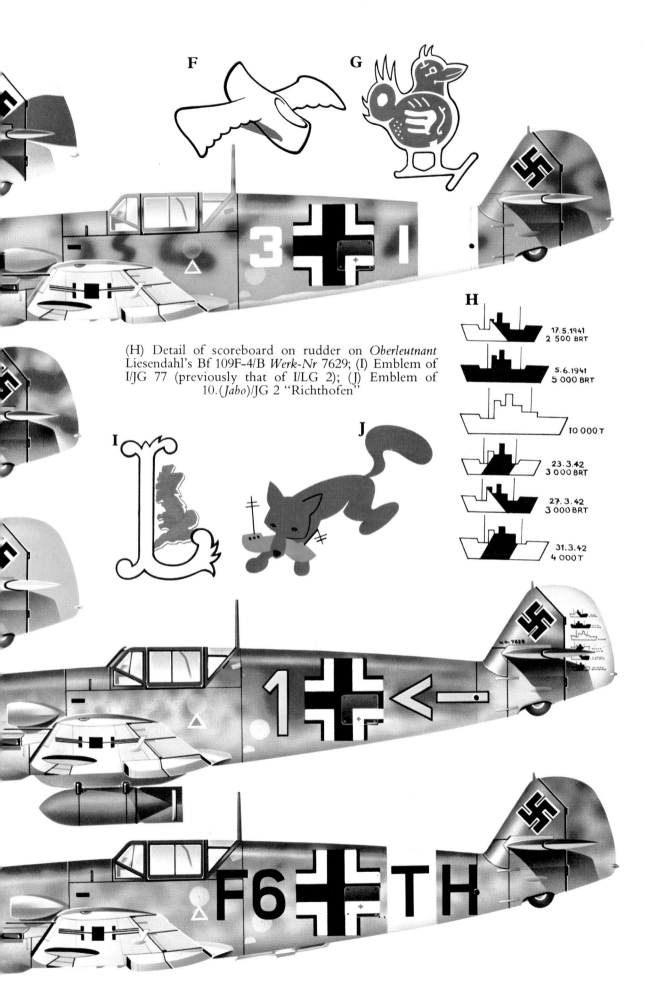

(H) Detail of scoreboard on rudder on *Oberleutnant* Liesendahl's Bf 109F-4/B *Werk-Nr* 7629; (I) Emblem of I/JG 77 (previously that of I/LG 2); (J) Emblem of 10.(*Jabo*)/JG 2 "Richthofen"

H

17.5.1941
2 500 BRT

5.6.1941
5 000 BRT

10 000 T

23.3.42
3 000 BRT

27.3.42
3 000 BRT

31.3.42
4 000 T

(1) Bf 109F-4 of the *ungarische Jagdstaffel* (1./1 *vadasz század*) on Stalingrad Front, late 1942; (A) Emblem of Finnish HLeLv 34; (B) Emblem of Finnish HLeLv 24

(2) Bf 109G-4/R6 of the *Corpul 1 Aerian* of the Royal Rumanian Air Force; (C) Emblem of the Slovakian Insurgent Air Force applied to two Bf 109G-6s in October 1944; (D) Emblem of 14th Slovakian Fighter Squadron; (3) Bf 109G-6 of 14th Slovakian Fighter Squadron, Crimea, spring 1943

(4) Bf 109G-2 of HLeLv 34, summer 1943; (E) Emblem of the 102/2 Squadron of the Hungarian Air Force; (F) Emblem of the Hungarian 5/1 "Puma" Fighter Group; (5) Bf 109G-6 of the Hungarian 102 Independent Fighter Group, summer 1944

E

F

G

H

(G) Bulgarian national insignia; (H) Emblem of the Bulgarian 6th Fighter Regiment's "Wildcat" Squadron; (6) Bf 109G-6 of the Bulgarian 6th Fighter Regiment, Wrasdebna, April 1944

(1) Bf 109G-2/Trop of II/JG 51 "Mölders" at Casa Zeppera, Sardinia,
summer 1943; (A) Emblem of JG 51 "Mölders"; (2) Bf 109G-6 of I/JG 52
at Leipzig (Rumania), summer 1944

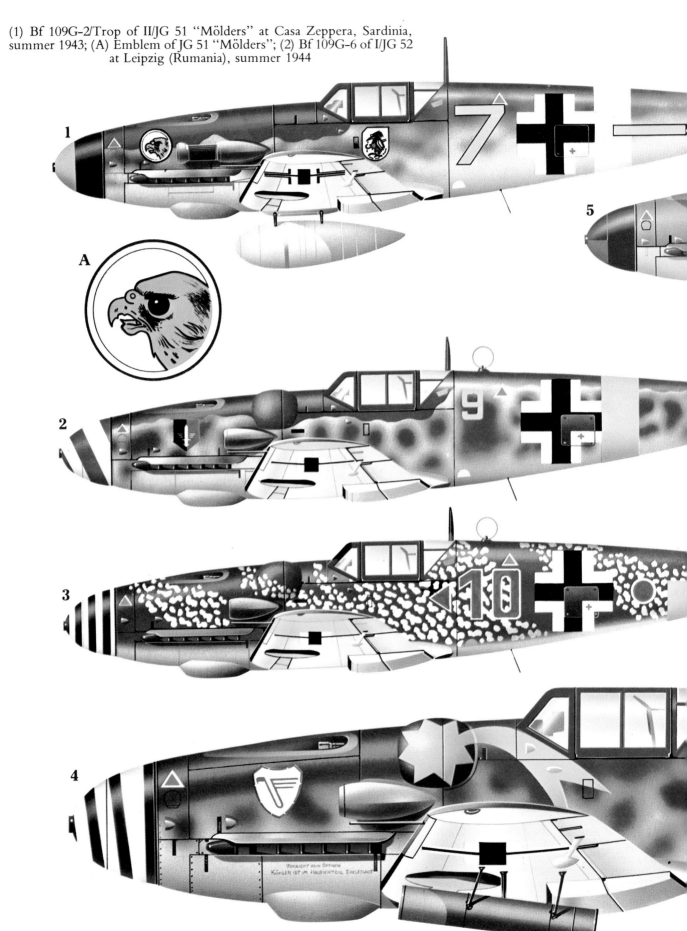

(5) Bf 109G-2 of II/JG 54 "Grünherz" at Siverskaya, autumn 1942

**B**

**C**

**D**

**E**

**F**

(B) Emblem of II/JG 51 "Mölders"; (C) Emblem of II/JG 54 "Grünherz"; (D) Emblem of JG 54 "Grünherz"; (E) Emblem of JG 52; (F) Emblem of JG 3 "Udet"

(3) Bf 109G-6 of IV/JG 5 at Petsamo, winter 1943-44; (4) Bf 109G-6/R2 of III/JG 3 "Udet" at Bad Wörishofen, spring 1944

# Messerschmitt Bf 109G-14/U4 Cutaway Drawing Key

1 Starboard navigation light
2 Starboard wingtip
3 Fixed trim tab
4 Starboard Frise-type aileron
5 Flush-riveted stressed
  wing-skinning
6 Handley Page leading-edge
  automatic slot
7 Slot control linkage
8 Slot equalizer rod
9 Aileron control
  linkage
10 Fabric-covered
  flap section
11 Wheel fairing
12 Port fuselage
  machine-gun
  ammunition-feed fairing
13 Port Rheinmetall Borsig
  13-mm MG 131 machine
  gun
14 Engine accessories
15 Starboard machine-gun
  trough

16 Daimler Benz DB 605AM
  twelve-cylinder inverted-vee
  liquid-cooled engine
17 Detachable cowling panel
18 Oil filter access
19 Oil tank
20 Propeller pitch-change
  mechanism
21 VDM electrically-operated
  constant-speed propeller
22 Spinner
23 Engine-mounted cannon
  muzzle
24 Blast tube
25 Propeller hub
26 Spinner back plate
27 Auxiliary cooling intakes

28 Coolant header tank
29 Anti-vibration rubber
  engine-mounting pads
30 Elektron forged engine bearer
31 Engine bearer support strut
  attachment
32 Plug leads
33 Exhaust manifold fairing strip
34 Ejector exhausts
35 Cowling fasteners

36 Oil cooler
37 Oil cooler intake
38 Starboard mainwheel
39 Oil cooler outlet flap
40 Wing root fillet
41 Wing/fuselage fairing
42 Firewall/bulkhead
43 Supercharger air intake
44 Supercharger assembly
45 20-mm cannon magazine
  drum
46 13-mm machine-gun
  ammunition feed
47 Engine bearer upper
  attachment
48 Ammunition feed fairing
49 13-mm Rheinmetall Borsig
  MG 131 machine gun
  breeches
50 Instrument panel
51 20-mm Mauser MG 151/20
  cannon breech
52 Heelrests
53 Rudder pedals
54 Undercarriage emergency
  retraction cables
55 Fuselage frame
56 Wing/fuselage fairing

57 Undercarriage emergency
  retraction handwheel
  (outboard)
58 Tail trim handwheel (inboard)
59 Seat harness
60 Throttle lever
61 Control column
62 Cockpit ventilation inlet
63 Revi 16B reflector gunsight
  (folding)
64 Armoured windshield frame
65 Anti-glare gunsight screen
66 90-mm armourglass
  windscreen
67 'Galland'-type clear-vision
  hinged canopy
68 Framed armourglass
  head/back panel
69 Canopy contoured frame

70 Canopy hinges
  (starboard)
71 Canopy release catch
72 Pilot's bucket-type seat (8-mm
  back armour)
73 Underfloor contoured fuel tank
  (88 Imp. gal/400 l of 87 octane
  B4

74 Fuselage frame
75 Circular access panel
76 Tail trimming cable conduit
77 Wireless leads
78 MW 50 (methanol/water) tank
  (25 Imp. gal/114 l capacity)
79 Handhold
80 Fuselage decking
81 Aerial mast
82 D/F loop
83 Oxygen cylinders (three)
84 Filler pipe
85 Wireless equipment packs
  (FuG 16ZY communications
  and FuG 25a IFF)
86 Main fuel filler cap
87 Aerial
88 Fuselage top keel (connector
  stringer)
89 Aerial lead-in
90 Fuselage skin plating sections
91 'U'-stringers
92 Fuselage frames (monocoque
  construction)
93 Tail trimming cables

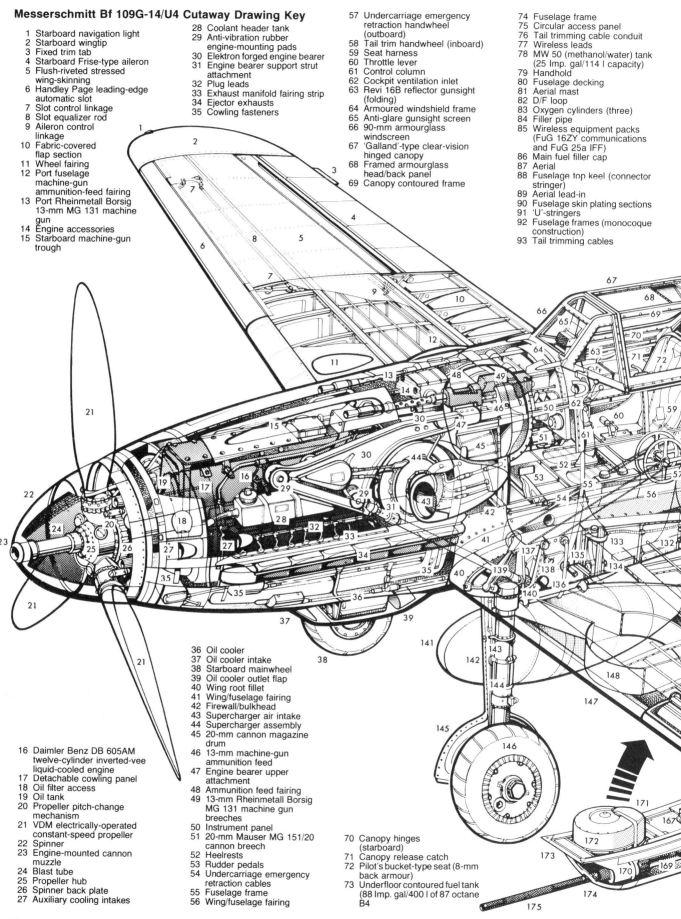

104

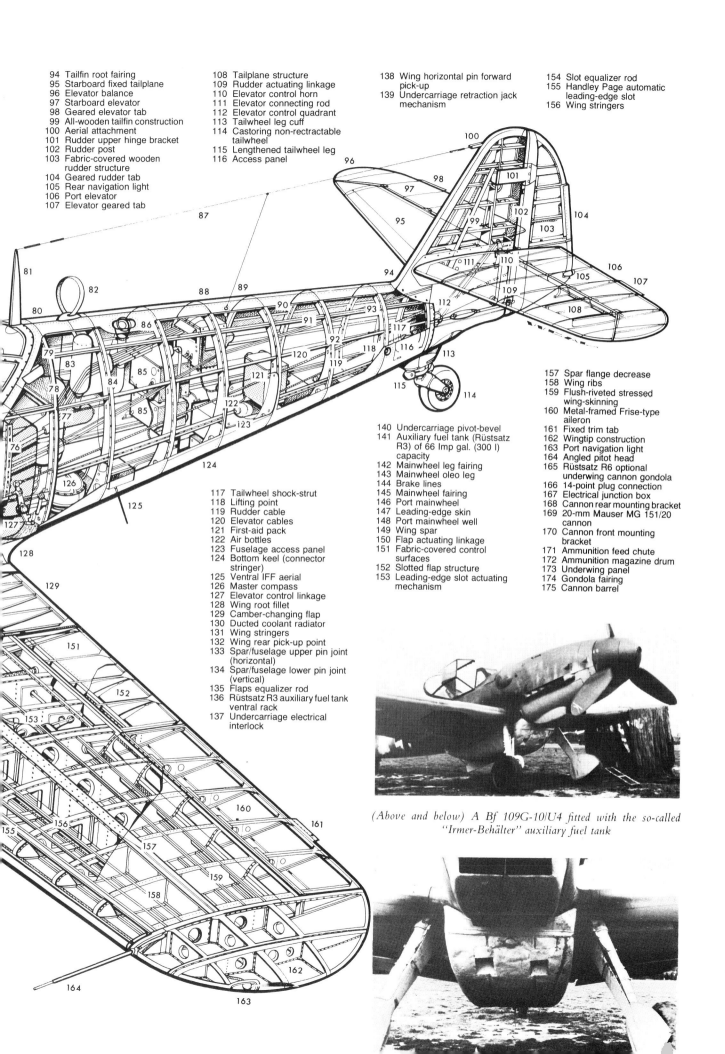

94 Tailfin root fairing
95 Starboard fixed tailplane
96 Elevator balance
97 Starboard elevator
98 Geared elevator tab
99 All-wooden tailfin construction
100 Aerial attachment
101 Rudder upper hinge bracket
102 Rudder post
103 Fabric-covered wooden rudder structure
104 Geared rudder tab
105 Rear navigation light
106 Port elevator
107 Elevator geared tab

108 Tailplane structure
109 Rudder actuating linkage
110 Elevator control horn
111 Elevator connecting rod
112 Elevator control quadrant
113 Tailwheel leg cuff
114 Castoring non-rectractable tailwheel
115 Lengthened tailwheel leg
116 Access panel

138 Wing horizontal pin forward pick-up
139 Undercarriage retraction jack mechanism

154 Slot equalizer rod
155 Handley Page automatic leading-edge slot
156 Wing stringers

117 Tailwheel shock-strut
118 Lifting point
119 Rudder cable
120 Elevator cables
121 First-aid pack
122 Air bottles
123 Fuselage access panel
124 Bottom keel (connector stringer)
125 Ventral IFF aerial
126 Master compass
127 Elevator control linkage
128 Wing root fillet
129 Camber-changing flap
130 Ducted coolant radiator
131 Wing stringers
132 Wing rear pick-up point
133 Spar/fuselage upper pin joint (horizontal)
134 Spar/fuselage lower pin joint (vertical)
135 Flaps equalizer rod
136 Rüstsatz R3 auxiliary fuel tank ventral rack
137 Undercarriage electrical interlock

140 Undercarriage pivot-bevel
141 Auxiliary fuel tank (Rüstsatz R3) of 66 Imp gal. (300 l) capacity
142 Mainwheel leg fairing
143 Mainwheel oleo leg
144 Brake lines
145 Mainwheel fairing
146 Port mainwheel
147 Leading-edge skin
148 Port mainwheel well
149 Wing spar
150 Flap actuating linkage
151 Fabric-covered control surfaces
152 Slotted flap structure
153 Leading-edge slot actuating mechanism

157 Spar flange decrease
158 Wing ribs
159 Flush-riveted stressed wing-skinning
160 Metal-framed Frise-type aileron
161 Fixed trim tab
162 Wingtip construction
163 Port navigation light
164 Angled pitot head
165 Rüstsatz R6 optional underwing cannon gondola
166 14-point plug connection
167 Electrical junction box
168 Cannon rear mounting bracket
169 20-mm Mauser MG 151/20 cannon
170 Cannon front mounting bracket
171 Ammunition feed chute
172 Ammunition magazine drum
173 Underwing panel
174 Gondola fairing
175 Cannon barrel

*(Above and below) A Bf 109G-10/U4 fitted with the so-called "Irmer-Behälter" auxiliary fuel tank*

(1) Bf 109G-5 of *Hauptmann* Carganico, *Kommandeur* of II/JG 5, Arctic, autumn 1942; (2) Bf 109G-6 of II/JG 77, Northern Italy, late 1943

Defence of the Reich fuselage bands allotted to Bf 109 *Jagdgruppen*: (A) II/JG 2; (B) II and III/JG 3; (C) III/JG 4; (D) I and II/JG 5; (E) III/JG 6; (F) JG 7; (G) II/JG 11; (H) III/JG 26; (I) I and III/JG 51; (J) JG 52; (K) JG 53; (L) JG 54; (M) JG 77; (N) I/JG 300; (O) II/JG 301

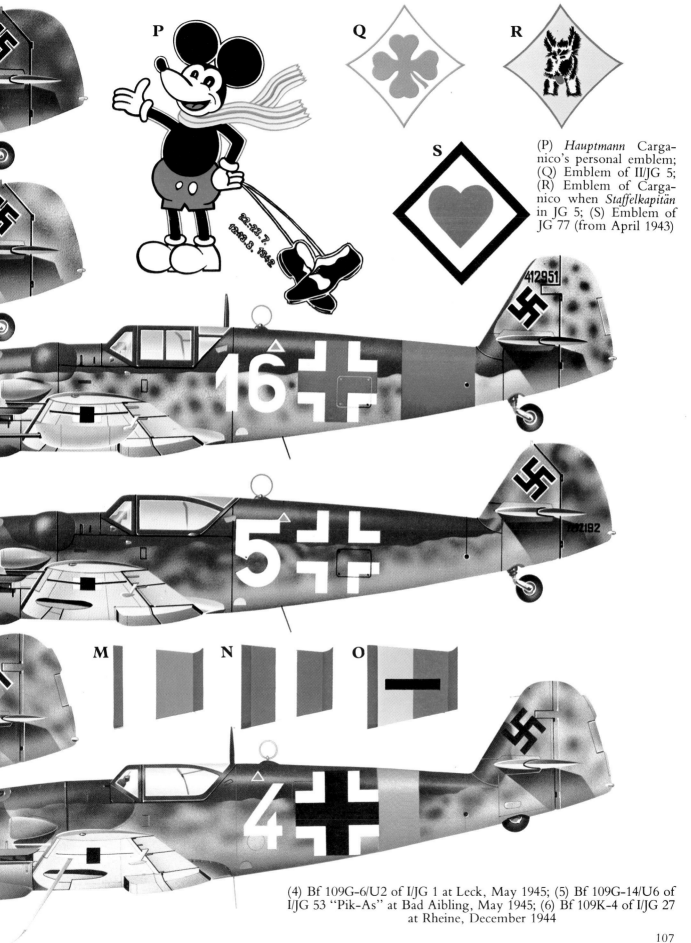

**P**  **Q**  **R**

**S**

(P) *Hauptmann* Carganico's personal emblem;
(Q) Emblem of II/JG 5;
(R) Emblem of Carganico when *Staffelkapitän*
in JG 5; (S) Emblem of
JG 77 (from April 1943)

412951

**M**   **N**   **O**

(4) Bf 109G-6/U2 of I/JG 1 at Leck, May 1945; (5) Bf 109G-14/U6 of
I/JG 53 "Pik-As" at Bad Aibling, May 1945; (6) Bf 109K-4 of I/JG 27
at Rheine, December 1944

(1) Bf 109G-6 of II° *Gruppo Caccia Terrestre* (3ª *Squadriglia* "Diavoli") at Villafranca, Verona, October 1944; (A) Emblem of the 3ª *Squadriglia*; (B) Emblem of *Fliegerkompagnie* 7; (2) Bf 109G-6 of *Fliegerkompagnie* 7; (C) RSI fuselage and tail insignia; (D) RSI wing insignia

(3) Bf 109G-5/U2 of HLeLv 31, Finnish Air Force, Utti, 1948; (4) Bf 109G-10/U4 of *kroat. Jagdstaffel* at Eichwalde, November 1944 (this Croatian unit operating under the command of the *Jagdfliegerführer Ostpreussen*); (5) Bf 109G-14/U2 of the Hungarian 101 Fighter Group, South Germany, April 1945. Note non-standard spinner, lack of dorsal radio mast and provision of FuG 16ZY Morane antenna; (E) Alternative styles of Hungarian national insignia applied to Bf 109s

**C**

**D**

**E**    **E**    **E**

J-706

MT-422

7

(1) Czechoslovak-assembled Bf 109G-14 (S 99) of the National Air Guard, 1947; (A) Emblem of Israeli No 101 Squadron; (B) National insignia as applied to S 99 fighters of the Czechoslovak National Air Guard; (2) S 199 of No 101 Squadron of the *Chel Ha'avir* at Herzaleah, 1948

(C) Emblem of *Ala 7 de Cazabombardeo*; (D) Emblem carried by some HA-1112-M1Ls of the *Ala 46 Mixta*; (3) HA-1112-M1L of the 71 *Escuadron* of *Ala 7 de Cazabombardeo*

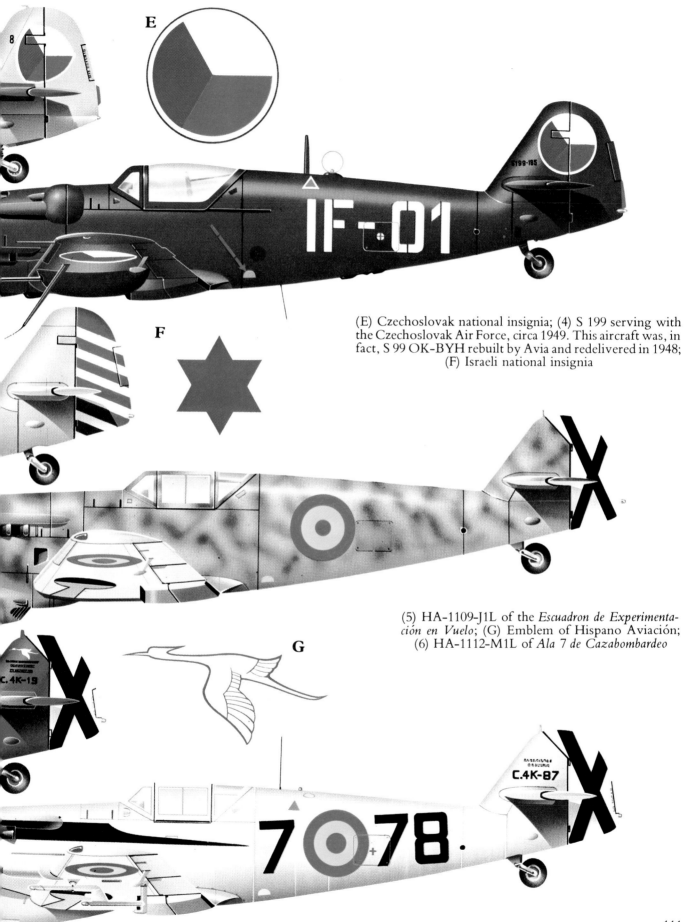

(E) Czechoslovak national insignia; (4) S 199 serving with the Czechoslovak Air Force, circa 1949. This aircraft was, in fact, S 99 OK–BYH rebuilt by Avia and redelivered in 1948; (F) Israeli national insignia

(5) HA-1109-J1L of the *Escuadron de Experimentación en Vuelo*; (G) Emblem of Hispano Aviación; (6) HA-1112-M1L of *Ala 7 de Cazabombardeo*

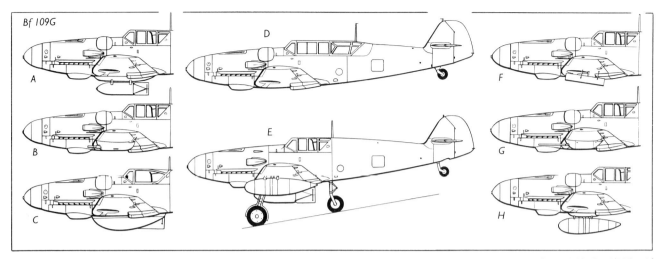

*(A) SC 250 bomb carried by G-6/R1, G-10/R6, G-14/R1 and G-16; (B) Underwing MK 108 cannon on G-6/R4; (C) G-10/U4 with "Irmer-Behälter" tank; (D) G-12 tandem two-seater; (E) G-2/R1 with SC 500 bomb and auxiliary wheel; (F) Wfr.Gr. 21 mortar carried by G-5/R2, G-6/R2 and G-10/R2; (G) MG 151 underwing cannon of G-6/R6, G-10/R6 and G-14/R6; (H) 66 Imp. gal. (300 l) drop tank*

*Continued from page 97*

in the year) were equipped exclusively with the Bf 109G, although III/JG 26 was operating a mix of Bf 109G-3s and Fw 190As, and a few Bf 109Gs were included on the strengths of 1. and 3.(F) *Staffeln* of each of *Aufklärungsgruppen* 33 and 123.

On the Eastern Front, units operating the Bf 109 under *Luftflotte Ost*, which included the I and V *Fliegerkorps*, comprised II/JG 3, II, III and V/JG 51, I, II and III/JG 54, 5. and 6./JG 77, and III/JG 77, and to the south under *Luftflotte* 4, with forces from the IV and VIII *Fliegerkorps*, were III/JG 3, I/JG 4, I, II and III/JG 52, and I/JG 53.

With *Luftflotte* 2 were I, II and III/JG 27, III/JG 53, and the *Jabo-Staffel Afrika* under the *Fliegerführer Afrika*; II/JG 53 and I/JG 77 under II *Fliegerkorps* (Sicily), and *Jagdkommando* 27 under X *Fliegerkorps* (Greece and Crete). Under *Luftflotte* 5 (*Ost*) in the Far North were II/JG 5 and 9./JG 5, and for home defence under the *Luftwaffenbefehlshaber Mitte* were I and III/JG 1, the last-mentioned *Gruppe* also operating Fw 190As.

The more specialized roles that had been assigned the Bf 109G-6 by 1943 dictated the *Rüstsatz* fitted. With a ventral ETC for a 551-lb. (250-kg) SC 250 bomb and a bomb-fusing battery box in the fuselage, the basic aircraft became the Bf 109G-6/R1. For the "*Pulk-Zerstörer*" ("Formation Destroyer") role with a pair of Wfr.Gr. 21 mortars beneath the wings it was designated Bf 109G-6/R2. The 21-cm mortar shells were intended to break up the tight defensive boxes adopted by the bombers of the 8th Air Force so that the waves of interceptors following the mortar-carrying *Gustavs* could get at the individual bombers. The 21-cm shells had a ±23-ft. (7,00-m) vertical deviation and a ±130-ft. (40,00-m) horizontal deviation over a distance of 3,280 ft. (1 000 m), and could be launched outside the range of the bombers' defensive fire. The mortar-equipped *Gustav* was first used in some numbers over Schweinfurt on October 14, 1943, and of the 228 U.S.A.A.F. bombers in the attacking force, 62 were lost during the action, 17 crashed after crossing the British coastline, and a further 121 were damaged of which some 30 per cent proved total write-offs.

For the *Zerstörer* role with two additional 30-mm MK 108 cannon carried in underwing gondolas the *Gustav* became the Bf 109G-6/R4, and with the underwing MK 108s replaced by 20-mm MG 151s it was known as the Bf 109G-6/R6. The *Rüstsatz* 2 was also retrospectively applied to some examples of the Bf 109G-5 which thus became the Bf 109G-5/R2. In addition to the various *Rüstsätzen*, certain *Umrüst-Bausätze* (Factory Conversion Sets) were also applied to the Bf 109G-6. Follow-

ing earlier experiments with a wooden tailplane on the G-5/U2, the G-6/U2 introduced in addition a wood-formed fin-and-rudder assembly. Taller than the standard metal unit, which had remained virtually unchanged during the entire life of the Bf 109, the new rudder employed a morticed balance in place of the more familiar oblique tip balance, and incorporated an inset trim tab. Designed to alleviate the take-off swing which had become progressively more pronounced with the application of engines of increased power, the larger wooden surfaces had the added advantage of conserving metals that were steadily becoming shorter in supply. The greater weight of the wooden units, however, precluded a proposal to enlarge the tailplane, although some tests were carried out. The Bf 109G-6/U4 featured a semi-retractable tailwheel (tested earlier on examples of the Bf 109G-2), but as drag reduction proved marginal, relatively few aircraft were so modified.

A Bf 109G-6/U2 with *Rüstsatz* 2 (*Werk-Nr*. 41 2951) which landed at Manston in error on July 21, 1944, was flown (as TP814) during the summer and autumn of that year for tactical trials with the Spitfire IX, the Spitfire XIV, and the Mustang III by a pilot of No. 1426 Flight. The trials were conducted by the Air Fighter Development Squadron, and were somewhat protracted owing to the frequent unserviceability of the *Gustav*, but the qualities of the fighter were summarized as follows:

**Flying characteristics:** The rudder was fairly heavy but not uncomfortably so, and as no rudder trimming device was provided it was necessary to apply right rudder for take-off and left rudder at high speeds. The ailerons became increasingly stiff as speed was increased and were especially so at speeds in excess of 350 m.p.h. (563 km/h) indicated. At speeds below 180 m.p.h. (290 km/h) indicated, the ailerons were not positive and became non-effective as the stall was approached. The elevators also became increasingly difficult to operate as speed increased, and above 350 m.p.h. (563 km/h) indicated, this unpleasantness was accentuated as the elevator trim was practically impossible to operate.

The forward view for taxiing was very poor and was little improved in flight owing to the gun magazine bulges on the engine cowling and the thickness of the windscreen framing. The brakes were positive but the tailwheel did not castor easily, and sharp turns on the ground were difficult. At all times when the engine was running at low revs, the pilot suffered acute discomfort from fumes in the cockpit. Unless taking-off directly into wind, the aircraft had a strong tendency to swing

into wind, and the throttle had to be opened slowly. The tailwheel locking device on this particular Bf 109G-6 had been disconnected, and this increased the tendency to swing. When taking-off directly into wind, however, the aircraft presented no control problems.

**Comparison with the Spitfire L.F.IX:** The Bf 109G-6 was compared with a Spitfire L.F.IX for speed and all-round man-oeuvrability at altitudes up to 25,000 ft. (7 620 m), and it was found that up to 16,000 ft. (4 877 m) the Spitfire possessed a slight speed advantage when using 18 lb. (8,16 kg) boost. Between this altitude and 20,000 ft. (6 096 m) the Bf 109G possessed a slight edge in speed, but above 20,000 ft. (6 096 m) the Spitfire regained the speed advantage to the extent of approximately 7 m.p.h. (11 km/h). When 25 lb. (11,3 kg) boost was employed by the Spitfire it was about 25 m.p.h. (40 km/h) faster at altitudes below 15,000 ft. (4 570 m) and some 7 m.p.h. (11 km/h) faster above this height.

The climb of the Spitfire was superior to that of the Bf 109G at all altitudes, and the British fighter enjoyed a particularly marked advantage below 13,000 ft. (3 960 m) when using 18 lb. (8,16 kg) boost, this naturally being even more pronounced when 25 lb. (11,3 kg) of boost was employed. When both aircraft pulled up into a climb from a dive their performances were almost identical, but when climbing speed was attained the Spitfire slowly pulled away. Comparative dives showed that the Bf 109G could leave the Spitfire without any difficulty, but the turning circle and roll rate of the Spitfire were markedly superior to all speeds.

*The Bf 109G-6/U2 (TP814) used for tactical trials with the Spitfire*

**Comparison with the Spitfire XIV:** The Bf 109G-6 was compared with a fully operational Spitfire XIV and, using

### Messerschmitt Bf 109G-6 Cockpit Instrumentation Key:

1 Undercarriage emergency lowering handwheel
2 Tailplane trim wheel
3 Seat height adjustment handle
4 Tailplane incidence indicator panel
5 Fuel injection primer pump
6 Fuel Cock lever
7 Throttle
8 Throttle-mounted propeller pitch control thumbswitch
9 Dust filter handgrip
10 Canopy lever
11 Undercarriage switches
12 Undercarriage position indicators
13 Start plug cleansing switch
14 Starter switch
15 Panel light
16 Main line switch
17 Ignition switch
18 Frame struts
19 Armoured glass windscreen
20 Revi 16B reflector gunsight
21 Armament switch
22 Ammunition counters
23 Clock
24 Repeater compass
25 Artificial horizon/turn-and-bank indicator
26 Fine and coarse altimeter
27 Airspeed indicator
28 Gunsight padding
29 Manifold pressure gauge
30 Tachometer
31 AFN 2 Homing indicator (FuG 16ZY)
32 Mechanical propeller pitch indicator
33 Tumbler switch
34 Combined coolant exit and oil intake temperature indicator
35 Fuel warning lamp
36 MK 108 cannon breech
37 Rudder pedals
38 Firing trigger
39 Gun charging knob
40 Control column
41 Pilot's seat
42 Undercarriage emergency release
43 Electric fuel contents guage
44 Dual oil and fuel pressure guage
45 Auxiliary fuel contents indicator
46 Panel light
47 Coolant radiator control
48 Oxygen supply indicator
49 Oxygen pressure guage
50 Radio switch panel
51 Oxygen supply
52 Radio tuner panel

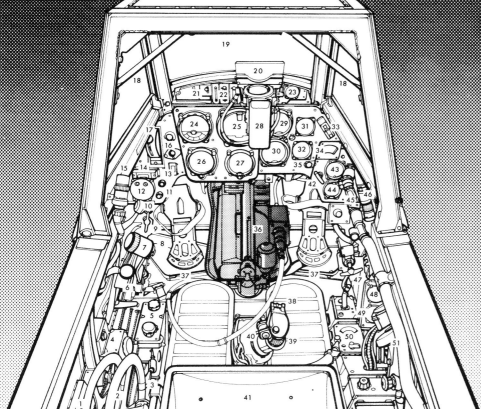

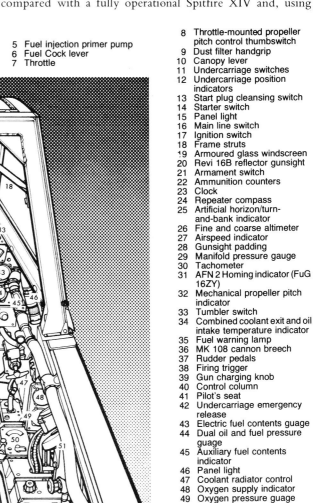

*(Above and below) The experimental Bf 109G-2/R1 converted by Škoda to Fieseler designs*

18 lb. (8,16 kg) of boost, it was found that the Spitfire possessed an advantage in speed of 25 m.p.h. (40 km/h) at altitudes up to 16,000 ft. (4 877 m) – the rated altitude of the Bf 109G – at which the advantage to the Spitfire was reduced to 10 m.p.h. (16 km/h). Above 16,000 ft. (4 877 m) the speed advantage of the Spitfire XIV increased progressively with altitude, being 50 m.p.h. (80 km/h) faster at 30,000 ft. (9 144 m).

At the rated altitude of the Bf 109G there was little to choose between the two fighters in climbing performance, but at all other altitudes the Spitfire possessed a marked advantage in rate of climb. When both aircraft were put into a dive with engine throttled back and then pulled into climbing attitude, their rate

*A Bf 109G-6/R4 with 30-mm MK 108 cannon beneath the wings and a lengthened tailwheel leg*

of climb was identical, but when using maximum power in the dive the Spitfire easily left the Bf 109G behind in the subsequent climb. Comparative dives revealed that the Bf 109G possessed a slight initial advantage but this was lost at speeds in excess of 380 m.p.h. (610 km/h) indicated. The Spitfire XIV had no difficulty in out-turning the Bf 109G in either direction, but the advantage was more marked when turning to the right, this being due to the greater power of its Griffon engine at full throttle and to the use of contra-props.

**Comparison with the Mustang III (P-51C):** By comparison with the Bf 109G the Mustang III possessed a clear speed advantage at all altitudes, this being some 30 m.p.h. (48 km/h) greater at the Bf 109G's rated altitude and increasing to 50 m.p.h. (80 km/h) at 30,000 ft. (9 144 m). The Bf 109G had a slightly better climb rate up to 20,000 ft. (6 096 m), but between this altitude and 25,000 ft. (7 620 m) the Mustang had a very slight advantage. When the two aircraft were dived and subsequently climbed there was very little to choose between their performances. The comparison of the respective merits of the two aircraft in dives proved that the Bf 109G was steadily out-dived by the Mustang III, and the longer the dive the greater the gain of the latter. The Mustang III had no difficulty in out-turning the Bf 109G in either direction, and the rate of roll of the two fighters was almost identical.

It had been planned to perform comparative trials between the Bf 109G-6/U2 and the Tempest V, but on November 23, 1944, before these could be undertaken, the *Gustav* crashed during a take-off from Wittering. However, trials had been conducted some months earlier between the Tempest V and a Bf 109G-2 (*Werk-Nr.* 10 639), which, captured in Sicily, freighted to Britain and taken on charge in February 1944 by No. 1426 Flight, was subsequently allocated the serial RN228. These trials had indicated that the Tempest V using 9 lb. (4,1 kg) of boost possessed a speed advantage of 40–50 m.p.h. (64–80 km/h) over the earlier *Gustav* at altitudes up to 20,000 ft. (6 096 m) but that the speed advantage diminished rapidly above that altitude. The climb rate of the Bf 109G-2 was superior to that of the Tempest at all altitudes, although this advantage was not pronounced at heights below 5,000 ft. (1 524 m), but in comparative dives the Tempest proved capable of pulling away from the Messerschmitt. The turning circle of the Tempest was marginally superior to that of the Bf 109G-2, and there was little to choose between the two aircraft in the roll rate at speeds below 350 m.p.h. (563 km/h), but above this speed the Tempest could out-manoeuvre its opponent by making a quick change of bank and direction.

During the early summer of 1943, *Major* Hajo Herrmann had proposed new nocturnal defensive tactics in which single-seat fighters could be used to intercept bombers visually over their targets where they were frequently silhouetted by target markers, searchlights and fires. This form of "unfettered pursuit", which was to be dubbed *Wilde Sau* (Wild Boar), held sufficient promise for a new *Jagdgeschwader*, JG 300, to be formed on Bf 109G-6s to evaluate *Major* Herrmann's tactics, and the unit came into existence on June 27, 1943.

Previously, all night fighters had been tied to the confines of their *Himmelbett* zones forming the "Kammhuber Line", but when, in the following month, the R.A.F. began dropping metal foil strips as a radar countermeasures device, thus rendering *Himmelbett* control inoperative, the *Wilde Sau* tactics offered an immediate temporary expedient pending the availability of radar impervious to the *Düppel*, as the metal foil strips had become known. On July 29, *Oberst* von Lossberg of the *Generalstab* proposed that all night fighters should switch to the *Wilde Sau* tactics, these proposals being accepted on the following day, and the decision was taken to make JG 300 the nucleus of a complete *Jagddivision*.

At this time, the three *Gruppen* of JG 300 at Bonn-Hangelar, Rheine and Oldenburg were only in the initial phases of night flying training, but two additional *Geschwader* were rapidly formed, these being JG 301, at Neubiburg, near Munich, and JG 302 at Döberitz, near Berlin, the three *Geschswader* forming 30.*Jagddivision* under the command of Hajo Herrmann who was promoted to *Oberstleutnant*. Only one *Gruppe* in each *Geschwader* possessed its own aircraft, the other two *Gruppen* utilizing the aircraft of the day fighter *Gruppen* whose bases they shared, and thus the 30.*Jagddivision* operated a variety of versions of the *Gustav* and Fw 190A.

Initially, the 30.*Jagddivision* enjoyed considerable success, but with the onset of winter attrition rose alarmingly, and even when the Bf 109G-6s were fitted with FuG 25a I.F.F. (which homed on to ground beacons) and FuG 16zy R/T (which, in addition to providing plane-to-plane and plane-to-ground communications, afforded direction and range measuring facilities), landing in inclement weather was extremely hazardous, and more and more pilots felt themselves compelled to bale out rather than make what would probably be a lethal attempt to land, even when they *could* find their airfield.

Early in 1944, a further modification of the Bf 109G-6 intended specifically for nocturnal *Wilde Sau* tactics made its appearance. In addition to anti-glare shields, exhaust flame dampers, FuG 16zy, FuG 25a and *Rüstsatz* 6 armament (i.e. two 20-mm MG 151 cannon in underwing gondolas supplementing the standard MK 108 and twin MG 131s), this variant, the Bf 109G-6/N, was equipped with FuG 350 *Naxos Z* which could pick up emissions from the H2S radar of R.A.F. pathfinders, and the rotating antenna for which was installed in a domed transparent housing immediately aft the cockpit.

In the event, the Bf 109G-6/N was destined never to serve with the 30.*Jagddivision* which was dissolved on March 16, 1944, its component *Gruppen* retraining as conventional day fighter units, and the few examples of the Bf 109G-6/N that *were* completed were employed for a brief period by one of the two *Gruppen* of NJG 11 formed with a cadre of experienced *Wilde Sau* pilots before the *Gustav*'s brief incursion in the realm of nocturnal interception finally terminated.

During the early months of 1943, proposals to standardize *Umrüst-Bausätze* 2 and 4 were agreed, and although this "standard model" was assigned the designation Bf 109G-7, the wide dispersal of the Bf 109 manufacturing complex presented various problems preventing promulgation of the standardization order, and this sub-type failed to reach the assembly lines. The Bf 109G-8, manufactured in relatively small numbers, was a specialized reconnaissance-fighter version of the Bf 109G-6 powered by either the DB 605A-1 or DB 605AS engine. The fuselage-mounted MG 131 machine guns were dispensed with, armament being restricted to the single engine-mounted 30-mm MK 108 (replaced in some examples by a 20-mm MG 151), and provision was made for a single Rb 12,5/7 or Rb 32/7 camera. The Bf 109G-8/U2 was provided with GM 1, the G-8/U3 had MW 50, and the G-8/R5 was equipped with FuG 16zs R/T, but by 1944 two new models, the G-10 and G-14, were being developed. The G-14 represented an attempt to standardize all the progressive refinements that had been applied to DB 605A- and AM-engined models, while the higher-performance G-10, which, in the event, *followed* the G-14 into squadron service in the latter half of the year, was delayed by problems with the new DB 605D engine.

During the course of 1943, production of the Bf 109 had risen by leaps and bounds. From 258 Bf 109Gs accepted in January, acceptances in March rose to 500, the peak output for the year being attained in July when no fewer than 725 Bf 109Gs were accepted. By this time, the Hungarian aircraft industry had phased into the Bf 109G programme, the Györi Vagongyár (Gyor Wagon Factory) being primarily responsible for airframe production, with the Magyar Állami Vaggon és Gépgyár (Hungarian State Wagon and Engineering Factory), or MAVAG, contributing some assemblies, and the Manfréd Weiss concern manufacturing the DB 605 engines.

Production of the Bf 109G was undertaken in Hungary under the German-Hungarian Mutual Armament Programme signed in June 1941, the plan calling for an output of 50 fighters per month by the end of 1943, Hungarian-built fighters being divided between the *Luftwaffe* and the *Magyar Királyi Légierö* on the basis of two-thirds for the former and one-third for the latter, and deliveries to the *Luftwaffe* began in June 1943, production commencing with the Bf 109G-2 but soon switching to the Bf 109G-6. Only 92 Bf 109Gs were manufactured in Hungary during the course of 1943, of which 39 went to the *Luftwaffe*, the *Magyar Királyi Légierö* having earlier received 59 Bf 109G-2s from German production.

Late in 1943, when initial production difficulties appeared to have been resolved, it was decided to increase planned Hungarian Bf 109G production to 75 per month and the total on order to 900, and in March 1944 production of the Me 210C was stopped by the Duna Repülögépgyár in order that it could join with the Györi Vagongyár and the Wiener-Neustädter Flugzeugwerke (WNF) to form a so-called *Arbeitsgemeinschaft* concentrating solely on Bf 109G production. Simultaneously, the Manfréd Weiss concern formed another *Arbeitsgemeinschaft* with Daimler-Steyr-Puch for DB 605 engine production.

It was anticipated that the airframe *Arbeitsgemeinschaft* would produce 500–550 Bf 109G fighters per month, but Allied bombing frustrated this programme, and in the summer of 1944, the German authorities decided to transfer all undamaged Bf 109G jigs and tools to the cellars of a brewery in Köbánya, a suburb of Budapest. In October 1944, by which time the Bf 109G-6 had given place to the Bf 109G-14 on the Hungarian assembly line, the first deliveries were made from the Köbánya brewery, output attaining one fighter per day, but in mid-December the jigs and tools were removed and the factory evacuated, thus bringing Hungarian Bf 109G production to an end. Of the 516 Bf 109G-6s and G-14s manufactured in Hungary during 1944, a total of 270 was delivered to the *Luftwaffe*.

Licence manufacture of the Bf 109G-2 was also initiated in 1943 by the Industria Aeronautica Romana factory at Brasov, but after the assembly of 30 Bf 109G-6s from imported components and sub-assemblies, the Brasov factory was destined to complete only 16 additional examples. On April 16, 1944, the Brasov factory received its first visit from the bombers of the U.S. 15th Air Force, suffering some damage, and as a result of a second visit on May 6 was largely gutted. Total German Bf 109G production for 1943 amounted to 6,379 aircraft, almost double the output of the Fw 190, and 66 per cent of all single-seat fighters manufactured by the aircraft industry.

*Bf 109G-6/R6 fighters on the hard standing of a shadow factory during acceptance testing prior to delivery to operational units*

# Gustav in foreign plumage

By the beginning of 1943, the *Gustav* had appeared in service with Germany's allies, one of the first recipients being the Finnish air arm, *Ilmavoimat*. Towards the end of 1942, there had been a noticeable improvement in the quality of the Soviet aircraft by which the Finns found themselves opposed, and as the ageing Finnish fighters were decidedly outclassed by the Lavochkin La-5, a "*Mersu Laivue*" (Messerschmitt Squadron) was formed on January 23, 1943, within *Lentorykmentii* (Flight Regiment) 3 under the designation HLeLv 34. An initial batch of 16 Bf 109G-2s was ferried from Wiener-Neustadt to Malmi, reaching Finland on March 13, and a further batch of 12 followed on May 16 when HLeLv 34 attained operational status with a strength of 28 aircraft under *Majuuri* Eino Luukkanen who had been appointed when the first commander, *Majuuri* Erkki Ehnrooth, was killed in an accident.

Of the Regiment's component squadrons, 1/LeLv 34 was deployed with seven aircraft at Malmi-Helsinki for the defence of the Finnish capital, 2 and 3/LeLv 34 operating from Utti. In June, 1/LeLv 34 was transferred to Suulajärvi, being replaced at Malmi-Helsinki by 3/LeLv 34, and on August 2 the HLeLv 34 Headquarters and 2/LeLv 34 were transferred to Kymi, near Kotka. During its first four months of combat flying with the Bf 109G-2 (May 19 to September 11, 1943) HLeLv 34 was to be officially credited with the destruction of 100 Soviet aircraft for the loss in combat of only six of its own fighters and four pilots.

Before the violent defensive battles of the summer of 1944 on the Karelian Isthmus, *Ilmavoimat* had begun to take delivery of further batches of *Gustavs*. The Finns had requested supplies of the Bf 109G-6, and the first batch of 15 fighters of this sub-type reached HLeLv 34 in April 1944, the Regiment passing its 15 surviving Bf 109G-2s to HLeLv 24 to supplement this unit's ageing Brewster 239s. During the course of May and June additional supplies of *Gustavs* reached *Ilmavoimat*, but as a result of the deteriorating situation within the German aircraft industry, these included not only Bf 109G-6s and G-6/R6s, on which *Ilmavoimat* had planned to standardize, but Bf 109G-5/U2s and Bf 109G-10s, which, together with three Bf 109G-8s for the tactical reconnaissance role, were to be supplemented in the following August by Bf 109G-14s.

Although all these various *Gustav* sub-types were described as Bf 109G-6s, a designation which thus became generic in so far as the Finns were concerned, component and accessory commonality was extremely limited, and inadequate spares backing for this variety owing to the worsening war situation was to provide *Ilmavoimat* with acute embarrassment and result in low serviceability. By June 12, 1944, HLeLv 34 had 36 fighters ostensibly on operational strength, and HLeLv 24, which had transferred eight surviving Bf 109G-2s to HLeLv 28, was partly operational on later *Gustav* fighters, the preponderance being Bf 109G-6s, and was joined at Lappeenranta on June 16 by HLeLv 34. Within two days, however, the two units combined could not muster more than two or three airworthy fighters, the remainder being grounded by lack of spares.

The situation improved slowly, and on June 21, HLeLv 34 was able to transfer to Taipalsaari with nine airworthy fighters, and part of HLeLv 24 was deployed to Utti. By July 15, HLeLv 34 was maintaining an average of 24 *Gustavs* at constant readiness for intercept, escort and reconnaissance missions, and by September 4, when Finland was forced to accept Soviet surrender terms, this principal *Ilmavoimien* Bf 109G unit had claimed 270 "kills" for the loss in combat of 22 aircraft and 11 pilots. Five of its pilots had received the *Mannerheimin Risti*, the highest Finnish decoration of which no more than 15 were awarded the entire air arm throughout the conflict.

Excluding the initial batch of Bf 109G-2s, *Ilmavoimat* received a total of 132 *Gustav* fighters, but the survivors of the conflict with the Russians did not, owing to their inadequate range, participate in the Finnish campaign against German forces in Lapland which had been dictated by the preliminary Armistice terms. However, Bf 109Gs remained in service at Utti with HLeLv 31 and 33, as HLeLv 24 and 34 had been respectively redesignated in December 1944, and the Messerschmitt fighter was destined to soldier on in Finnish service until finally phased out in 1954.

In Hungarian service, the 1/1 *vadasz század* (Fighter Squadron), which had been operating Bf 109F-4s on the Russian Front under German command as the *ungarische Jagdstaffel* from October 1942, had been redesignated 5/1 *vadasz század* and re-equipped with Bf 109G-2s, being joined by a second squadron the 5/2 *vadasz század* which had also completed conversion to the Bf 109G-2 by May 1943, to form the 5/1 *vadasz osztaly* (Fighter Group) operating under the VIII *Fliegerkorps*.

In November 1943, the 5/1 *szlazad* was withdrawn from operations on the Russian Front, by which time the Bf 109G-2s of the 5/1 *osztaly* claimed 70 "kills", despite having been confined largely to escort, fighter-bomber and strafing tasks, and the 5/2 *század* became the 102 *önálló vadasz század* (Independent Fighter Squadron). In May 1944, this squadron was

*A Bf 109G-6 at Malmi in the summer of 1944. In addition to G-6s, Finland received the G-5/U2, G-10 and G-14 versions of the Gustav, all of which were referred to generically as "Bf 109G-6s"*

*(Above) Bf 109G-6s in postwar service with the Finnish air arm and (below right) a Bf 109G-2 flown by Majuuri Eino Luukkanen from Utti in the spring of 1944 as commander of HLeLv 34*

incorporated into the Hungarian *Fliegerführer* 102 *Ungarn*, which controlled all Hungarian units under the VIII *Fliegerkorps*, and became 102/1 when joined by a second Hungarian squadron, 102/2, on Bf 109G-6s to form the 102 *vadasz osztaly* (Fighter Group).

In the spring of 1944, only two Bf 109G-equipped squadrons, 101/1 and 101/2, were based in Hungary for home defence, but with the commencement of U.S.A.A.F. bombing attacks on Hungarian targets in April, a third squadron was formed on Bf 109G-6s, the three becoming the 101/1 *vadasz osztaly*, and within two months this Group had been expanded to six squadrons as the 101 *vadasz ezred* (Fighter Regiment). Until the end of August 1944, no *Luftwaffe Jagdstaffeln* were based in Hungary, and thus the 101 *vadasz ezred* had to bear the full brunt of the steadily escalating 15th Air Force attacks.

The 102/1 and 102/2 squadrons continued operations on the Russian front as the 1. and 2.*ungarische Jagdstaffeln* until the revolt in Rumania in August 1944 when the I *Fliegerkorps* retreated into Hungary, the two Hungarian squadrons falling back on Munkacs. By October, the *Fliegerführer* 102 *Ungarn* had been transferred to I *Fliegerkorps*, the 102/1 and 102/2 squadrons being based at Felsöabrany, and in the following month these were placed under 8.*Jagddivision*.

By December, I *Fliegerkorps* had retreated to Budapest, and a completely new command structure was established, all fighter units based in Hungary, including those of the *Luftwaffe*, coming under the newly-established *Jagdabschnittsführer Ungarn* (Fighter Sector Leader Hungary). The two Bf 109G-6-equipped squadrons of the 102 *vadasz osztaly*, together with a new squadron (101/9), were attached to the 101 *vadasz ezred* as the Regiment's third Group (101/III), bringing strength to nine Bf 109G-6 squadrons

More than half of Hungary had now been occupied by Soviet forces, and a Soviet-sponsored government under the leadership of General Miklós Bela had been established at Debrecen, this government signing an armistice with the Allies on January 20, 1945, but the 101 *vadasz ezred* fought on, the Bf 109Gs being switched from bomber interception to ground strafing until March when the last Hungarian territory, western

*(Below) One of the most successful Finnish pilots of the Gustav, Majuuri Eino Luukkanen*

Transdanubia, was occupied. The surviving elements of the Regiment continued operations from Austrian bases under the 8.*Jagddivision* as part of the *Luftflotte Reich*, and the end of hostilities found the remnants based near Linz where the last *Gustavs* were destroyed before the surrender to American forces.

The Rumanian air arm, the *Fortelor Regal ale Aeriene Româna*, began to receive Bf 109G-2s early in 1943, at which time most fighter formations were operating the indigenous IAR 80 in defence of the oilfields and refineries. Later in 1943, the Rumanian *Corpul 1 Aerian* (1st Air Corps), on the Russian Front as a component of the *Luftwaffe*'s I *Fliegerkorps*, received

*Bf 109G-6 fighters of the Hungarian 102. Independent Fighter Group operating in the early summer of 1944 under the command of the Fliegerführer 102 Ungarn. This group comprised two squadrons, the 1. and 2.ungarische Jagdstaffeln*

Bf 109G-6s plus a few Bf 109G-8s to equip the four-*escadrila* (Nos. 45, 46, 47 and 48 *escadrile*) fighter component which was based at Mariupol (Zhdanov) in the Ukraine.

The 1st Air Corps was fully operational by the end of June when attention was directed to the reorganization of the fighter defences of metropolitan Rumania, further Bf 109G-6s being supplied for the re-equipment of some *Fortelor Aeriene* units defending the oil installations. By the beginning of 1944, the Rumanian contingent in Russia had declined considerably in strength, and, with the progressive withdrawal of units, only one Rumanian Bf 109G squadron remained by February, and this, the 49 *escadrila* (*rum.*49.J.St.) based at Saki on the Crimea, possessed a strength of only some five aircraft.

By the time of the Rumanian *coup d'état* on August 23, 1944, *Fortelor Aeriene* units based in Rumania with Bf 109Gs comprised the 51 and 52 *escadrile*, at Tepes-Voda and Mamaia respectively, which also operated a number of IAR 80s under the *Jagdabschnittsführer Rumänien* in conjunction with *Luftwaffe* units and the independent II and VII Groups of the *Corpul 1 Aerian* equipped exclusively with the *Gustav*. By the beginning of September, the Rumanian *Gustav* units were back in operation but in support of the *Soviet* offensive across the River Pruth, participating in the fighting against the German forces in the vicinity of Klausenburg.

Other recipients of the *Gustav* included Bulgaria, Croatia, Italy, Slovakia, Spain and Switzerland. The Royal Bulgarian

*Rumanian "ace", Captain Alexandre Serbanesco, with his Bf 109G-6/R6 after a successful sortie*

Air Force's 6 *Polk* (Regiment) began to receive Bf 109G-2s and G-6s early in 1944, supplemented later by G-10s, to replace its obsolescent equipment, which included Avia B-534 biplanes. The Bf 109Gs were used primarily for the defence of Sofia, but in August 1944 some Bf 109Gs from the Bulgarian 6 *Polk* were deployed in the defence of the Ploesti oilfields. By the following month only some 30 of the 145 Bf 109Gs delivered to the 6 *Polk* remained airworthy, and based at Karlovo, these were knocked out by an R.A.F. attack on the airfield.

The fighter component of the Croatian Legion in Russia, 15.(*kroat.*)/JG 52 under *Luftflotte* 4, had converted from Bf 109E-7s to Bf 109G-2s in July 1942, but by November 1943, this unit, which, in the meantime, had converted to the Bf 109G-6, had been reduced to six aircraft of which only three were serviceable. By February 1944, 15.(*kroat.*)/JG 52 was based at Karankut in the Crimea with only four machines on strength. Personnel for two further Croatian Legion fighter squadrons had trained on Bf 109Gs in France during the previous year, returning to Velika Goritse in Croatia at the beginning of January 1944.

As no *Gustavs* were available to equip the two new units, which were designated the 2nd and 3rd Fighter Squadrons of the Croatian Legion, it was decided that they should operate Fiat G.50s and Macchi C.202s until Messerschmitts could be delivered. However, several casualties were suffered during conversion and neither unit achieved operational status until the summer of 1944, by which time the 1st Fighter Squadron (formerly 15.(*kroat.*)/JG 52 and subsequently referred to in German records simply as *kroat.*J.St.) had re-equipped with the Bf 109G-10, this unit continuing operations alongside the *Luftwaffe* until shortly before the end of hostilities.

With the establishment of the *Aviazione della Repubblica Sociale Italiana* following the Italian capitulation of September 8, 1943, the I° and II° *Gruppi Caccia Terrestre* were activated in November and December at Turin and Milan respectively, their component *squadriglie* operating Fiat G.55s, Macchi C.202s and 205s, and Reggiane Re 2001s, By July 1944, the II° *Gruppo* had begun conversion to the Bf 109G-6, both the 1ª and 2ª *Squadriglie* being operational on the German fighter by September 1944 when the I° *Gruppo* had begun conversion.

Some pilots of the I° *Gruppos's* 1ª *Squadriglia* were converting to the Bf 109G-6 and G-10 in Germany in November 1944, and by the following month the entire *Gruppo* was completing conversion at Memmingen, becoming operational at Holzkirchen by January 1945, and continuing operations until

*Bf 109G-6s of the II° Gruppo Caccia Terrestre of the Italian Aviazione della RSI in the late summer of 1944. It was joined on operations late in 1944 by the similarly-equipped I° Gruppo; (Below right) A non-standard Bf 109G-2 in Rumanian service to which Rüstsatz 2 (two 20-mm MG 151s underwing) was applied*

disbanded at Gallarate on April 29, the II° *Gruppo* being disbanded on the previous day at Udine. The *Aviazione della RSI* had activated another fighter unit, the III° *Gruppo*, at Fossano in March 1944, this being transferred to Holzkirchen in January 1945 for Bf 109G conversion which was still in process when hostilities terminated.

Early in 1943, the Slovakian air arm, the *Slovenské vzdusné zbrane*, received 15 Bf 109G-6s, these equipping 13.*stíhací letka* (Fighter Squadron). As the *slowak.Jagdstaffel*, or 13.(*slowak.*)/JG 52, this unit was attached to the so-called Slovak Fast Division during the fighting in the Crimea, and subsequently flew in defence of Bratislava. The 11.*stíhací letka* had also re-equipped with the Bf 109G-6 by July 26, 1944, when, shortly before the Slovakian uprising, the unit took off from Piestany to intercept a strong U.S.A.A.F. B-17 force escorted by P-38 Lightnings. In the mêlée that followed the entire complement of the Slovakian squadron was lost.

Previously, in 1942, the Spanish *Ministerio del Aire* and the *Reichsluftfahrtministerium* had reached an agreement concerning the licence manufacture of the Bf 109G-2 in Spain for the *Ejército del Aire*. Under this agreement Germany was to supply

25 airframes broken down into main assemblies, together with pattern drawings, jigs and tools, following these with DB 605A engines, airscrews, and armament for a further 200 aircraft, the airframes of which were to be manufactured by Hispano-Aviación. In the event, the deteriorating war situation resulted in only incomplete drawings reaching Spain, and the 25 airframes lacked tail assemblies, power plants and armament. Nevertheless, the airframes were assembled and adapted to take the Hispano-Suiza 12Z 89 engine, the first being flown on July 10, 1947 (see page 134).

*A Bf 109G-6/R6 of the slowak.Jagdstaffel, or 13.(slovak)/JG 52, which was attached to the so-called Slovak Fast Division until April 1944 when it was transferred to Piestany in western Slovakia for the defence of Bratislava*

(Left and above) Bf 109G-6s serving with Fliegerkompagnie 7 of the Swiss Fliegertruppe in 1944. These aircraft were found to suffer numerous defects, the Swiss being reimbursed with 50 per cent of the original purchase price as a result of these. (Foot of page) Elaborate "nose art" applied to a Bf 109G-5/U2 in Finnish service in 1948

Switzerland's *Fliegertruppe*, anxious to make good attrition suffered by its Bf 109E-equipped *Fliegerkompagnien*, obtained 12 Bf 109G-6s in 1944 as a result of a somewhat unusual bargain. On the night of April 28, 1944, R.A.F. Bomber Command had attacked Friedrichshafen, and a Bf 110G-4b night fighter flown by the *Staffelkapitän* of the newly-formed 5./NJG 5 pursued a Lancaster into Swiss air space. The port engine of the Messerschmitt began to lose oil and overheat. This necessitated cutting the engine and feathering the airscrew. Although the pilot, *Oberleutnant* Wilhelm Johnen, attempted to return to base on one engine, he became disorientated after being caught in a cone of searchlights and was forced to land on Dübendorf airfield, near Zürich.

The Bf 110G-4b was equipped with FuG 220 *Lichtenstein*

SN 2 radar and the *Schräge Musik* oblique gun installation, and as Switzerland was swarming with agents of all the combatants and a serious risk existed of details of the fighter's equipment falling into Allied hands, the German Ambassador demanded that the aircraft should be returned to Germany immediately. As such action would have contravened Swiss neutrality, the demand was refused, the Germans then proposing that the aircraft be burned in the presence of embassy officials, and in return for this concession the Swiss government would be permitted to purchase 12 Bf 109G fighters for the *Fliegertruppe*. Agreement was reached on this basis, and on May 20, 1944, the first six Bf 109G-6 fighters landed at Dübendorf, the remaining six following two days later, these replacing the Bf 109E-3s of *Fliegerkompagnie* 7 in which they were joined by a Bf 109G that had landed at Samaden on the previous March 29. A further Bf 109G was to be acquired later in the year, on December 17, when it landed at Affeltraagen, being duly impressed by the *Fliegertruppe*.

The Swiss were initially delighted with the Bf 109G-6, but after a mere 15 hours' flying serious defects began to appear, reflecting the falling standards of workmanship in the German aircraft industry. Considerable effort was expended in endeavouring to rectify the deficiencies of the fighters but this was only partially successful and representations to the parent company eventually resulted in agreement to reimburse 50 per cent of the purchase price. Despite their shortcomings, the Bf 109Gs were retained in service with *Fliegerkompagnie* 7, although flying hours were severely restricted. Restrictions notwithstanding, the unit suffered casualties, one such occurring on May 29, 1946, when *Leutnant* Zweiacker, who, incidentally, was flying the Bf 109G-6 that had been impressed after landing at Samaden in March 1944, disappeared during a training flight between Emmen and Locarno. An extensive search failed to locate the wreckage and, shortly afterwards, the Bf 109G-6s were withdrawn from service and scrapped in the following year. Seven years after the disappearance of *Leutnant* Zweiacker, on September 4, 1953, the wreckage of his aircraft was discovered by alpinists on the Pizzo di Rodi.

# The Eagle ages

The prodigious strides of 1943 in Bf 109 output were as nothing compared with those taken in 1944. Acceptances of the fighter rose almost 120 per cent to 13,942 aircraft (excluding Hungarian and Rumanian production) despite the constant aerial attack to which the German aircraft industry was by now subjected. This immense increase in output was widely attributed to the efforts of the *Jägerstab* (Fighter Staff) which had been established within the *Reichskriegsministerium* on March 1, 1944, under the leadership of Party Leader Otto Saur.

The primary task of the *Jägerstab* was that of boosting fighter output in the shortest possible time, and Saur, a protégé of Albert Speer, had the full backing of the Minister of Armaments as well as the personal power of the *Führer* behind all steps that he considered necessary to fulfil this task. The steps taken by the *Jägerstab* were impressive, although it was unrealistic to believe that any major increase in the production of so sophisticated an item of weaponry as a fighter could be achieved rapidly merely by administrative changes. The apparent success of the *Jägerstab* was largely due to programmes promulagated on August 15 and October 1, 1943, long before the creation of Saur's organization, these having provided for major acceleration of fighter production, materials and components having been ordered on the basis of this accelerated output.

However, Allied bombing attacks in the late autumn of 1943 had primarily affected final assembly, and one result had been an accumulation of materials, components and subassemblies. What the *Jägerstab* succeeded in doing was to expedite the release of this accumulated potential and remove bottlenecks by the application of emergency priorities and the threatening of plant managers with Dachau.

The *Jägerstab* was faced with conflicting demands simultaneously: that for increased fighter output, and the need for increased dispersal to reduce the effects of the Allied bombing offensive. The average working week was raised from 50–60 to 72 hours and coupled with the incentive of increased rations; couriers were employed to rush shipments of urgently-needed components or equipment from plant to plant; special brigades were formed for immediate despatch to bombed plants to rally the management and put into effect emergency steps to resume operations; Saur's personal representatives were placed in every factory where the efficiency of the management was suspect, and arrests were made for any failure to meet schedules. So terrified of the *Jägerstab* was the management of certain Ruhr steelmills that a long-standing bottleneck in Bf 109G wing spar caps was overcome in a matter of days.

The natural tendency of this campaign was to transfer emphasis from the earlier stages of fighter production to the later stages, bleeding the pipeline of components and subassemblies, but the results were undeniable. Bf 109G acceptances of 1,006 in April 1944 rose to 1,348 in July and 1,605 in September. However, the *Jägerstab* minimized the distribution of spares in order to maximize the number of complete aircraft rolling off the assembly lines. Furthermore, as Göring was to state subsequently, dispersal had a deleterious effect on quality. Components frequently failed to meet tolerances, and as there were several production sources of each component interchangeability suffered.

Spares shortages and unsatisfactory component interchangeability were reflected by the fact that, despite the greatly increased production of the Bf 109 fighter, there was no conspicuous increase in the number of serviceable Bf 109s on the operational strength of the *Jagdflieger*. Dr. Frydag, Director of the Main Committee for Airframes, constantly raised the question of why, when the aircraft industry was making such strenuous efforts to increase fighter output, the number of serviceable aircraft with the operational units appeared to remain virtually unchanged, but he was never to receive a satisfactory answer.

Production of the DB 605 engine for the Bf 109G had, like the airframe, shown a persistent rise despite Allied bombing, but from April 1944, direct and indirect effects of the assault began to result in a decline. The principal DB 605 manufacturing plant at Genshagen was badly damaged in July 1944, although output did not fall below 40 per cent of the maximum previously achieved. Nevertheless, the vulnerability of the factory dictated the immediate removal of the machine shop to a gypsum mine at Neckar-Els, near Heidelberg, known as the *Goldfisch* plant, but unnumerable problems arose. The dampness was detrimental to the machine tools, the high humidity made working conditions almost unbearable, and the power supply, which also supplied the local community, was frequently interrupted as a result of bombing, and under such conditions it proved almost impossible to undertake precision work on DB 605 components.

Attacks on the Büssing DB 605 licensee did not seriously reduce output because of successful dispersal, but an attempt by the Büssing-Werke to move part of its DB 605 production into a saltmine was largely frustrated owing to corrosion of the precision machine tools as a result of humidity. The attacks on Henschel at Kassel, where DB 605s were also being produced, were more effective, but as a result of dispersal,

*(Above) Late production Bf 109s: a Bf 109G-14/U2 with wooden tailplane and enlarged and redesigned wooden vertical surfaces, and (in background) a Bf 109G-10 found intact by the advancing Allied forces in the spring of 1945*

*The Bf 109G-14/U4 illustrated above was one of the very few late production Gustavs captured during the closing stages of hostilities in Europe to be taken to the UK for flight testing*

the output by December 1944 was as high as it had ever been.

## A surfeit of suffixes

As previously mentioned, by early 1944, two new sub-types were scheduled to enter production – the G-10 (DB 605D) and G-14 (DB 605AM). Delays resulted in the G-10 actually *succeeding* the G-14 in production, and it was thus to become the definitive G-series fighter in quantity service, although it will be treated here in sub-type numerical order. The Bf 109G-10 was intended to standardize on the DB 605D series engine on which an increased-diameter supercharger had been fitted and compression ratio raised from 7·3/7·5 to 8·3/8·5. The standard DB 605D engine, using 87 octane B4 fuel and methanol-water (MW 50) injection, provided 1,850 h.p. for take-off and 1,600

h.p. at 19,685 ft. (6 000 m); using 96 octane C3 fuel (DB 605DB) 1,800 h.p. was available for take-off with 1,530 h.p. at 19,685 ft. (6 000 m), and with C3 fuel plus MW 50 (DB 605DC) 2,000 h.p. was afforded for take-off and 1,800 h.p. at 16,730 ft. (5 100 m). A 20-mm MG 151 with 150 rounds or a 30-mm MK 108 with 60 rounds was optional as an engine-mounted weapon, and was combined with two 13-mm MG 131 machine guns in the top cowling with 300 r.p.g. A *Revi* 16B reflector sight on a folding bracket replaced the *Revi* 12C or 12D; it was intended to standardize on FuG 16zy and FuG 25a radio, and provision was made for a 66 Imp. gal. (300 l) Junkers drop tank.

In clean condition and with a DB 605DC engine, the Bf 109G-10 was the fastest of the G-series fighters, and at 6,834 lb. (3 100 kg) possessed a maximum speed ranging from 342 m.p.h. (500 km/h) at sea level to 426 m.p.h. (685 km/h) at 24,280 ft. (7 400 m), an altitude of 19,685 ft. (6 000 m) being attained in 5·8 min. Unfortunately, from the performance aspect, the Bf 109G-10 rarely reached service status before the application of one or another of the various *Rüstsätzen*. For example, the Bf 109G-10/R1 had a ventral ETC for a single 551-lb. (250-kg) bomb or four 110-lb. (50-kg) SC 50 bombs, bomb-fusing battery box and selector switch panel, and 5-mm armour protection for the oil coolers, radiator and fuel pump.

The Bf 109G-10/R2 was a DB 605DB-powered reconnais-

*(Above right and below) The prototype of the tandem two-seat Bf 109G-12 converted from a standard Bf 109G-5 single-seat fighter. A number of G-1, G-5 and G-6 airframes were converted to G-12 standards for the Jagdfliegerschulen*

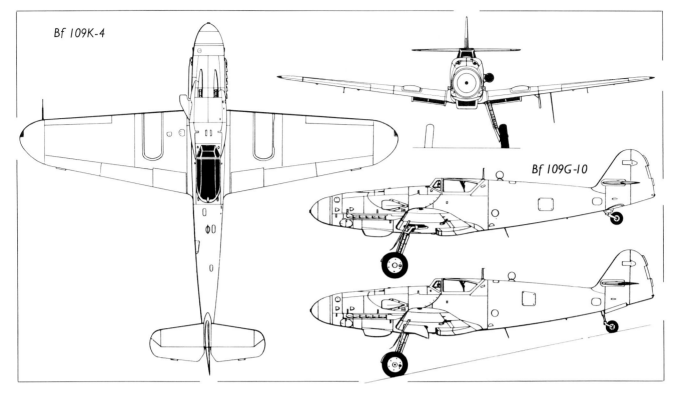

Bf 109K-4

Bf 109G-10

*The general arrangement drawing illustrates the Bf 109K-4, showing main and tailwheel door closures, long tailwheel leg, relocated D/F loop, fuel filler and rear fuselage access panel, these features contrasting with the otherwise similar late-production G-10 illustrated for comparison purposes by upper sideview*

sance fighter with MG 131s removed, provision for a single Rb 50/30 or 75/30 camera and a loaded weight (including a 66 Imp. gal./300 litre drop tank) of 7,280 lb. (7 198 kg) at which a maximum speed of 404 m.p.h. (650 km/h) could be attained at 29,530 ft. (9 000 m), range being 526 miles (850 km) at 388 m.p.h. (624 km/h) at 27,230 ft. (8 300 m); the Bf 109G-10/R4 was a DB 605D-engined variant with a pair of 30-mm MK 108 cannon in underwing gondolas, and the Bf 109G-10/R6 was similar apart from having 20-mm MG 151s beneath the wings with 120 r.p.g.

As the DB 605D engine, like the DB 605AS, used the enlarged supercharger, all G-10s displayed the overall fairing described for the DB 605AS-powered G-6, but with added "chin" blisters forward of the oil cooler to cover the larger oil sump of the DB 605D. By late 1944, when the first G-10s were

entering service, the application of *Umrüst-Bausätzen* 2 and 4 (wooden tail unit) had become standard, as had the "Galland" hood, long-stroke fixed tailwheel unit with narrow tyre, and the reinforced pilot armour. New features were the further deepening of the oil cooler scoop and the attachment of the FuG 16zy "Morane" mast beneath the port wing. Final production G-10 models embodied some features of the subsequent Bf 109K – firstly a further increase in mainwheel tyre width, resulting in long fairings over the wing enclosing the wheel recesses, and secondly the addition of external rudder trim plates above and below the inset tab. A short tailwheel leg was standard on this model and the rudder base of all G-10s terminated in a sharp point.

Although it would be an exaggeration to suggest that the innumerable suffix numerals and letters that accompanied the

*A Bf 109G-14 believed to belong to I/JG 3 taxying from dispersal in the late autumn of 1944. Note the clear vision canopy and short radio mast*

*A Bf 109G-6 of the Combined Squadron, Czechoslovak Insurgent Air Force photographed at the Tri Duby (Three Oaks) airfield, Central Slovakia, during the Slovak national uprising of September 1944. Note the insurgent markings under the port wing*

application of the various *Rüstsätzen* and *Umrüst-Bausätzen* led to chaos, the lack of standardization undoubtedly complicated the spares supply situation, and contributed in no small measure to the steadily reducing serviceability returns of the *Gustav*-equipped *Jagdgruppen*. From mid-1944, the situation was aggravated by the disruption of the German transportation system by air attack, the wide dispersal of the Bf 109G manufacturing complex resulting in frequent bottlenecks in certain items of equipment or sub-assemblies, and although the special committee intended to co-ordinate the work of the various main assembly plants for the Bf 109G, and the numerous sub-contractors feeding these plants, arranged interchange of the items in short supply, transportation difficulties and lack of co-ordination in manufacturing standards frequently defeated such arrangements.

The *Jägerstab* made a determined effort to rationalize production and reduce the number of sub-types being manufactured simultaneously. This was to be effected by standardizing on a new basic model, the Bf 109K, which embodied many of the progressive changes incorporated in the G-series as *Umrüst-Bausätze*. The "standardization" programme was initiated in the late summer of 1944, but evidence that it had barely left the ground by the end of the year may be seen from the fact that of nearly 14,000 Bf 109s manufactured by the German aircraft industry during the course of 1944, only 754 were Bf 109Ks.

Prior to the initiation of the Bf 109K programme, another G-series variant, the Bf 109G-12 tandem two-seat conversion trainer, had made its début. The Messerschmitt bureau had first initiated studies for a two-seat version of the basic Bf 109 late in 1940 as the Bf 109S (the suffix letter indicating *Schule*), but the *Jagdfliegerschulen* saw little need for such an aircraft, and the study was not resurrected until 1942 when fighter pilot training was accelerated with a general lowering of standards and, in consequence, a markedly higher accident rate during conversion training. The first pre-production Bf 109G-0 (*Werk-Nr*. 14

0001 VJ + WA) was therefore fitted with a mock-up of an elongated cockpit canopy for aerodynamic trials. The success of these tests resulted in the conversion of a standard Bf 109G-5 (CJ + MG) as a prototype two-seater.

Provision for cabin pressurization was removed, a second cockpit was inserted immediately aft of the fuel tank, this necessitating some equipment repositioning, and a lengthened canopy was provided, this incorporating two sections hinging to starboard. The forward hinged section, enclosing the pupil's cockpit, was identical to that of the standard single-seater, but the aft section was bulged on both sides to provide the instructor with a measure of forward vision for take-off and landing. Full dual controls were fitted, and full armament was normally retained owing to the considerable change in the c.g. position that would have accompanied its removal, the reduction in weight forward being coupled with the increased weight aft with the insertion of the instructor's cockpit.

A substantial number of Bf 109G-1, G-5 and G-6 single seaters were converted to two-seat Bf 109G-12 standard by maintenance units, and these began to reach the *Jagdfliegerschulen* from late 1943. A number were issued in 1944 to the *Schuljagdgeschwader*, including JG 101, JG 102, JG 106 and JG 107, and many saw operational service during the final stages of the fighting in Europe.

Despite the decision of the *Jägerstab* to standardize production on the Bf 109K, some time had to elapse before this could be implemented. In the interim and in fact preceding the G-10 previously described, the Bf 109G-14 was rolling off the lines from the spring of 1944. Earlier, geared tabs had been fitted to the ailerons and elevators in order to lighten the controls, but delays in deliveries of the modified elevators had led to some aircraft reaching service units with only the aileron tabs fitted. This resulted in an unacceptable difference between the effort required from the pilot by the ailerons and the elevators, and instructions were therefore issued to disconnect the aileron tabs and lock them by means of riveted dural strips.

The Bf 109G-14 closely paralleled the G-6 and was an attempt to standardize the refinements thereon. Like the G-6/U2, the G-14/U2 adopted the wooden tail unit, and as with the late-production G-6, the late G-14 forsook the DB 605AM for the DB 605AS and its accompanying wide cowling. This last model could be distinguished from the late G-6, however, by the extra deep oil cooler intake (as for the G-10) and by the unique belly-mounted position of the FuG 16zy mast. The "Galland" hood and fixed short-leg tailwheel were standard on all G-14s, as was also an armament of one 20-mm MG 151 and two 13-mm MG 131s. The metal tail unit was retained by early production examples only. The Bf 109G-16 was essentially similar to the basic G-14, apart from having a DB 605D engine and armoured oil cooler and radiators, the ventral bomb rack (*Rüstsatz* 1) and gondola-mounted MG 151 cannon (*Rüstsatz* 6) being installed as standard on the assembly line. Few were produced.

Although the Bf 109 manufacturing complex had largely switched to the production of K-series fighters by the beginning of 1945, the transition had by no means been completed when the assembly lines finally came to a halt, and of 2,970 Bf 109 fighters accepted by the *Luftwaffe* during the months of 1945 prior to the final defeat of the Third Reich, more than half were of the G-10 and G-14 sub-types.

When, on January 1, 1945, the *Luftwaffe* undertook its last concerted offensive action of W.W. II, Operation *Bodenplatte*, in which 700–800 fighters made a surprise attack on Allied airfields in France, Belgium and the Netherlands, the bulk of 12 *Gruppen* of BF 109G-6s, G-10s and G-14s, plus five *Gruppen* that had largely re-equipped with the Bf 109K-2 and K-4, participated in this desperate attempt to reduce Allied air supremacy (I and III/JG 3; I, III and IV/JG 4; II/JG 11; I, II, III and IV/JG 27; I, II, III and IV/JG 53, and I, II and III/JG 77).

The *Bodenplatte* assault was a success in that it obtained for the hard-pressed ground forces a temporary respite from constant harassment by Allied tactical air power, 465 Allied aircraft being destroyed or damaged on the 27 bases attacked. But although enemy air power was temporarily paralysed by *Bodenplatte*, the Allies could replace their losses quicker than could the *Luftwaffe*, which had sacrificed most of its remaining fighter reserves, and the *Jagdgruppen* were never to recover from the loss of some 150 pilots which was the price they paid for what was to provide barely a week's suspension of the Allied aerial onslaught.

According to the *Luftwaffe* Quartermaster-General's strength returns for January 10, 1945, nine days after Operation *Bodenplatte*, fewer than 1,000 Bf 109s remained on the strength of operational units and of these some 700 were serviceable. The Bf 109-equipped and part-equipped units with the various *Luftflotten* at that time were as follows (initial figure indicating total strength being followed by a figure indicating the number of aircraft serviceable):

**Luftflotte 1** (Courland and the Gulf of Riga area): A small number of Bf 109Gs were in operation alongside Fw 189s with *Nahaufklärungsgruppe* 5 and were mixed with Fw 190s in the *Stabschwarm* of *Jagdgeschwader* 51.

**Luftflotte 2** (Northern Italy): Both Bf 109Gs and Fw 190s were serving with *Nahaufklärungsgruppe* 11.

**Luftflotte 3** (Western Front): The 2. and 3.*Staffeln* of *Nahaufklärungsgruppe* (NAGr) 1 (15/8); NAGr 13 (42/31); I and III/JG 3 (63/48); I, III and IV/JG 4 (80/60); II/JG 11 (37/31); I, II, III and IV/JG 27 (110/89); II, III and IV/JG 53 (131/88), and I, II and III/JG 77 (85/51).

**Luftflotte 4** (Hungary and Yugoslavia): NAGr 12 (11/7); NAGr 14 (33/26); II/JG 51 (36/26); II/JG 52 (34/30) and I/JG 53 (19/18).

**Luftflotte 5** (Norway and Finland): Few Bf 109Gs operated alongside Fw 190s with 1.(H) *Staffel* of *Aufklärungsgruppe* 32 and with the *Stabschwarm* and III and IV *Gruppen* of JG 5 (combined strength of Bf 109Gs and Fw 190s being 113/88).

**Luftflotte 6** (East Prussia to the Carpathians): NAGr 2 (mixed with Fw 190s 35/30); NAGr 3 (mixed with Fw 189s 57/46); NAGr 4 (mixed with Fw 189s 23/21); NAGr 8 (mixed with Fw 189s 24/16); NAGr 15 (mixed with Fw 189s 20/13); I, III and IV/JG 51 (108/78); I and III/JG 52 (76/70); *Nachtjagdgeschwader* 5 (mixed with Ju 88s 51/41).

**Luftflotte Reich:** I and III/JG 300 (101/75), and I/NJG 11 (mixed with Ju 88s 43/30).

## The last of the wartime Eagles

The final production version of the Bf 109 was primarily the result of the rationalization policy of the *Jägerstab* which was determined to reduce the number of sub-types and modifications of the fighter and standardize on the basic model to

*A Bf 109K-2 believed to have belonged to I/JG 51 photographed in May 1945. Note the "Defence of the Reich" fuselage bands, those of I (and III) Gruppe of JG 51 being green-white-green*

which all plants engaged in Bf 109 production would progressively convert. This, the Bf 109K (the letter "I" not being employed by the RLM to distinguish between variants of a basic design, and "J" having been assigned to the Hispano-built model), was based on the Bf 109G-10 but embodied as standard certain of the progressive changes incorporated in the G-series as *Umrüst-Bausätze* as well as some aerodynamic refinements.

The first pre-production Bf 109K-0 fighters appeared in September 1944, and differed externally from the definitive Bf 109G-10 in some undercarriage refinements. Doors were fitted to cover the retracted mainwheels (although often removed in service), and doors also enclosed the fully-retracting long-stroke tailwheel. The longer tailwheel leg was introduced, incidentally to raise the tailplane into the slipstream and thus ease take-off. Some relocation of radio and fuel equipment in the rear fuselage resulted in the D/F loop being moved aft one fuselage frame, the fuel filler cap being moved forward. The inspection panel was also moved forward and upward in the fuselage portside and was re-shaped. The position of this panel and the D/F loop, together with the presence of undercarriage doors, in fact provided the only sure means of recognizing a Bf 109K from a late production G-10.

The pre-production Bf 109K-0 was powered by the DB 605DB, but production models used the DB 605DCM and standard features included the overall cowl fairing, "chin" blisters, deep oil cooler, tall tail with fully-tabbed rudder, "Galland" hood and the long chordwise wing fairings associated with the larger mainwheels. Proposals to fit an enlarged tailplane and also to install Flettner integrally-balanced ailerons were not proceeded with. As introduced on the Bf 109G-6, the standard armament continued to be the engine-mounted MK 108 cannon which was employed in concert with the fuselage-mounted MG 131s, but the wing structure was modified to allow for the *internal* mounting of either the MG 151 or MK 108. The initial models, which began to leave the assembly lines in October 1944, were the Bf 109K-2 and K-4, these differing only in that the latter had provision for cabin pressurization, and among the first *Jagdgruppen* to receive these were II/JG 11, II and III/JG 27, and II/JG 53, all of which participated in Operation *Bodenplatte* against Allied airfields on January 1, 1945.

Later production Bf 109K-4s introduced an engine-mounted 30-mm MK 103 cannon in place of the standard MK 108, but the 2·5-in. (6,50-cm) diameter outer sheath enclosing the barrel of this weapon rendered a barrel change under operational conditions a somewhat onerous task. By comparison with the MK 108, the MK 103 was a far superior weapon, offering a higher muzzle velocity and a very flat trajectory, and was less prone to jamming, but it possessed the disadvantage of being appreciably heavier. Variants included the Bf 109K-4/R2 reconnaissance fighter which reverted to the engine-mounted MK 108, was equipped with FuG 16zs, and had provision for an Rb 50/30 or Rb 75/30 camera, and the Bf 109K-4/R6 bad weather fighter. The MK 103 was also adopted for the next K-series variant, the Bf 109K-6, which, intended primarily as an anti-bomber weapon, carried the two usual MG 131 cowl guns, plus two (internally-mounted) wing MK 108 cannon, or, alternatively, a pair of MK 103s or MK 108s in underwing gondolas.

Deliveries of the Bf 109K-6 to the *Jagdgruppen* began in January 1945, but relatively few had attained operational status by the time Germany's Third Reich finally collapsed, and with a loaded weight of 7,928 lb. (3 596 kg) and somewhat unwieldy in consequence, this was perhaps fortunate for the *Jagdflieger* operating under conditions of complete Allied air supremacy. A few examples of the Bf 109K-8 were also completed. This was a photographic reconnaissance model with either an Rb 32 camera in the rear fuselage or an Rb 50/30 aft of the cockpit. Cowl guns were deleted and the armament comprised an MK 103 hub and two MG 151 or MK 108 internal wing cannon.

Even fewer examples of the last K-series production models, the Bf 109K-10 and Bf 109K-14, were destined to see operational service, as deliveries began during the last two weeks of the conflict, and the *Gruppe Stab* of II/JG 52 is the only unit recorded as having taken the last-mentioned version on strength. Whereas the Bf 109K-10 retained the DB 605D-series engine (being a heavy interceptor with an armament of one engine-mounted MK 103, two fuselage-mounted MG 131s, and two wing-mounted MG 151/15s), the Bf 109K-14 was powered by the long-awaited DB 605L with a two-stage mechanical supercharger. A chance bomb dropped on a target of opportunity had hit the high-altitude test chamber of the DB

*A Bf 109G-14 of the kroat. Jagdstaffel which was surrendered by its pilot at Falconara, near Ancona, in April 1945. This unit had operated under the command of the Jagdfliegerführer Ostpreussen and prior to its demise was equipped with a mix of Bf 109G-10/U4 and Bf 109G-14/U2 fighters. Note the aft cowling bulges, long tailwheel leg (fixed) and wooden fin-and-rudder assembly characteristic of late examples of this sub-type*

605L in the previous year, and the consequent delay was an important factor in the postponement of the use of this engine in the Bf 109K. The DB 605L, using 96 octane C3 fuel and MW 50 boost, provided 1,700 h.p. for take-off and 1,725 h.p. at 4,900 ft. (1 495 m). At 31,400 ft. (9 570 m) maximum output was 1,350 h.p. with 1,150 h.p. available for climb and combat, and the maximum speed of 452 m.p.h. (727 km/h) attained by the Bf 109K-4 at 19,685 ft. (6 000 m) could be reached by the Bf 109K-14 at 37,730 ft. (11 500 m). This formidable performance was accompanied by a somewhat less formidable armament, however, this being restricted to a single engine-mounted 30-mm calibre weapon (either MK 103 or MK 108 could be installed) and two 13-mm MG 131 machine guns.

The equipment of all K-series fighters was basically similar, and included a *Revi* 16B reflector sight and FuG 16zy and FuG 25a radio, a D/F loop behind the cockpit and the usual radio mast being supplemented by a whip antenna under the port wing. It had been planned to replace the FuG 16zy by FuG 15 from July 1945, *Egon B* (Lorenz) procedure being used for distance measurement during fighter control as FuG 15 did not permit retention of the standard *Y* procedure, but by that time those Bf 109 assembly lines that *did* still exist had long since come to a standstill.

When the Allies crossed the Rhine, the number of Bf 109s remaining at the disposal of the *Luftwaffe* was still quite impressive, some 800 being on the operational strength of the *Jagdgruppen*, and, divided almost equally between G- and K-series aircraft, more than 80 per cent of them were listed as serviceable, but their operations were being progressively reduced as the remaining stocks of fuel dwindled and bases were overrun by the Allies.

Few more weeks of operational service, at least in the insignia of the *Luftwaffe*, remained to the Bf 109 on April 7, 1945. On that date, a few months short of the full decade since the first

prototype had been rolled out at Augsburg, the *Jagdgruppen* still flying its last wartime descendants (the number on strength and the number serviceable being indicated in parentheses) were as follows:

*Luftwaffenkommando West*, which had withdrawn into Bavaria, included the *Stabschwarm* and II, III and IV/JG 53 (134/76) and 1./NJG 11 (16/15); *Luftflotte* 4 included II/JG 51 (7/5), II/JG 52 (43/29) and I/JG 53 (27/27); *Luftflotte* 6 had II and III/JG 3 (98/95), III/JG 6 (21/17), the *Stabschwarm* and I and III/JG 52 (80/74), the *Stabschwarm* and I, II and III/JG 77 (101/82), and II and IV (*Einsatz*)/JG 1 (109/97); *Luftflottenkommando Ostpreussen* included I and III/JG 51 (33/15), and *Luftflotte Reich* had III/JG 4 (61/56) and 4. and 7./NJG 11 (35/26).

---

### Bf 109K-4 Specification

**Power Plant:** One Daimler-Benz DB 605DCM 12-cylinder inverted-vee liquid-cooled engine rated at 2,000 h.p. for take-off, 2,030 h.p. at 1,640 ft. (500 m), and 1,800 h.p. at 16,400 ft. (5 000 m).
**Performance:** (At 6,834 lb./3 100 kg) Maximum speed, 378 m.p.h. (608 km/h) at sea level, 452 m.p.h. (727 km/h) at 19,685 ft. (6 000 m), 435 m.p.h. (700 km/h) at 24,610 ft. (7 500 m); range at 6,834 lb. (3 100 kg), 356 mls. (573 km) at 19,685 ft. (6 000 m); initial climb rate, 4,820 ft./min. (24,5 m/sec); time to 16,400 ft. (5 000 m), 3·0 min., to 32, 810 ft. (10 000 m), 6·7 min., to 39,370 ft. (12 000 m), 10·2 min.; service ceiling at 7,440 lb. (3 374 kg), 41,000 ft. (12 500 m).
**Weights:** Empty, 4,886 lb. (2 380 kg); normal loaded, 7,440 lb. (3 374 kg); maximum overload, 7,937 lb. (3 600 kg).
**Dimensions:** Span, 32 ft. 8½ in. (9,97 m); length, 29 ft. 7½ in. 9,03 m); height, 8ft. 2½ in. (2,50 m); wing area, 173·299 sq. ft. (16,1 m²).
**Armament:** One 30-mm Rheinmetall Borsig MK 103 or MK 108 engine-mounted cannon with 60 rounds and two 13-mm Rheinmetall Borsig MG 131 fuselage-mounted machine guns with 300 r.p.g.

---

# High-flying and Double-headed Eagles

While the Bf 109K was the last model of Messerschmitt's fighter to reach the assembly lines during W.W. II, a wide variety of derivatives of the basic design had been proposed from time to time for specialized roles, but only the Bf 109H high-altitude fighter and the "Siamese Twin" heavy *Zerstörer* Bf 109Z were actually built, and the latter was never to fly.

As combat altitudes had risen with the progress of the air war, emphasis on effective ceiling had increased accordingly in fighter requirements, and by the beginning of 1943, an interim *Hochleistungsjäger* (High-performance Fighter) based on the Bf 109F but intended to offer a substantially improved combat ceiling had assumed considerable importance. Designated Bf 109H, this proposal had been tendered to the *Technischen Amt* of the RLM to meet the requirements of the first phase of a *Hochleistungsjäger* development programme. This phase, which was referred to as the *Sofort-Programm* (Immediate Programme), envisaged the development of a fighter which, offering a more effective ceiling, would be based on an existing series of production airframe, and would provide interim equipment pending availability of the progeny of the second phase, or *Vorrücken-Programm* (Advanced Programme), calling for an *extremen Höhenjäger* (Extreme Altitude Fighter) for delivery from the end of 1944.

As originally conceived, the Bf 109H was essentially a Bf 109F airframe with a higher-rated DB 601 engine and a parallel-chord centre section inserted in the wing to increase overall span to 39 ft. 1¼ in. (11,92 m). However, the *Technische Amt* progressively raised its sights regarding altitude performance, calling for service ceilings of from 42,650 to 49,200 ft.

(13 000 to 15 000 m), the changes in the required performance necessitating commensurate changes in the Bf 109H concept.

Work was proceeding in parallel at this time on the Me 209/II as a potential production successor for the Bf 109, and on April 23, 1943, the Messerschmitt bureau submitted a proposal to the *Technischen Amt* for an *extremen Höhenjäger* version of the Me 209-II as a replacement for the Bf 109H development. This, the *Projekt 1091a*, foresaw the use of either the DB 628A engine which had been evolved specifically for high-altitude operation, or the DB 603U which was basically a DB 603E fitted with a TKL 15 turbo-supercharger.

It was estimated that the *Projekt 1091a* would have a maximum ceiling of 57,400 ft. (17 500 m), but it was obvious to the *Technischen Amt* that the fighter now proposed by Messerschmitt could not be ready for series production much before the end of 1944, and the exigencies of the air war demanded that a fighter capable of operation at extreme altitudes be made available to the *Jagdfliegern* as quickly as possible. Messerschmitt was therefore instructed to revert to the basic Bf 109H concept but embody some of the features envisaged for the *Projekt 1091a*, including the DB 628 engine.

To finalize the DB 628 engine installation for the Me 209-II, a Bf 109G-5 airframe (*Werk-Nr.* 16 281) had already been fitted with a mock-up of the power plant as the Bf 109 V49, and having completed bench running, the DB 628 was installed for flight testing in a Bf 109G-3 airframe (*Werk-Nr.* 15 338), and flown for the first time on May 18, 1943, as the Bf 109 V50 by *Flugkapitän* Wendel. Although similar in general arrangement to the DB 605A, the DB 628A, which had an induction cooler

127

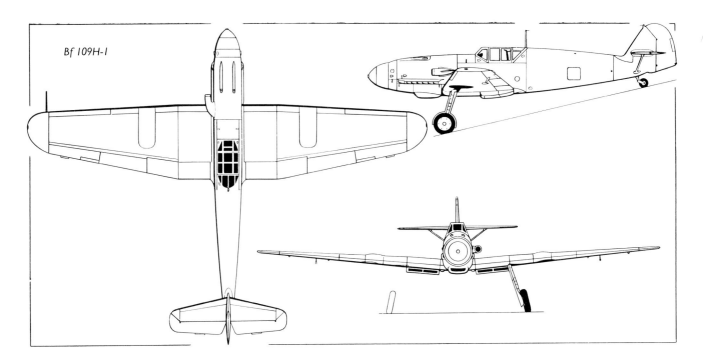

Bf 109H-1

and two-stage mechanical supercharger, possessed larger overall dimensions and was some 375 lb. (170 kg) heavier. A ducted spinner and broad-bladed airscrew were fitted, but the installation dictated a 2 ft. 6¾ in. lengthening of the forward fuselage which, necessitating balance weights in the rear fuselage of the Bf 109 V50 to restore the c.g., was to be compensated for in the revised Bf 109H by moving the wing attachment points forward 10¼ in. (25,50 cm) and substantially enlarging the tail surfaces.

After brief flight testing at Augsburg, the Bf 109 V50 was transferred to the Daimler-Benz test centre at Echterdingen, south of Stuttgart, where test pilots completed two 30-hour flight test programmes during which the maximum altitude attained was 50,850 ft. (15 500 m). It was calculated that, from a take-off output of 1,490 h.p., the series production DB 628A engine would deliver 1,580 h.p. at 6,550 ft. (2 000 m), 1,480 h.p. at 21,000 ft. (6 400 m), 1,350 h.p. at 31,400 ft. (9 570 m), and 1,130 h.p. at 39,400 ft. (12 000 m). While Daimler-Benz was performing engine flight trials with the Bf 109 V50, a Bf 109G-5 airframe was also being fitted with the DB 628, together with the additional parallel-chord wing centre section and commensurately enlarged tail surfaces, this flying for the first time early in June 1943 as the Bf 109H V54 (DV + JB). Simultaneously, work was proceeding on the adaptation of several Bf 109F-4 airframes for development tasks under the designation Bf 109H-0.

Apart from the addition of the parallel-chord wing centre section, the transfer of the main undercarriage attachment points to the outer extremities of this section, and the provision of bracing struts for the extended tailplane, the Bf 109H-0 was similar to the Bf 109F-4/Z, retaining the DB 601E-1 engine and nitrous oxide (GM 1) injection system, and armament of one 20-mm MG 151 cannon and two 7,9-mm MG 17 machine guns. It was intended primarily for the investigation of the problems of flying at extreme altitudes, and the development of suitable equipment. The Bf 109H-1s that followed were intended for service evaluation, being based on the Bf 109G-5 airframe with its pressurized cockpit, employing a DB 605A engine with GM 1 power boosting, and possessing a similar armament to that carried by the Bf 109H-0 but having provision for an Rb 20/30, 50/30 or 75/30 camera in the rear fuselage.

Several Bf 109H-1s were delivered to an experimental service evaluation unit based at Guyancourt, near Paris, early in 1944, and although the general characteristics of the fighter were found to be satisfactory, and its service ceiling to be of the order of 47,500 ft. (14 480 m), some wing flutter was encountered in diving at speeds in excess of 455 m.p.h. (732 km/h). A series of diving trials with the Bf 109H-1 were initiated at Augsburg by *Flugkapitän* Wendel, but on April 14, 1944, after commencing a dive at 16,400 ft. (5 000 m), the wing began to flutter at 9,850 ft. (3 000 m) and 497 m.p.h. (800 km/h) indicated, and as soon as Wendel pulled back on the stick the port wing parted company with the fuselage.

Although limited additional testing was undertaken, the further development of the Bf 109H was abandoned shortly afterwards in favour of the Ta 152H. In the meantime, however, several proposals had been made for further variants of this *Höhenjägers*, and on December 22, 1943, another prototype, the Bf 109H V55 (*Werk-Nr.* 15 709 DV + JC), had flown. Flight testing of the Bf 109H V54 had revealed a serious stability problem which stemmed largely from the design of the extended forward fuselage, and the Bf 109H V55 (construction of which had been initiated as the Me 209 V6 but the airframe being transferred to the Bf 109H programme with the cancellation of further development of the Me 209), while retaining the lengthened fuselage, had a DB 605B engine with the larger DB 603 supercharger.

## Bf 109H V55 Specification

**Power Plant:** One Daimler-Benz DB 605B 12-cylinder inverted-vee liquid-cooled engine rated at 1,600 h.p. for take-off
**Performance:** Maximum speed, 427 m.p.h. (687 km/h) at full boost altitude, 367 m.p.h. (590 km/h); service ceiling, 44,290 ft. (13 500 m).
**Weights:** Empty equipped, 6,338 lb. (2 875 kg); normal loaded, 7,804 lb. (3,540 kg).
**Dimensions:** Span, 43 ft. 6 in. (13,26 m); length, 33 ft. 7½ in. (10, 55 m); height, 10 ft. 7½ in. (3,24 m); wing area 235·729 sq. ft. (21,9 m²).
**Armament:** One 30-mm Rheinmetall Borsig MK 108 engine-mounted cannon with 60 rounds and two 20-mm Mauser MG 151/20 wing-mounted cannon with 200 r.p.g.

Other changes included extended wingtips similar to those intended for the *Höhenjäger* variant of the Me 209 and which increased overall wingspan to 43 ft. 6 in. (13,26 m), lengthened leading-edge slots and ailerons, and redesigned vertical tail surfaces. The intended power plant had been the DB 603G, but owing to delays in the delivery of this engine, the proposed production derivative of the Bf 109H V55 was to receive the Junkers Jumo 213E with GM 1 injection.

Development ended with the V55, however, which was, itself, totally destroyed in an air attack on Augsburg on February 25, 1944, its DB 628-powered predecessor, the Bf 109H V54, being destroyed six months later, on August 14, 1944, in a bombing attack on Daimler-Benz's Echterdingen flight test centre.

Perhaps the most intriguing variant of the basic Bf 109 actually built was the *Zwilling*, or "Siamese Twin" version derived from two standard Bf 109F airframes. The *Zwilling* concept originally stemmed from *Generaloberst* Udet who, during 1940, had proposed the marriage of two He 111H bombers to provide an adequately powerful towplane for the immense Me 321 and Ju 322 gliders then under development. The success of this "marriage of convenience" led to a study by the Messerschmitt bureau of the possibility of a similar combination of two Bf 109 fighters to provide a heavy *Zerstörer* while avoiding the disruption of production lines that would inevitably result from an attempt to introduce an entirely new design.

This proposal aroused considerable interest in the *Technischen Amt* as it offered a substantial advance in performance over existing aircraft in the *Zerstörer* category yet conformed with the RLM policy of restricting production to a relatively small number of basic types. For test purposes two Bf 109F airframes were allocated for conversion to *Zwilling* configuration late in 1942.

The two fuselages, complete with DB 601E-1 engines, were virtually unchanged apart from the introduction of a keel member in each fuselage to carry the main undercarriage attachment points (which were moved inboard to the centrelines of the fuselages), and an ETC 250 rack. One set of port and starboard wings was retained, but the repositioning of the main undercarriage members necessitated some revision of the structure forward of the mainspar to provide for the new wheel wells. These components were married by means of a parallel-chord wing centre section (embodying twin radiator baths, a central strong point capable of lifting a single 1,102-lb/500-kg bomb, and flaps), and a parallel-chord tailplane.

While work was proceeding on the prototype Bf 109

*Zwilling*, the Messerschmitt bureau undertook studies for production models based on the Bf 109G airframe and powered by either the DB 605A or Jumo 213E engine. These envisaged a cannon armament of two engine-mounted 30-mm MK 108s, two similar weapons in gondolas beneath the outer wing panels, and a single 30-mm MK 103 slightly to starboard of the centreline in the wing centre section. For the fast bomber role a 1,102-lb. (500-kg) bomb was to be carried by the centreline rack and a 551-lb. (250-kg) bomb beneath each fuselage, and it was proposed that only the port cockpit be retained, the starboard cockpit providing space for additional fuel.

The prototype *Zwilling* was completed in 1943, and weighing some 13,000 lb. (5 900 kg) in loaded condition, had an overall span of 43 ft. 5½ in. (13,24 m), the distance between the fuselage axes being 10 ft. 11½ in. (3,34 m). Preparations for flight trials were allegedly being made when the prototype suffered damage during the course of an air attack and, in consequence, no testing had been undertaken when the development programme was abandoned in 1944. By coincidence, a similar development of the North American P-51 Mustang was conceived late in 1943, eventually emerging in April 1945 as the P-82 Twin Mustang.

---

### Bf 109 Zwilling Specification
**(Based on manufacturer's estimates for proposed production model)**

**Power Plant:** Two Junkers Jumo 213E 12-cylinder inverted-vee liquid-cooled engines each rate at 1,750 h.p. for take-off and 1,320 h.p. at 29,530 ft. (9 000 m).

**Performance:** (Without external stores) Maximum speed, 374 m.p.h. (602 km/h) at sea level, 462 m.p.h. (743 km/h) at 26,250 ft. (8 000 m), (with single 1,102-lb./500-kg bomb and gun armament reduced to two 30-mm MK 108 cannon) 366 m.p.h. (590 km/h) at sea level, 455 m.p.h. (732 km/h) at 26,250 ft. (8 000 m); maximum continuous cruise, 418 m.p.h. (673 km/h); maximum economical cruise, 354 m.p.h. (570 km/h); range, 1,050 mls. (1 690 km) at 418 m.p.h. (673 km/h), 1,240 mls. (1 995 km) at 354 m.p.h. (570 km/h); initial climb rate (without external stores), 5,080 ft./min. (25,56 m/sec).

**Weights:** Normal loaded 16,050 lb. (7 280 kg); maximum loaded, 17,882 lb. ( 8 110 kg).

**Dimensions:** Span, 43 ft. 5½ in. (13,24 m); length, 28 ft. 2 in. (8,89 m); height 8 ft. 10 in. (2,69 m); wing area, 249·72 sq. ft. 23,2 m².

**Armament:** Four 30-mm Rheinmetall Borsig MK 108 and one 30-mm MK 103 cannon, plus one 1,102-lb. (500-kg) and two 551-lb (250-kg) bombs.

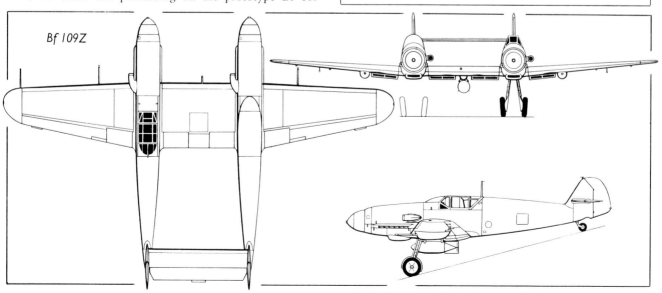

Bf 109Z

# The Eagle flies on

The end of W.W. II spelled *finis* for virtually every combat aircraft that had seen birth in Germany's Third Reich during the 12 years of its existence, but *not* for the Messerschmitt Bf 109. Indeed, this fighter, born on the drawing boards of the Bayerische Flugzeugwerke in Augsburg more than a decade before Adolf Hitler's Germany was to be finally defeated, was destined to outlive its erstwhile opponents both in production and service.

Switzerland's *Flugwaffe*, as the *Fliegertruppe* became in 1946, included five Bf 109-equipped *Fliegerstaffeln* on its strength, one of which was operating the Bf 109G-6 and the remainder the Bf 109E, and these continued to provide the backbone of the *Flugwaffe* interceptor force until the acquisition of surplus North American P-51D Mustangs from 1948 permitted the progressive phase out of the ageing Messerschmitts with the last example being retired, as previously recorded, on December 28, 1949.

The Bf 109 was to survive still longer in Finnish service for, by 1948, nearly 100 Bf 109Gs remained in the *Ilmavoimien* inventory, including G-5s, G-6s, G-10s and G-14s, and the *Gustav* was considered standard fighter equipment, serving *Lentorykmentit* (Flight Regiments) 1 and 3, each of which possessed two squadrons, the former comprising HLeLv 11 and 13 and the latter HLeLv 31 and 33. When the *Lentorykmentit* were disbanded and replaced by *Lennostot* (Wings) on November 31, 1952, *Gustavs* remained in service with a *Hävittäjälentu* (Fighter Flight) at Luonetjärvi with the 1.*Lennosto*, and with *Hävittäjälaivue* (Fighter Squadron) 31 and 33 at Utti with the 3.*Lennosto*, until, in 1954 they were finally phased out of the Finnish inventory.

In Rumania, with the declaration of a People's Republic, the air arm became the *Fortele Aeriene ale Republicii Populare România* (Air Forces of the Rumanian People's Republic) and continued to operate Bf 109G-6s, -10s and -14s – many of which had been taken over from the *Luftwaffe* in August 1944 – until 1948, when deliveries commenced of 100 Yak-9s and some 40 La-7s from the Soviet Union for the re-equipment of the fighter element. With the liberation of Yugoslavia and the creation of a new Yugoslav air arm, the *Jugoslovensko ratno vazduhoplovstvo*, the Messerschmitt fighter once again flew in Yugoslav colours. As the *Wehrmacht* retreated, many Bf 109Gs of both the *Luftwaffe* and the Croatian air arm had been abandoned on Yugoslav airfields owing to lack of fuel or spares, and those that could be made airworthy were incorporated in the JRV, these later being supplemented by between 50 and 60 Bf 109G-2s, -6s, -10s and two-seat -12s which had served with the Royal Bulgarian Air Force and which were "presented" to Yugoslavia as war reparations, these serving for several years.

*A Bf 109G-6 in postwar Yugoslav service originally acquired from Bulgaria*

But the Swiss, Finnish, Rumanian and Yugoslav air forces were not to provide the *final* refuges for this most longevous of warplanes, for after the last Bf 109s had been grounded by these services, the Messerschmitt fighter was still to be seen over Czechoslovakia sporting the insignia and civil registrations of the para-military Czechoslovak National Air Guard. In 1944, with the progressive dispersal of the German aircraft industry, the Bf 109 manufacturing complex was expanded to absorb a number of small factories in the vicinity of Prague, these producing components for assembly by the Avia factory at Čakovice. The sub-types assembled at Čakovice were the Bf 109G-12 two-seater and the Bf 109G-14 single-seater, but relatively few had been accepted by the *Luftwaffe* when the approach of Soviet forces necessitated the German withdrawal from Prague, leaving, surprisingly, the physical capacity for the manufacture of the Messerschmitt fighter virtually intact.

With the end of hostilities all Bf 109 components were gathered from the numerous Czechoslovak sub-contractors and from elsewhere in Eastern Europe, the assembly line at Čakovice was reactivated and a second assembly line set up at the Letov factory at Letnany. Two Bf 109G-12s and 20 Bf

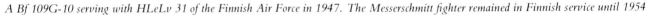

*A Bf 109G-10 serving with HLeLv 31 of the Finnish Air Force in 1947. The Messerschmitt fighter remained in Finnish service until 1954*

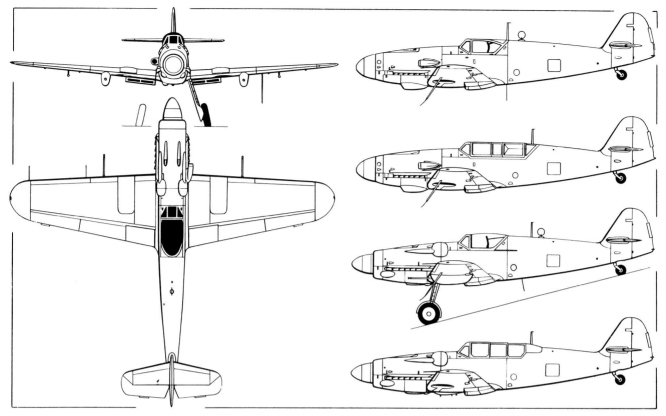

*The plan and front views above depict the definitive production S 199, and the sideviews depict (from top to bottom) the S 99, the CS 99, the S 199 and the CS 199*

109G-14s that had reached an advanced stage of assembly on the Čakovice line when German forces withdrew were completed after careful examination for sabotage, and eventually issued to the National Air Guard, the single seater being designated S 99 and the two-seater CS 99. Plans to assemble the Bf 109G-14 in substantially larger numbers for the equipment of the fighter element of Czechoslovakia's re-established air arm, the *Ceskoslovenské vojenské letectvo*, received a serious setback in September 1945 when a sugar refinery at Krasno Bresno being used to store ammunition was set ablaze. The refinery also housed the entire available stock of DB 605AM engines!

The only 12-cylinder inverted-vee liquid-cooled engines readily available in substantial numbers in Czechoslovakia were the 1,340 h.p. Junkers Jumo 211F and the 1,420 h.p. Jumo 211J intended for installation in the Heinkel He 111H bomber and by no means ideal as fighter engines. Nevertheless, hundreds of Bf 109G airframes were available, together with very large stocks of spares, offering the prospect of rapid and inexpensive production, and the *Gustav* was adapted to take the Jumo which drove a paddle-bladed VS 11 wooden propeller. This "marriage of convenience" was designated S 199, a tandem two-seat model being known as the CS 199, and the appellation bestowed upon the Jumo-engined fighter by the Czechoslovak pilots who found themselves flying the aircraft was anything but complimentary, the S 199 being promptly dubbed *Mezec* (Mule), for its behaviour was little short of "mulish".

The prototype S 199 conversion undertaken by the Avia factory at Prague-Čakovice airfield was flown for the first time on March 25, 1947, by Petr Široký, and deliveries to the *vojenské letectvo* commenced in February 1948, series aircraft receiving both the Jumo 211F and Jumo 211J. The tandem two-seat advanced training version, the CS 199, flew initially on January 24, 1949, with A. Kraus at the controls, and 58 examples of this model were to be built, the last of these being

test flown on September 12, 1950, and during the course of production, the original side-hinging cockpit canopies were replaced by aft-sliding canopies and the angle of the wheel axis was changed.

The handling characteristics of the S 199 were described by some pilots as unpleasant and by others as vicious. The big paddle-bladed airscrew was responsible for a dangerous tendency to swerve as soon as the tailwheel left the ground during take-off, necessitating the constant application of rudder. Once in the air control tended to be over-sensitive, demanding the constant attention of the pilot. Acceleration was sluggish,

*(Above) One of two CS 99 (Bf 109G-12) two-seaters completed, and (below) an S 99 (Bf 109G-14)*

*A small number of production S 199 fighters were completed with a pair of 13-mm MG 131 machine guns in the wings in place of the two gondola-mounted 20-mm cannon, one of these being illustrated above*

and a successful landing demanded even more skill than the take-off. Standard armament comprised a pair of 13-mm MG 131 machine guns in the forward fuselage and the *Rüstsatz 6* arrangement of two gondola-mounted 20-mm MG 151 cannon under the wings, although some examples had the underwing weapons replaced by a pair of 13-mm MG 131s or 7,9-mm MG 17s mounted within the wings. While a maximum speed of 367 m.p.h. (590 km/h) was claimed for the fighter, the production model barely managed to exceed 340 m.p.h. (547 km/h) in level flight.

In view of the obvious shortcomings of the S 199, it is perhaps surprising that the Czechoslovak aircraft industry succeeded in exporting this fighter, but the purchaser had little choice. In March 1948, two months before, on May 14, a resolution of the United Nations brought the State of Israel *officially* into existence, an Israeli air arm, the *Chel Ha'avir*, had been created clandestinely. The prospective government of the new State was well aware that, with official recognition for Israel, attack by the Arab states would not be long delayed, and word had already gone out through Zionist organizations that the fledgling *Chel Ha'avir* would need experienced combat pilots. It was obvious that there would be no shortage of volunteers, but pilots without aircraft to fly were of little use, and Israeli representatives approached the Czechoslovak government with a view to the purchase of fighters. Despite the embargo imposed on arms to the Middle East, the Czechoslovak government agreed to the export of the fighters – the Israelis were offering U.S. dollars and Czechoslovakia was

*(Above left and below) S 199.185 rebuilt from a DB 605-engined S 99 (Bf 109G-14) OK-BYH (see page 131) of the National Air Guard and re-delivered by Avia late in 1948. This particular aircraft eventually became a static display example and was scrapped in 1959*

desperately short of hard currency. Thus, on April 23, 1948, an initial contract for the supply of 10 S 199 fighters at a unit price, including spares and ammunition for the guns, of $190,000 was signed in Prague by Israeli representatives, and on the day that the State of Israel came into existence the fighters were ready for delivery.

Arms were being flown into Israel under the code-name *Operation Balak*, and the first S 199 was loaded aboard a privately-chartered DC-4 in Prague on May 20, 1948, and, as "Balak Flight No. 5", was flown into Israel that night. On the same day negotiations began with the Czechs for the supply of a further 15 S 199 fighters, and all 25 aircraft were dis-assembled, loaded aboard the DC-4, and flown one by one into Israel. In the meantime, volunteer pilots were being secretly flown to Rome where a clandestine military flying school known as *Alica* and staffed largely by U.S. instructors had been established to train pilots for the *Chel Ha'avir*. From Rome volunteers with fighter experience were sent to Czechoslovakia for a rudimentary two-week conversion course on the S 199. The future *Chel Ha'avir* pilots were soon echoing the sentiments expressed by the Czech pilots concerning the Jumo-engined Bf 109.

Nevertheless, the first Israeli fighter unit, No. 101 Squadron, was formed on the S 199 and began operations on the evening of May 19, 1948, from Ekron with a strafing attack by four aircraft on a stalled Egyptian armoured column two miles north of Ashdod. One of the S 199s was shot down by ground fire and another, badly damaged, crashed on landing at its home base. On the following day, another S 199 was lost in an attack on the Iraq Suweidan fortress, but on June 3, the CO of No 101 Squadron, Modi Alon, destroyed two Egyptian C-47s, which, adapted for the bombing role, were attempting an attack on Tel Aviv, these being the first two of the very few "kills" achieved with the S 199. The Czechoslovak-built Messerschmitts continuously suffered technical problems and there were rarely more than a half-dozen airworthy at any one time. Attrition resulting from accidents was extremely serious. For example, of four S 199s despatched to attack an Egyptian concentration on July 8, one crashed on take-off and another was lost as a result of engine failure. Ten days later, what was probably the last recorded combat between the Messerschmitt and its principal W.W. II antagonist, the Spitfire, took place when three S 199s, returning to base after attacking Egyptian armour near Bir Aslu, encountered two Egyptian Spitfires, Modi Alon accounting for one of these.

Soon after joining combat, No 101 Squadron was transferred from Ekron to Herzlea, north of Tel Aviv, and while the S 199 proved little more than worthless as a fighter, as a morale-booster it was invaluable. Only four or five survived until

*The tandem two-seat version of the S 199, the CS 199, which was built in small numbers for conversion training*

fighting terminated in January 1949, and these – by that time incorporated with Spitfires in a composite unit designated No. 105 Squadron – were only kept airworthy by dint of cannibalization, the remainder having been lost for the most part in accidents. The S 199 was anything but popular with *Chel Ha'avir* pilots. The seat was non-adjustable and appeared to have been designed for a slim pilot not exceeding 5 ft. 8 in.

*(Above right and below) Early production S 199 fighters in service with No. 101 Squadron of the Chel Ha'avir which began operations in June 1948. Although effective as a morale-booster, the S 199 proved virtually useless as a combat aircraft*

*The Bf 109E-1 (illustrated above and below left) was originally delivered to the Legion Condor at Zaragoza early in 1939, eventually being used by Hispano Aviación and the Instituto Nacional de Técnica Aeronautica as a test-bed for the Hispano-Suiza 12Z-89 engine eventually utilized by the HA-1109-J1L and K1L, and HA-1112-K1L version of the Bf 109*

(1,73 m) in height, and the taller, shorter, or fatter pilot had problems other than those resulting from the handling characteristics of the aircraft. The rudder control and brakes were on the same plate, depending on the application of toe or heel, a system which created more than its share of difficulties. A number of S 199s were lost as a result of too harsh application of brakes which was invariably followed by violent swinging, and it was by no means uncommon for the S 199 to turn over during take-off. As the cockpit canopy was locked from the outside this sometimes resulted in the pilot being trapped in the cockpit into which petrol was pouring.

## The end of the Eagle

It was perhaps fitting that Messerschmitt's remarkable fighter should finally end its long service career in the same skies in which it first fired its guns in anger. As previously related, under a 1942 agreement between Spain's *Ministerio del Aire* and the RLM a manufacturing licence for the Bf 109G-2 was acquired, but various problems arose to delay the initiation of the Spanish production programme, and by the time Germany began the delivery of the 25 dismantled aircraft called for under the agreement and intended to provide the Spanish licensee with assembly experience, the war was going so badly for the Third Reich that after the arrival in Spain of the 25 airframes, which lacked tail assemblies, power plants and armament, no further deliveries materialized. Thus, with only incomplete manufacturing drawings, Hispano Aviación found itself in the position of having to manufacture the Messerschmitt fighter for Spain's *Ejército del Aire* without any of the promised jigs or tools, let alone the DB 605 engines, armament, instrumentation and airscrews.

The Hispano-Suiza 12Z 89 12-cylinder vee engine rated at 1,300 h.p. for take-off had just entered production in Barcelona, and as, by the end of 1944, it was obvious that the promised DB 605 engines would never reach Spain, a Bf 109E-1 airframe was fitted with the Hispano-Suiza engine for flight testing by both Hispano Aviación and the *Instituto Nacional de Técnica Aeronautica*. Although these tests did not produce entirely satisfactory results, no alternative power plant immediately presented itself, and preparations were made at Seville for the assembly of the 25 Bf 109G-2s and installation of the HS 12Z 89 engine. The prototype conversion, which had flown on March 2, 1945, as the HA-1109-J1L, was initially fitted with a VDM airscrew which necessitated a reduction in maximum permissible engine r.p.m. from 2,800 to 2,600, this, coupled with somewhat ungainly, drag-producing carburettor air intake and oil cooler, resulted in a disappointing performance.

Somewhat surprisingly, in view of the fact that the original Bf 109 vertical tail surfaces were designed as aerofoil sections to counter the torque of the engine by "sideways lift", no attempt was made to redesign the surfaces for the Hispano engine rotating in the opposite direction, the changed torque being compensated for in flight simply by maintaining the rudder a few degrees to starboard. The underwing radiators and engine

---

### S 199 Specification

**Power Plant:** One Junkers Jumo 211F 12-cylinder inverted-vee liquid-cooled engine rated at 1,340 h.p. for take-off and 1,060 h.p. at 17,390 ft. (5 300 m).

**Performance:** (At 7,054 lb./3 200 kg) Maximum speed, 366 m.p.h. (590 km/h) at 19,685 ft. (6 000 m), 322 m.p.h. (518 km/h at sea level; maximum continuous cruise, 287 m.p.h. (462 km/h); economical cruise, 248 m.p.h. (400 km/h); range with 66 Imp. gal. (300 l) drop tank, 528 mls. (850 km) at 248 m.p.h. (400 km/h); maximum climb rate, 2,695 ft./min. (13,7 m/sec); service ceiling, 31,170 ft. (9 500 m).

**Weights:** Empty equipped, 5,732 lb. (2 600 kg); maximum loaded, 8,236 lb. (3 736 kg).

**Dimensions:** Span, 32 ft. 6½ in. (9,92 m); length, 29 ft. 4 in. (8,94 m); height, 8 ft. 6 in. (2,59 m); wing area, 173·299 sq. ft. (16,1 m²).

**Armament:** Two 13-mm Rheimetall Borsig MG 131 fuselage-mounted machine guns and two 20-mm Mauser MG 151/20 wing-mounted cannon. Provision for one 551-lb. (250-kg) bomb or four 154-lb (70-kg) bombs beneath the fuselage.

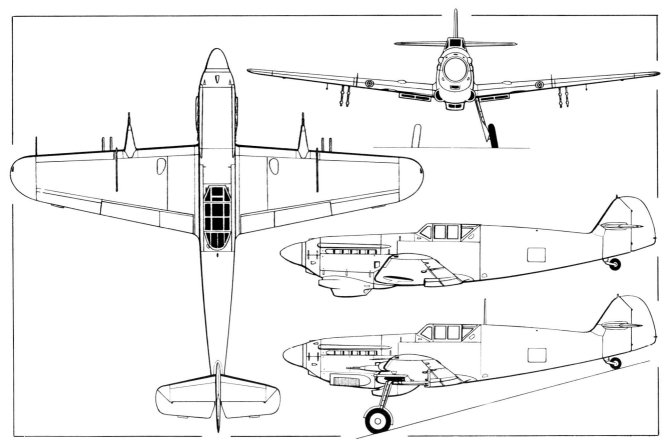

*The general arrangement drawing above depicts the HA-1112-K1L, the upper sideview illustrating the HA-1109-J1L for comparison purposes. (Immediately right) An HA-1109-J1L. (Below right centre) An HA-1112-K1L and (foot of page) an HA-1109-K1L operated by the Escuadron de Experimentación en Vuelo*

bearer pick-up points proved amenable to the new upright-vee engine, and from the outset it was intended to replace the VDM airscrew with a Swiss Escher-Wyss unit which was eventually fitted to the prototype by the INTA (*Instituto Nacional de Técnica Aeronautica* or National Institute of Technical Aeronautics), flight testing with the new airscrew commencing in January 1946.

The first of the 25 Bf 109G airframes to be fitted with the HS 12Z 89 engine and Escher-Wyss airscrew was flown on July 10, 1947, and the remaining 24 airframes were assembled over the following 18 months, but owing to the unsatisfactory characteristics of the power plant the 25 HA-1109-J1L fighters were never issued to the *Ejército del Aire* which continued to soldier on with its surving Bf 109Es and 109Fs, the HS-1109-J1Ls being grounded after limited flying trials.

Meanwhile, Hispano Aviación had begun preparations at Seville for the construction of a series of 200 HA-1109 fighters. The possibility of installing the French-manufactured Hispano-Suiza 12Z 17 fuel-injection engine was investigated, and this was eventually mounted in the 10th HA-1109-J1L as the prototype HA-1109-K1L which flew in May 1951 for the first time. The HS 12Z 17 was rated at 1,300 h.p. at 2,650 r.p.m. and 1,150 h.p. at 2,400 r.p.m., and drove a de Havilland Hydromatic PD-63-335-1 airscrew, and the HA-1109-K1L proved to possess markedly superior characteristics to those of the HA-1109-J1L. Production deliveries began in 1952, although the aircraft was considered by the *Ejército del Aire* more in the light of an operational trainer than as a front-line combat aircraft.

*The HA-1109-M1L prototype for the Merlin-engined production HA-1112-M1L which was the first Spanish-built version of the Messerschmitt fighter to see service in any substantial quantities. Flight testing of the HA-1109-M1L commenced in 1954*

Production of the HA-1109-K1L at the Seville factory was maintained at an extremely low tempo, the relatively few aircraft of this type completed being delivered for the most part without armament, although one aircraft was experimentally fitted with a 12,7-mm Breda-SAFAT machine gun in a fairing beneath each wing. In 1954 the first production example was fitted with two 12,7-mm Breda-SAFAT machine guns over the engine and underwing launchers for eight 80-mm Oerlikon rockets as the HA-1109-K2L, while the sixth aircraft was flown with rocket launchers but without gun armament as the HA-1109-K3L.

Earlier, in 1953, the last HA-1109-J1L, which had been re-engined with the HS 12Z 17, was modified to take two wing-mounted 20-mm Hispano HS-404 cannon and rocket launchers, thus becoming the prototype HA-1112-K1L, and with the standardization of this armament, the remaining Hispano-Suiza-engined aircraft were delivered to the *Ejército del Aire* as HA-1112-K1Ls. The year 1953 had also seen the flight testing of two prototypes of the tandem two-seat HA-1110-K1L, development of which had begun in 1951. The standard seat was moved forward slightly and a second seat inserted aft, the two seats being enclosed by a continuous canopy. The 88 Imp. gal. (400 l) fuselage fuel tank of the single-seater was replaced by three smaller fuselage tanks and two wing tanks with a total capacity of 93 Imp. gal. (423 l), endurance being 1 hr. 45 min., and empty and loaded weights being 5,388 lb. (2 444 kg) and 6,373 lb. (2 891 kg) respectively.

During the course of 1953 the decision was taken to adapt the basic Bf 109 airframe to take the Rolls-Royce Merlin, the HS 12Z 17 having, in the meantime, gone out of production, and most Hispano-Suiza-engined aircraft were subsequently to be re-engined.

*(Below) One of the two tandem two-seat HA-1110-K1L conversion trainers built by Hispano Aviación, and (above left) the prototype HA-1109-K1L originally the 10th HA-1109 J1L*

136

*HA-1112-M1L fighters of the 71 Escuadron of Ala 7 de Cazabombardeo. Dubbed Buchón, the HA-1112-M1L was the final production version of the Bf 109 fighter, and was phased out of service with Spain's Ejército del Aire in 1967.*

When, in 1954, the HA-1109-M1L took-off on its maiden flight from San Pablo airport, on the outskirts of Seville, the full circle had turned for Messerschmitt's Bf 109 fighter. Almost exactly 19 years had elapsed since its first prototype had climbed out of the Augsburg–Haunstetten airfield on the power of a Rolls-Royce engine, and once again, after nearly two decades, the Bf 109 was Rolls-Royce powered, the Merlin 500-45 having been selected as the definitive engine for Spanish-built fighters.

The prototype conversion, originally the eleventh HA-1109-J1L and thus basically a German-built airframe, revealed extremely pleasing characteristics during flight trials, this most famous of German fighter aircraft proving perfectly amenable to the installation of the power plant that had equipped its principal wartime antagonists which it had outlived in production. While the marriage of the British engine and German airframe nearly 10 years after hostilities in Europe had ceased was perhaps not inappropriate, the use of the appellation *Buchón* (a high-breasted pigeon common to Seville), engendered by the deeper, more rotund nose resulting from the installation of the Merlin engine was somewhat less appropriate for this ageing eagle from Augsburg.

The Merlin 500-45 with automatic two-speed supercharger

*(Immediately below) A close-up view of the nose of the HA-1109-K1L, and (foot of page) the starboard HS-404 cannon and rocket rails of the HA-1112-K1L*

## HA-1112-K1L Specification

**Power Plant:** One Hispano-Suiza HA 12Z 17 12-cylinder vee liquid-cooled engine rated at 1,300 h.p. for take-off.
**Performance:** (At 6,304 lb./2 860 kg) Maximum speed, 382 m.p.h. (615 km/h) at 13,780 ft. (4 200 m), 346 m.p.h. (557 km/h) at sea level; maximum economical cruise, 277 m.p.h. (446 km/h) at 9,840 ft. (3 000 m); endurance, 1 hr. 17 min.; time to 6,560 ft. (2 000 m), 1·57 min.; service ceiling 32,800 ft. (10 000 m).
**Weights:** Empty equipped, 5,456 lb. (2 520 kg); maximum loaded, 6,834 lb. (3 100 kg).
**Dimensions:** Span, 32 ft. 6½ in. (9,92 m); length, 29 ft. 6⅓ in. (8,99 m); height, 8 ft. 6½ in. (2,6 m); wing area, 173·299 sq. ft. (16,1 m²).
**Armament:** Two 20-mm Hispano HS-404 or HS-808 wing-mounted cannon and (close support) eight 80-mm Oerlikon rockets.

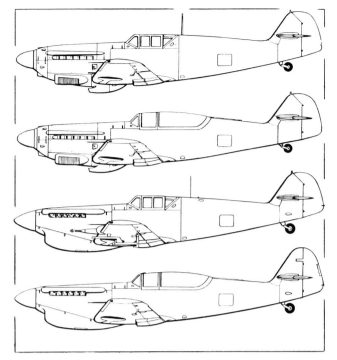

and driving a four-bladed Rotol airscrew was rated at 1,610 h.p. for take-off, affording a noteworthy improvement in performance, and examples of the HA-1112-K1L, HA-1109-K2L and HA-1109-K3L (respectively the fourth, seventh and eighth Spanish-built aircraft) were converted to take the Merlin engine as HA-1112-M1L, HA-1109-M2L and HA-1109-M3L prototypes, but production standardized on the HA-1112-M1L which was, in fact, the first version of the Spanish-built Bf 109 to see service in any numbers with the *Ejército del Aire*, being operated by 71 and 72 *Escuadrones* of *Ala 7 de Cazabombardeo* formed in 1956. Production at Seville finally phased out in 1958, a total of 239 Bf 109s having been built in Spain of which 170 were powered by the Merlin. In the previous year the two two-seat HA-1110-K1Ls had been re-engined with the Merlin as HA-1112-M4Ls, these subsequently serving with *Ala 47 de Misiones Varias* which, together with *Ala 36 Mixta*, was for long the principal operator of *Buchones* which remained in the inventory of the *Ejército del Aire* until 1967. Twenty-seven HA-1112-M1L single-seaters and one HA-1112-M4L two-seater held in storage in Spain were purchased for use in the epic film *The Battle of Britain*, a fitting swansong for this venerable eagle.

### HA-1112-M1L Specification

**Power Plant:** One Rolls-Royce Merlin 500-45 12-cylinder vee liquid-cooled engine rated at 1,610 h.p. for take-off, 1,635 h.p. at 2,250 ft. (690 m), and 1,510 h.p. at 9,250 ft. (2 820 m).
**Performance:** Maximum speed, 419 m.p.h. (674 km/h) at 13,120 ft. (4 000 m); maximum economical cruise, 318 m.p.h. (512 km/h); initial climb rate, 5,581 ft./min. (29,53 m/sec); maximum range, 476 mls. (766 km/h); service ceiling, 33,450 ft. (10 195 m)
**Weights:** Empty equipped, 5,855 lb. (2 656 kg); maximum loaded, 7,011 lb. (3 180 kg).
**Dimensions:** Span 32 ft. 6½ in. (9,92 m); length, 29 ft. 10 in. (9,10 m); height, 8 ft. 6½ in. (2,6 m); wing area, 173·299 sq. ft. (16,1 m²).
**Armament:** Two 20-mm Hispano HS-404 or HS-808 wing-mounted cannon and (close support) eight 80-mm Oerlikon rockets.

*The sideview drawings depict (top to bottom) the HA-1109-K1L, the HA-1110-K1L, the HA-1112-M1L, and the HA-1112-M4L. (Left) An HA-1112-M1L in service with the 71 Escuadron of Ala 7 de Cazabombardeo, and (below) one of the two two-seat HA-1112-M4Ls in service with the same unit*

# General Index

# Index of Aircraft, Engines and Units

JG 334, 39
JG 433, 40
J.Gr.101, 43, 44, 48
J.Gr.102, 43, 44, 48, 49, 50
J.Gr.126, 43, 44
J.Gr.152, 43,44
J.Gr.176, 43, 44
III/KG 66, 92
IV/KG 101, 91, 92
II/KG 200, 91, 92
LG 2, 44
I(*Jagd*)/LG 2, 48, 58, 75, 76, 79, 87, 99
11.(*Nacht*)/LG 2, 44
II(*Schlacht*)/LG 2, 44, 49, 72, 75, 76
*Luftflotte* 1, 44, 87, 125
*Luftflotte* 2, 44, 72, 73, 74, 75, 87, 112, 125
*Luftflotte* 3, 44, 72, 73, 74, 75, 88, 97, 125
*Luftflotte* 4, 44, 87, 112, 118, 125, 127
*Luftflotte* 5, 72, 83, 112, 125
*Luftflotte* 6, 125, 127
*Luftflotte Ost*, 112
*Luftflotte Reich*, 83, 117, 125, 127
*Luftgaukommando* VI, 75
*Luftgaukommando* XI, 75
*Luftgaukommando Holland*, 75
*Luftwaffenkommando Ostpreussen*, 48, 127
*Luftwaffenkommando West*, 127
*Luftkreiskommando* II, 50
*Luftwaffen Lehrdivision*, 44
NAGr.1, 125
NAGr.2, 125
NAGr.3, 125
NAGr.4, 125
NAGr.5, 125
NAGr.8, 125
NAGr.11, 125
NAGr.12, 125
NAGr.13, 125
NAGr.14, 125
NAGr.15, 125
NJG 5, 120, 125
NJG 11, 125, 127
Sch.G.1, 63
SKG 210, 61, 62
St.G.77, 49
*Trägergruppe* 186, 40, 82
ZG 1, 40, 43, 44, 48, 49, 63
ZG 2, 43, 44, 48, 49, 50
ZG 26, 40, 43, 44, 48, 49, 53
ZG 52, 40, 43, 44
ZG 76, 40, 43, 44, 48, 49

# Flying Units: Non German

## American

U.S. Army 8th Air Force, 96, 112
U.S. Army 15th Air Force, 115, 117

## British

No 9 Sqn, 48
No 37 Sqn, 48
No 149 Sqn, 48
No 150 Sqn, 48
No 1426 (Enemy Aircraft) Flight, 70, 94, 112, 114

## Bulgarian

6th Royal Bulgarian Fighter Rgt, 81, 101, 118

## Croatian

1st Fighter Sqn (*kroat.J.St.*), 108, 118, 126
2nd Fighter Sqn, 118
3rd Fighter Sqn, 118

## Czechoslovakian

Combined Sqn, Insurgent Air Force, 124
National Air Guard, 110, 130, 131

## Finnish

1st Wing, 130
3rd Wing, 130
Flight Rgt 1, 130
Flight Rgt 3, 130
HLeLv 11, 130
HLeLv 13, 130
HLeLv 24, 100, 116
HLeLv 28, 116
HLeLv 31, 108, 116, 130
HLeLv 33, 116, 130
HLeLv 34, 100, 101, 116, 117

## Hungarian

5/1 Fighter Group, 116
101/1 Fighter Group, 108, 117
102 Fighter Group, 107, 118
101 Fighter Rgt, 117
102 Independent Fighter Sqn, 101, 116
1/1 Fighter Sqn, 101, 116
5/1 Fighter Squadron "Puma", 101, 116
5/2 Fighter Sqn, 116

## Israeli

No 101 Sqn, 110, 133
No 105 Sqn, 133

## Italian (*Regia Aeronautica*)

3° *Gruppo Caccia Terrestre*, 89, 90
150° *Gruppo Caccia Terrestre*, 90
*Gruppo XXIII "Asso di Bastoni"*, 36

## Italian (RSI)

I° *Gruppo Caccia Terrestre*, 118, 119
II° *Gruppo Caccia Terrestre*, 108, 118, 119

## Rumanian

1st Air Corps, 100, 117, 118
1st Fighter Group, 80
*Flotila 1V*, 60
II Independent Group, 118
VII Independent Group, 118

## Slovakian

11th Fighter Sqn, 81
13th Fighter Sqn, 119
14th Fighter Sqn, 100
Slovakian Insurgent Air Arm, 100

## Spanish Nationalist

*Ala 36 Mixta*, 138
*Ala 46 Mixta*, 110
*Ala 47 MV*, 138
*Escuadron Azul*, 81, 89
*Escuadron Experimentacion en Vuelo*, 111, 135
*Escuela de Caza*, 40, 44, 50
*Grupo 1-E-2*, 25
*Grupo 2-E-2*, 25
*Grupo 3-E-2*, 25
*Grupo 5-E-5*, 38
*Grupo 6-G-6*, 40
25 *Grupo/23 Regimiento*, 40, 44, 53, 89
71 *Escuadron/Ala 7*, 110, 111, 137, 138
72 *Escuadron/Ala 7*, 138

## Spanish Republican

1ª *Escuadrilla* I-16, 35
2ª *Escuadrilla* I-16, 36
3ª *Escuadrilla* I-16, 35, 36
4ª *Escuadrilla* I-16, 35, 36
5ª *Escuadrilla* I-16, 36
1ª *Escuardilla de Moscas*, 27
*Escuadra num* 11, 26, 27
*Grupo num* 21, 26
*Grupo num* 26, 26

## Swiss

*Fliegerkompagnie* 6, 45, 60, 61, 77
*Fliegerkompagnie* 7, 77, 78, 108, 120
*Fliegerkompagnie* 8, 77
*Fliegerkompagnie* 9, 77
*Fliegerkompagnie* 15, 33, 45, 60, 77
*Fliegerkompagnie* 21, 45, 77

## Yugoslavian

31st Fighter Group, 77
32nd Fighter Group, 76, 77
51st Fighter Group, 76
52nd Fighter Group, 77
2nd Fighter Rgt, 77
6th Fighter Rgt, 44, 45, 76, 77
Independent Sqn/Fighter Training School, 77